KT-471-869

INSTANT REFERENCE
EUROPEAN HISTORY

TEACH YOURSELF ®

For UK orders: please contact Bookpoint Ltd, 78 Milton Park, Abingdon, Oxon OX14 4TD.
Telephone: (44) 01235 400414, Fax: (44) 01235 400454. Lines are open 9.00–6.00, Monday
to Saturday, with a 24-hour message answering service.
E-mail address: orders@bookpoint.co.uk

For USA and Canada orders: please contact NTC/Contemporary Publishing, 4255 West
Touhy Avenue, Lincolnwood, Illinois 60646-1975, USA. Telephone: (847) 679 5500, Fax:
(847) 679 2494.

Long renowned as the authoritative source for self-guided learning – with more than 40
million copies sold worldwide – the *Teach Yourself* series includes over 200 titles in the fields
of languages, crafts, hobbies, business, computing and education.

British Library Cataloguing in Publication Data
A catalogue record for this title is available from the British Library.

Library of Congress Catalog Card Number: On file

First published in UK 2000 by Hodder Headline Plc, 338 Euston Road, London NW1 3BH.

First published in US by NTC/Contemporary Publishing, 4255 West Touhy Avenue,
Lincolnwood (Chicago), Illinois 60646-1975, USA.

The 'Teach Yourself' name and logo are registered trademarks of Hodder & Stoughton.

Picture credits:
With special thanks to AKG:
22, 23, 31, 38, 39, 47, 49, 74, 76, 78, 84, 99, 115, 118, 126, 128, 132, 136, 141, 146, 161,
163, 164, 171, 174, 177, 193, 196

Text editor: Malcolm Chandler
Typeset by TechType, Abingdon, Oxon
Printed in Great Britain for Hodder & Stoughton Educational, a division of Hodder Headline
Plc, 338 Euston Road, London NW1 3BH, by Cox & Wyman Ltd, Reading, Berkshire

Impression number   10 9 8 7 6 5 4 3 2 1
Year   2006   2005   2004   2003   2002   2001   2000

Contents

Bold type in the text indicates a cross reference. A plural, or possessive, is given as the cross reference, i.e. is in bold type, even if the entry to which it refers is singular.

Abyssinian Crisis

Political crisis caused by the successful invasion of Abyssinia (Ethiopia), East Africa, by the Italian dictator Benito Mussolini in October 1935. The Italian forces used poison gas to overcome resistance.

Italy's attempt in 1895 to invade Abyssinia had ended in defeat at the Battle of Aduwa and Italian national pride had not recovered from this humiliating blow. **Mussolini** wanted revenge.

- With his domestic policies in tatters by 1935, an invasion of Abyssinia was seen by Mussolini as a way of boosting his popularity at home.

- Mussolini also had ambitions of a revived Roman empire and saw Abyssinia as an easy target. The Italians had occupied the neighbouring African country of Eritrea since 1889.

Britain and France opposed real sanctions because they were trying to keep Mussolini as an ally against the growing menace of **Hitler**. Britain and France put forward the **Hoare-Laval Pact** by way of compromise.

Mussolini's actions were condemned by the League of Nations, but Britain and France prevented oil being added to the list of sanctions proposed by the League, which would have forced Mussolini to withdraw. Consequently, Abyssinia remained under Italian control until 1941.

See also: *appeasement; Stresa Front.*

Adenauer, Konrad (1876–1967)

German Christian Democrat politician, chancellor of West Germany 1949–63. With the French president Charles de Gaulle he achieved the post-war reconciliation of France and Germany culminating in the reconciliation pact signed in Paris in 1963. He strongly supported all measures designed to strengthen the Western bloc in Europe.

- After the war Adenauer headed the Christian Democratic Union (CDU) and became chancellor, combining the office with that of foreign minister.

- He was re-elected chancellor in 1953 and retained the post of foreign minister until 1955.

- His visit to Moscow in 1955 resulted in the establishment of diplomatic relations between West Germany and the USSR and several thousand German prisoners, still held in the Soviet Union, were allowed home.

He was a strong advocate of West Germany's participation in the defence of Western Europe, and in 1955 the republic joined both **NATO** and the Western European Union (WEU), a forum for military issues among Western European governments.

- From 1958 onwards Adenauer endeavoured to make his country a dominant force in the **European Economic Community** (EEC).
- After de Gaulle was restored to power in France in 1958, Adenauer worked with him to forge closer links between both countries, ultimately bringing about the reconciliation treaty signed in Paris in January 1963.

Adenauer retired as chancellor in October 1963, but remained chair of the CDU until 1966.

❛A thick skin is a gift from God. ❜

Konrad Adenauer, German Christian Democrat politician,
New York Times, 30 December 1959.

Africa, the scramble for

Drive by European nations to establish colonies in Africa during the 19th century. Annexation of African territory by Europeans began in the 1880s and by 1914 only two African countries remained completely independent: Ethiopia (Abyssinia), which had been a kingdom for about 2,000 years; and Liberia, which had been established as a homeland for freed black slaves in 1822 by the American Colonization Society and declared an independent republic in 1847. The remaining countries in Africa came under the control of seven European powers: Belgium, Britain, France, Germany, Italy, Portugal, and Spain. France and Britain owned the most colonies.

- France controlled most of West and Equatorial Africa, and the island of Madagascar in the east.
- Britain seized territory in East and Central Africa, particularly Northern Rhodesia (Zambia) and Southern Rhodesia (Zimbabwe).
- Portugal took over Angola and Mozambique.
- Germany took territory in Southwest Africa and East Africa (now Namibia and Tanzania).
- Italy established colonies in what are now Libya, Eritrea, and Somalia.
- Spain held the northern part of Morocco, and the largely desert area of Western Sahara.

THE MAIN CAUSES FOR THE SCRAMBLE FOR AFRICA

- The opening up of vast areas of Africa by the pioneering expeditions of 19th-century explorers, including the Scottish missionary David Livingstone and the French naval officer Pierre de Brazza.
- The belief that Africa contained large supplies of minerals, including diamonds and gold, and other resources that could bring wealth to Europeans.
- The quest for imperial supremacy – each European country was anxious to build a bigger empire than its neighbours and the acquisition of African territory was a means to this end.

All the European colonies were relatively short-lived, and the majority achieved independence in the 1960s and 1970s.

Agadir Incident or the Second Moroccan Crisis
International crisis provoked by Kaiser **Wilhelm II** of Germany between July and November 1911 by sending the gunboat *Panther* to the port of Agadir in southwest Morocco, Africa. This was an attempt to increase German influence in the area and drive a wedge into the Anglo-French pact created by the **Entente Cordiale** in 1904. In fact, German aggression during this second of the **Moroccan Crises** merely served to reinforce Anglo-French fears of Germany's hostile intentions.

Alexander I (1777–1825)
Alexander was tsar of Russia from 1801. He was defeated by the French emperor **Napoleon I** at the Battle of **Austerlitz** in 1805 and subsequently signed a peace treaty at **Tilsit** in 1807. However, the economic crisis in Russia led to a break with Napoleon's **Continental System** of economic warfare with Britain, and Russia opened its ports to British trade. This led to Napoleon's ill-fated invasion of Russia 1812. After the Congress of Vienna in 1815, Alexander set up the **Holy Alliance** with Austria and Prussia, purporting to aspire to a new Christian order in Europe.

He imposed a new constitution on Poland, which fell to Russian control after the Congress of Vienna.

The first half of Alexander's reign was marked by several reforms and improvements: the abolition of torture, the creation of ministries and of the Council of State, the foundation of several universities and of an extensive state school system, and the liberation of serfs (men without land) in the Baltic provinces. However, Alexander's later policies became more reactionary, and counteracted the efforts of the first half of his reign.

> ❝ Napoleon thinks I am a fool, but he who laughs last laughs longest. ❞
>
> **Alexander I**, letter to his sister Catherine on 8 October 1808, after meeting Napoleon at Erfurt.

Alexander II (1818–1881)

Alexander II was tsar of Russia from 1855. Known as the 'Tsar Liberator', he embarked on reforms of the army, the government, education, local government, and of the law courts. In 1861 he announced the emancipation of the serfs, who hitherto had been bound to their lord and his land without privilege or pay. In practice, this proclamation had little effect since the serfs did not have the means to buy the land. Alexander retained all of his autocratic power, crushing the Polish revolt in 1863 with great severity. Many revolutionary groups were set up during his reign and these remained unsatisfied. Alexander became increasingly reactionary. He was assassinated by an anarchist terrorist group, the Nihilists.

Alexander's grandson, the future **Nicholas II**, was taken to see the mutilated body of his grandfather on his deathbed.

See also: *Crimean War.*

> ❝ It is better to abolish serfdom from above than to wait for it to abolish itself from below. ❞
>
> **Alexander II**, speech to the Moscow nobility, March 1856.

Algeciras Conference

International conference held between January and April 1906 after the first of the **Moroccan Crises**. France, Germany, Britain, Russia, and Austria–Hungary, together with the USA, Spain, the Low Countries, Portugal, and Sweden, met to settle the question of Morocco in north west Africa. The conference was held in response to increased German demands on in area traditionally seen as being under French influence. The conference resulted in a reassertion of Anglo-French friendship and underlined the isolation of Germany. France and Spain gained control of Morocco.

See also: *Agadir Incident; Wilhelm II.*

Alliance System

Network of alliances constructed by the German chancellor **Bismarck** after the defeat of France in the **Franco-Prussian War**. The alliances had three purposes:

- to isolate France and prevent it from gaining revenge by attacking Germany;
- to prevent the possibility of Germany facing a war on two fronts – this would only be possible if France became allied to Germany;
- to cement an alliance between Germany and **Austria–Hungary.**

THE ALLIANCES

- **1872** The **Dreikaiserbund,** signed by the respective emperors of Germany and Austria, and the tsar of Russia.
- **1879** The **Dual Alliance,** signed by Germany and Austria.
- **1881** The **Three Emperors League**, which included Germany, Austria-Hungary, and Russia. It was renewed in 1884, but Russia refused to sign in 1887. This led to the Reinsurance Treaty.
- **1882** The **Triple Alliance** which grew out of the Dual Alliance, extended to include Italy.
- **1887** The **Reinsurance Treaty**, which Bismarck quickly concluded with Russia to prevent Russia forming an alliance with France.

Through this system of alliances, Bismarck was able, until 1887, to keep all of the powers of Europe on the side of Germany, and France remained isolated. In 1890, however, Bismarck was forced to resign by the new Kaiser, Wilhelm II, and the alliances led to the creation of two power blocs, the **Triple Entente** (Britain and Russia) and the **Triple Alliance** (Germany, Austria-Hungary, and Italy). The alliances created by Bismarck now effectively divided Europe into two armed camps and suspicions between the two were a major cause of **World War I**.

- **1890** Russia refused to renew the Reinsurance Treaty. Instead, relations between Russia and France grew much closer.
- **1894** France and Russia signed the **Dual Entente**.
- **1904** Britain and France signed the **Entente Cordiale**, the 'friendly agreement'.
- **1907** Britain signed an entente with Russia, which became known as the **Triple Entente**.

Alsace-Lorraine

Area of northeast France, lying west of the River Rhine, which was part of the German empire until the 17th century. In 1648 part of the territory was ceded to France and in 1681 Louis XIV seized Strasbourg. The few remaining districts were occupied by France after the French Revolution. The area was taken by Germany after the **Franco-Prussian War**, 1870–71, chiefly for its iron ores. Disagreement over claims to the region was a major cause of **World War I**. It was regained by France in 1919, then again annexed by Germany in 1940 until it was liberated by the Allies in 1944.

> Sarah Berhhardt (1844–1923), the French actress, never once appeared in Germany. When a Berlin theatre manager asked her to name her price to appear in his theatre, she replied with a telegram It contained two words 'Alsace-Lorraine'.

The great prosperity and power built up by Germany after 1871 was largely due to its exploitation of the iron mines of Alsace-Lorraine. Without these resources Germany would have exhausted its capacity for turning out the essential materials of war long before 1918.

See also: *Bismarck.*

Ancien regime

The old order or the feudal, absolute monarchy in France before the French Revolution of 1789. There was no parliament, but the three estates of the church, the nobles, and the **third estate** (everybody else) met as the Estates General when summoned by the king. The Estates-General met in May 1789 (it had previously met in 1614). The meeting of 1789 led directly to the **French Revolution**.

See also: *Gabelle; Taille.*

Andropov, Yuri (1914–1984)

Soviet communist politician, president of the USSR 1983–84 who, as chief of the KGB (the secret police of the USSR) 1967–82, established a reputation for severe and efficient suppression of dissent.

Andropov was politically active from the 1930s. His part in quelling the Hungarian national uprising of 1956, when he was Soviet ambassador, brought him into the Communist Party secretariat in 1962 as a specialist on East European affairs. He became a member of the Politburo in 1973 and succeeded Leonid **Brezhnev** as party general secretary in 1982. Elected president in 1983, he instituted economic reforms, but died of kidney failure.

See also: *Chernenko.*

Anne of Austria (1606–1666)

Anne was Queen of France from 1615 and regent 1643–61. She was the daughter of Philip III (1578–1621) of Spain. She married Louis XIII (1602–1643) of France (whose chief minister, Cardinal **Richelieu**, conspired against her). On her husband's death she became regent for their son, Louis XIV, until he took complete power in 1661.

She was greatly influenced by Cardinal Mazarin (1602–1661), her chief minister, to whom she was supposed to be secretly married.

> ❢ God does not pay at the end of every week, but He pays. ❡
>
> **Anne of Austria**, Queen of France, to Cardinal Mazarin.

Anschluss

The annexation of Austria by Germany, accomplished by the German chancellor Adolf **Hitler** on 12 March 1938. By annexing Austria, Hitler realized an ambition he had held since 1933, fuelled by the fact

> The Anschluss was one of the worst planned invasions ever. German tanks had to stop at petrol stations in Austria in order to refuel.

that he was Austrian by birth. The Anschluss was banned by the terms of Treaty of **Versailles**, signed in 1919, but the failure of Britain and France to fully oppose Hitler's actions encouraged him to pursue his policy of aggression.

See also: *Schuschnigg; Seyss-Inquart.*

appeasement

The conciliatory policy adopted by the British government, in particular under Neville Chamberlain (1869–1940), towards the Nazi and Fascist dictators in Europe in the 1930s in an effort to maintain peace. Appeasement was based upon the idea that Germany had been treated too harshly at the Treaty of **Versailles** and that Hitler's actions were therefore justified. The high point of appeasement was the **Munich Agreement** in September 1938, when the Czech Sudetenland was handed over to Germany. The policy was widely supported in Britain, but strongly opposed by Winston Churchill (1879–1965). Appeasement ended when Germany occupied Bohemia-Moravia in March 1939 thus starting **World War II**.

See also: *Anschluss.*

aristocracy

Social elite that has traditionally based its power and influence upon landed wealth. Aristocracies are also usually associated with monarchy, but have frequently been in conflict with the sovereign over their rights and privileges. In Europe, their economic base was undermined during the 19th century by inflation and falling agricultural prices, leading to their demise as a political force after 1914.

The Prussian aristocracy (the Junker) based its power not only on landed wealth but also on service to the state.

Armed Neutrality

League of the northern powers of Europe, Russia, Denmark, and Sweden, formed in 1780. It was an attempt to prevent countries at war interfering with the ships of those countries that remained neutral. The League announced that 'free ships make free goods'. A proclamation of **Catherine the Great** of Russia laid down that:

- Neutral ships could sail freely from port to port and along the coasts of belligerents (those engaged in recognized conflict), so long as they did not carry contraband of war;
- Only real and effective blockade would be recognized.

The doctrine was accepted by Prussia and Austria treaty of 1781, but rejected by Britain. The League was suspended at the peace of 1783, but revived briefly in 1800. The settlement of the questions raised by the doctrines of the League was not achieved until 1856 at the Declaration of Paris.

Asiento, Treaty of

Agreement between Britain and Spain in 1713, whereby British traders were permitted to sell 144,000 black slaves in the Spanish-American colonies during the course of the following 30 years. In 1750 this right was bought by the Spanish government for $100,000.

Atlantic Wall

Fortifications built by the Germans in **World War II** on the North Sea and Atlantic coasts of France, Belgium, the Netherlands, Denmark, and Norway. They proved largely ineffective against the Allied invasion of 1944.

The defences extended 2,750 km/1,700 mi from the North Cape, off the north coast of Norway, to the Spanish frontier and did not actually form a continuous wall, but were grouped according to the likelihood of the area being used for landing. Millions of tons of concrete went into the construction of gun batteries, pillboxes, and obstacles against tanks.

Auschwitz

The site of a notorious extermination camp used by the Nazis in **World War II** to carry out the extermination of Jews and other political and social minorities, as part of the '**final solution**'. Each of the four gas chambers used to execute victims could hold 6,000 people.

The German commandant at Auschwitz was the infamous Rudolf **Hoess**, recognized for his discovery of Zyklon B gas which was used to kill the inmates.

Auschwitz was originally established as a transit camp but from March 1941 was expanded to a capacity of 130,000 to function as a labour camp: the nearby IG Farben factory took 10,000 Auschwitz prisoners as slave labour. In September 1941, mass executions began in the four gas chambers. Total numbers who died at Auschwitz are usually cited as between 1 million and 2.5 million, but some estimates reach 4 million.

See also: *Holocaust.*

Ausgleich
Compromise reached between Austria and Hungary in February 1867 establishing the Austro-Hungarian Dual Monarchy under Habsburg rule. It endured until the collapse of **Austria-Hungary** in 1918.

Austerlitz, Battle of
Battle on 2 December 1805 when the French forces of Emperor **Napoleon Bonaparte** defeated those of Alexander I of Russia and Francis II of Austria. The battle was one of Napoleon's greatest victories, and marked the end of the coalition against France. In the wake of their defeat, the Austrians signed the Treaty of Pressburg and the Russians withdrew to their own territory.

> ❧ Roll up that map; it will not be wanted these ten years. ❧
>
> **William Pitt, the Younger**, British Tory prime minister. Referring to map of Europe, after hearing of Napoleon's victory at Austerlitz 1805, in Stanhope's *Life of the Rt Hon William Pitt.*

Austria
Chronology

791	**Charlemagne** conquers Avars and establishes East Mark, nucleus of the future Austrian Empire.
1282	Holy Roman Emperor Rudolf of **Habsburg** seizes Austria and invests his son as its duke; for over 500 years most rulers of Austria are elected Holy Roman Emperor.
1519–56	Emperor **Charles V** is both archduke of Austria and king of Spain; the Habsburgs are dominant in Europe.

1618–48	**Thirty Years' War**: the Habsburgs are weakened by their failure to secure control over Germany.
1683	A Polish-Austrian force led by **John III** (John Sobieski) defeats the Turks at Vienna.
1699	Treaty of Karlowitz: the Austrians expel the Turks from Hungary, which comes under Habsburg rule.
1713	By the Treaty of **Utrecht**, Austria obtains the Spanish Netherlands (Belgium) and political control over most of Italy.
1740–48	The War of **Austrian Succession**: Prussia attacks Austria on the pretext of disputing the succession of **Maria Theresa** to the throne; Austria loses **Silesia** to Prussia.
1772	Austria plays an active part in the **partitions of Poland** and annexes Galicia.
1780–90	**Joseph II** tries to impose radical reforms.
1792	Austria goes to war against revolutionary France.
1804	Francis II takes the title emperor of Austria.
1806	The **Holy Roman Empire** is abolished.
1815	After the **Napoleonic Wars**, Austria loses the Netherlands but receives Lombardy and Venetia.
1848	There were liberal-nationalist revolts throughout the Austrian empire; Ferdinand I abdicates in favour of **Franz Joseph**; the uprisings are suppressed, but with difficulty.
1859	France and Sardinia forcibly expel Austrians from Lombardy.
1866	**Seven Weeks' War**: Prussia defeats Austria, Venetia ceded to Italy.
1867	Austria conceds equality to Hungary within the dual monarchy of **Austria-Hungary**.
1878	The Treaty of Berlin: Austria-Hungary occupies Bosnia-Herzegovina; annexed in 1908.
1914	Archduke **Franz Ferdinand**, the heir to the throne, is assassinated by a Serbian nationalist; Austria-Hungary invades Serbia, precipitating World War I.
1918	Austria-Hungary collapses in military defeat; the empire is dissolved and a republic is proclaimed.
1919	The Treaty of St Germain reduces Austria to its present boundaries and prohibits union with Germany.
1938	The Anschluss: Nazi Germany incorporates Austria into the Third Reich.
1945	Following World War II, the victorious Allies divide Austria into four zones of occupation (US, British, French, and Soviet).
1955	The Austrian State Treaty ends occupation; Austria regains independence on condition of neutrality.
1995	Austria becomes a full member of the European Union (EU).

Austrian Succession, War of

War 1740–48 between Austria (supported by England and Holland) and Prussia (supported by France and Spain). When the Holy Roman Emperor Charles VI (1685–1740) died, the succession of his daughter **Maria Theresa** was disputed by a number of European powers. **Frederick the Great** of Prussia seized Silesia from Austria.

- At Dettingen in 1743 an army of British, Austrians, and Hanoverians under the command of British king George II was victorious over the French.

  Dettingen was the last battle in which a reigning British monarch commanded the British forces.

- In 1746 an Austro-British army was defeated at Fontenoy but British naval superiority was confirmed, and there were gains in the Americas and India.

The war ended in 1748 by the Treaty of Aix-la-Chapelle and almost all conquests were returned.

Austro-Hungarian Empire

The Dual Monarchy established by the Habsburg emperor **Franz Joseph** in 1867 between his empire of Austria and his kingdom of Hungary (including territory that became **Czechoslovakia** as well as parts of Poland, the Ukraine, Romania, Yugoslavia, and Italy).

The Austro-Hungarian Empire came into being with an agreement known as the **Ausgleich**. The two countries retained their own legal and administrative systems but shared foreign policy. In 1910 the empire had an area of 261,239 sq km/100,838 sq mi with a population of 51 million.

It collapsed in the autumn of 1918 with the end of **World War I**. Only two king-emperors ruled: Franz Joseph and Charles, the last of the Habsburg emperors.

See also: *Franz Ferdinand.*

Axis

Alliance of Nazi Germany and Fascist Italy before and during **World War II**, which was formed by the **Rome-Berlin Axis** in 1936, when Italy was being threatened with sanctions because of its invasion of Ethiopia (see Abyssinian crisis). It became a full military and political alliance in May 1939. A ten-year alliance between Germany, Italy, and Japan (**Rome-Berlin-Tokyo Axis**) was signed September 1940 and was subsequently joined by Hungary, Bulgaria, Romania, and the puppet states of Slovakia and Croatia. The Axis collapsed with the fall of Italian dictator Benito **Mussolini,** and the surrender of Italy in1943 and Germany and Japan in 1945.

Balaclava, Battle of

A Russian attack on 25 October 1854, during the **Crimean War**, on British positions 10 km/6 mi southeast of the Black Sea port of **Sevastopol**. It was the scene of the ill-timed Charge of the Light Brigade of British cavalry against the Russian entrenched artillery. Of the 673 soldiers who took part, there were 272 casualties.

The Light Brigade was ordered to 'prevent the enemy carrying away the guns'. It seems that this order was intended to direct them to the hills where the Russians had captured some Turkish guns, but the order given to the cavalry was badly phrased and resulted in misunderstanding. The Light Brigade's commander, Lord Cardigan, assumed that his target was the Russian guns about half a mile away up the north valley. The battle ended with the Russians retaining their guns and their position.

The order to the Light Brigade was written in haste and the officer who carried it to Lord Cardigan was killed just before the charge. He may have been trying to tell Cardigan that he was charging the wrong guns.

❝ They dashed on towards that thin red line tipped with steel. ❞

William Russell, British journalist, describing the Russian attack at the Battle of Balaclava, in *The British Expedition in the Crimea.*

Balkans

Peninsula of southeastern Europe, stretching into Slovenia between the Adriatic and Aegean seas, comprising Albania, Bosnia-Herzegovina, Bulgaria, Croatia, Greece, Romania, the part of Turkey in Europe, and Yugoslavia. It is joined to the rest of Europe by an isthmus 1,200 km/750mi wide between Rijeka on the west and the mouth of the Danube on the Black Sea to the east.

Rivalries between Austria-Hungary and Russia in the Balkans were a major cause of **World War I**. Austrian ambition aimed to crush the state of

Serbia while the Russians supported the Serbs, who adhered to the Orthodox Church.

In 1919 the state of Yugoslavia was set up. This was occupied by Germany during **World War II**, but was reformed under the leadership of Josef **Tito** after the war in 1945. On his death in 1980, Yugoslavia, which was a federation of six republics, began to break up.

In the early 1990s Slovenia and Croatia, and then Bosnia-Herzegovina, battled to win independence from the Serb-dominated Yugoslav federation. Despite international recognition being awarded to all three republics in early 1992, fierce fighting between Serb, Croat, and Muslim factions continued in Bosnia-Herzegovina until 1994. Subsequently, Kosovo, an Albanian-dominated province of Serbia, also attempted to win its independence.

> ❝ Just because we cannot do everything for everyone does not mean we should do nothing for anyone. ❞
>
> **Bill Clinton**, President of the USA, forestalling demands for the withdrawal of US troops from the Balkans, MSNBC, 1 April 1999.

Balkan Wars

Two wars in 1912–13 and 1913 (preceding **World War I**) that resulted in the expulsion of Ottoman Turkey from Europe, except for a small area around Istanbul in Turkey, through the combined efforts of the Balkan states.

In the First Balkan War of 1912, Bulgaria, Serbia, Greece, and Montenegro fought against Turkey. By the Treaty of London, May 1913, Turkey retained only a small piece of eastern Thrace and the Gallipoli peninsula in Europe.

The Second Balkan War of June–July 1913 took place when the victors fought over acquisitions in Macedonia, from which most of Bulgaria was excluded. Bulgaria attacked Greece and Serbia, which were joined by Romania. Bulgaria was defeated, and Turkey retained Thrace. The result was an expanded Serbia that became the dominant power in the Balkans.

Barbarossa, Operation

The German code name, during **World War II**, given to the plan to invade the USSR that was launched on 22 June 1941.

The Germans utilized massive resources for the campaign, organized into three Army Groups. Some 3,330 German tanks were deployed, with four Luftwaffe air fleets providing total air superiority. Initial progress was rapid and the number of prisoners taken was high. Immense quantities of Russian equipment fell into German hands while most of the Soviet air force was destroyed on the ground. However, due to interference from Germany's dictator Adolf **Hitler**, the impetus of the drive towards Moscow was slowed, so that winter had set in

> The main cause of failure of Barbarossa was the late start due to delays caused by the Balkan campaign to support Mussolini. Hitler had originally planned to attack in April, but sent German forces to help Mussolini in Albania, Yugoslavia, and Greece. The attack eventually began on 20 June 1941.

before an invasion of the city was attempted. The failure to take Moscow marked the end of Barbarossa, with the German plan in ruins.

In December 1941 the Russian Red Army began a counterattack and the main German advance was then switched further south to prepare for an advance into the Caucasus region of southwest USSR.

See also: *Kursk; Stalingrad; Zhukov.*

Barras, Paul François Jean Nicolas (1755–1829)

Barras was a French revolutionary. He was elected to the National Convention in 1792 and helped to overthrow French Jacobin leader **Robespierre** in 1794. In 1795 he became a member of the ruling **Directory**. In 1796 he brought about the marriage of his former mistress, Joséphine de Beauharnais (1763–1814), to

> Barras had been looking for a way to get Josephine off his hands and subsequently rewarded Napoleon with command of the army of Italy.

French emperor **Napoleon I** and assumed dictatorial powers. After Napoleon's coup d'état of Brumaire, 19 November 1799, Barras fell into disgrace.

Bastille

Castle of St Antoine, built in about 1370 as part of the fortifications of Paris, and made into a state prison by Cardinal **Richelieu**. It was also used as a military arsenal and became a symbol of royal power. It was stormed by an angry mob in an effort to seize arms on 14 July 1789. The governor and most of the garrison were killed, and the Bastille was razed. This event emphasized the power of the Parisian mob and was the real starting point of the **French Revolution**.

> Only seven prisoners were found in the castle when it was stormed.

See also: *sans culottes.*

Beer-Hall Putsch or Munich Beer-Hall Putsch

Unsuccessful uprising in Munich on 9 November 1923 led by Adolf **Hitler,** leader of the newly formed Nazi Party, which attempted to overthrow the government of Bavaria. Hitler announced the plan in the 'Burgerbraukeller' on the night of 8 November. More than 2,000 Nazi demonstrators marched into Munich the following morning, but were met by armed police, who opened fire, killing 16 of Hitler's supporters. At the subsequent trial for treason, General **Ludendorff**, who had supported Hitler, was acquitted. Hitler was sentenced to five years in prison, where he wrote his political thesis, *Mein Kampf.*

One of the reasons for the failure of the putsch was that most of the Nazis in the 'Burgerbraukeller' got drunk on the night of 8 November. They smashed up the beer hall. The bill listed 2,372 pints of beer and 800 meals. The owner also claimed that they had stolen 144 sets of cutlery.

Belgium
Chronology

10th–11th centuries	Seven feudal states emerge: Flanders, Hainaut, Namur, Brabant, Limburg, and Luxembourg, all are nominally subject to the French king or Holy Roman Emperor, but in practice they remain independent.
12th century	The economy begins to flourish: textiles in Bruges, Ghent, and Ypres; copper and tin in Dinant and Liège.
15th century	One by one, the states come under the rule of the dukes of Burgundy.
1477	Belgium passes into **Habsburg** dominions through the marriage of Mary of Burgundy to **Maximilian**, Archduke of Austria.
1555	The division of Habsburg dominions; the Low Countries are allotted to Spain.
1648	The independence of the Dutch Republic is recognized; the south is retained by Spain.
1713	The Treaty of **Utrecht** transferrs the Spanish Netherlands to Austrian rule.
1792–97	The Austrian Netherlands are invaded by revolutionary France and finally annexed.
1815	The Congress of **Vienna** reunites the north and south Netherlands as one kingdom under the House of Orange.
1830	The largely French-speaking people in the south rebel against union with Holland and declare Belgian independence.
1831	Prince Leopold of Saxe-Coburg-Gotha becomes first king of Belgium as Leopold I.
1839	The Treaty of London recognizes the independence of Belgium and guarantees its neutrality.
1914–18	The Netherlands are invaded and occupied by Germany. Belgian forces under King Albert I fight in conjunction with the Allies.

1940	During the second invasion by Germany; King Leopold III orders the Belgian army to capitulate.
1944–45	Belgium is liberated from German control.
1948	Belgium forms the Benelux customs union with Luxembourg and the Netherlands.
1949	Belgium is a founding member of **NATO**.
1958:	Belgium is a founding member of the **European Economic Community** (EEC), which makes Brussels its headquarters.

See also: *European Union*

Benes, Edvard (1884–1948)

Czechoslovakian politician who worked with Tomás Masaryk towards Czechoslovak nationalism from 1918. He was foreign minister and representative at the **League of Nations** and then president of the republic from 1935 until forced to resign by the Germans. He headed a government-in-exile in London during **World War II**. He personally gave the order for the assassination of the German Nazi Reinhard **Heydrich** in Prague in 1942. Having signed an agreement with the Soviet dictator Joseph **Stalin**, he returned home as president in 1945 but resigned again after the communist coup in 1948.

> ❦ To make peace in Europe possible … the pre-war generation must die and take [their] pre-war mentality into the grave. ❦
>
> **Eduard Benes**, interview, December 1929.

Berchtesgaden

Village in southeastern Bavaria, Germany, site of the German dictator Adolf **Hitler's** country residence, the Berghof, which was captured and destroyed by US troops 4 May 1945 after Germany surrendered to the Allies towards the end of **World War II**.

Beresina, Battle of

Partial victory of Russian forces over the French army as it retreated from the French emperor **Napoleon I's** abortive attempt on Moscow in November 1812.

Two Russian armies attacked the French troops as they crossed the Beresina River on 28 November: one army fell on Napoleon, who had already crossed the river, while the other attacked Marshal Claude Victor's force which formed the rearguard and was just approaching the river. Napoleon managed to beat off the attack on his force, but Victor's troops were less fortunate: the Russians extracted a heavy toll of mainly stragglers and camp-followers, resulting in some 36,000 fatalities.

See also: *Borodino.*

Beriya, Lavrenti Pavlovich (1899–1953)

Georgian communist who was the USSR commissar (minister) for internal affairs 1938–45 and deputy prime minister under the Soviet dictator Joseph **Stalin**, in charge of security matters, 1941–53. In 1945 Beriya was made a marshal of the USSR. Beriya ended the Great Purge (a process of elimination of all opposition) by liquidating his predecessor Yezhov and many NKVD (Soviet secret police) officials, and organized the deportation of hundreds of thousands from eastern Poland, the Baltic States, and areas formerly occupied by the Germans. He was also in charge of the security police in the satellite states of Eastern Europe.

> Beriya was executed just as the *New Soviet Encyclopaedia* was about to be published. The entry for Beriya was hurriedly replaced by an entry for the Bering Sea.

In the struggle for power after Stalin's death Beriya was defeated, arrested, and shot as an 'imperialist agent'.

Berlin Blockade

The closing of all routes to Berlin from the west by road, rail, and canal by Soviet forces from June 1948 to May 1949. It was an attempt to prevent the other Allies (the USA, France, and the UK) unifying the western part of Germany. The Allies flew in food supplies daily with more than 272,000 flights being made during the Berlin Airlift.

The blockade was lifted in May 1949, but the airlift continued until September. The blockade marked the formal division of the city into Eastern and Western sectors. The three western sectors in West Germany became a 'Land' (province) of

> Gen Lucius Clay, the US commander in Berlin, offered to fight his way out, but was ordered not to by President Truman.

the Federal Republic of Germany in May 1949. The USSR created a separate municipal government in their sector; and in October 1949 East Berlin was proclaimed the capital of East Germany.

Berlin, Conference of

Conference 1884–85 of the major European powers (France, Germany, UK, Belgium, and Portugal) called by German chancellor Otto von

Bismarck to decide on the colonial partition of Africa. The conference agreed to:

- eliminate the slave trade
- allow free navigation on the Congo and Niger rivers
- recognize the Congo Free State.

Berlin, Congress of

Congress of the European powers (Russia, Turkey, **Austria-Hungary**, UK, France, Italy, and Germany) held in Berlin in 1878 to determine the boundaries of the Balkan states after the Russo-Turkish war of 1877–78. Britain and Austria objected to the creation of a 'Big Bulgaria' at the Treaty of San Stefano 1878. They believed that this would be dominated by Russia. The main result was that Bulgaria was broken up into three small states.

The Congress was part of German chancellor Otto von **Bismarck's** plans to create a balance of power in Europe and isolate France. He claimed to be the 'honest broker'.

The Balkans after the Congress of Berlin 1878–1913

land lost by Ottoman empire, with date

- 1830–1877
- 1878–1904
- 1905–1913

1878 date of independence
—— boundary 1914

RUSSIA

AUSTRO-HUNGARIAN EMPIRE

ROMANIA 1878

SERBIA 1878

BULGARIA 1878

Black Sea

1913

1913 1895 1913

1913 1389 MONTENEGRO

1913 1913 Constantinople

ALBANIA 1913

1913 Aegean Sea

OTTOMAN EMPIRE

Corfu 1864 1913

Ionian Islands 1863

GREECE 1830 Athens

Dodecanese (to Italy)

0 200 mi
0 400 km

Mediterranean Sea 1908

Crete

ITALY

Congress of Berlin *Map showing the division of the Balkan States following the Congress of Berlin.*

British prime minister Benjamin Disraeli (1804–1881) attended as the UK's chief envoy, and declared on his return to England that he had brought back 'peace with honour'.

Berlin Wall
Dividing barrier that existed from 1961 to 1989 between East and West Berlin. The city of Berlin had been divided between Britain, the US, France, and the USSR after **World War II** in 1945. The wall was erected by East Germany to prevent East Germans leaving for West Germany. Escapees were shot on sight.

From 13 August 1961, the East German security forces sealed off all but 12 of the 80 crossing points to West Berlin with a barbed wire barrier. It was reinforced with concrete by the Russians to prevent the escape of unwilling inhabitants of East Berlin to the rival political and economic system of West Berlin. The interconnecting link between East and West Berlin was **Checkpoint Charlie**, where both sides exchanged captured spies. On 9 November 1989 the East German government opened its borders to try to halt the mass exodus of its citizens to the West via other Eastern bloc countries, and the wall was gradually dismantled, with portions of it sold off as souvenirs.

Berlin Wall *Map showing the division of the city from 1945 to 1989*

Between 1949 and August 1961 about 2,500,000 people left East Berlin for the West. From August 1961 to November 1989 about 300 escaped, including one man in a flock of sheep.

Bernadotte, Jean-Baptiste Jules (1763–1844)
Marshal in French emperor Napoleon I's army who in 1818 became Charles XIV of Sweden. Hence, Bernadotte is the family name of the present royal house of Sweden.

&A Republican by principle and devotion, I will, until
my death, oppose all Royalists.9

Jean-Baptiste Bernadotte, letter to the French Directory, September 1797.

Bismarck, Otto Eduard Leopold von (1815–1898)

German politician chancellor of Prussia 1862–90, and chancellor of the German Empire 1871–90. He pursued an aggressively expansionist policy, waging wars against Denmark 1863–64, Austria 1866, and France 1870–71. He was largely responsible for the unification of Germany. He became prince in 1871.

1864	Bismarck secures Austria's support for his successful war against Denmark.
1866	Bismarck goes to war against Austria and its allies (the **Seven Weeks' War**), his victory forcing Austria out of the German federation.

Bismarck *Chancellor of Prussia and, from 1871, the German Empire.*

1867 He unifies the northern German states into the North German Confederation with himself as chancellor.

1870–71 Bismarck defeats France (under **Napoleon III)** in the **Franco-Prussian War** and annexes **Alsace-Lorraine**.

1873–87 He constructs the **Alliance System** in an effort to keep France isolated.

At home Bismarck ran into difficulties with the Roman Catholic Church and the socialist movement and was forced to resign by **Wilhelm II** on 18 March 1890.

Bismarck is credited with inventing *realpolitik*, but the first exponent was in fact **Cavour**, the Piedmontese prime minister

Bizonia

Name given to the unified US and British occupied zones of Germany after I January 1947. This was an attempt to get the German economy going again and aid recovery from the Second World War. Bizonia became Trizonia in April 1948 with the inclusion of the French zone.

Bizonia was a major factor in the breakdown of relations between East and West. The Allies had agreed that all decisions affecting the whole of Germany had to be unanimous.

Black Death

Great epidemic of bubonic plague that ravaged Europe in the mid-14th century, killing between one-third and half of the population (about 75 million people). At the time, people blamed strangers and stray animals, or believed that the plague was punishment from God. The real cause of the plague was a bacterium transmitted by fleas carried by migrating Asian black rats, which arrived in Europe on ships. The name 'Black Death' was first used in England in the early 19th century.

Amongst the reasons given for the outbreak of the Black Death were, strangers, stray animals, Jews, and God.

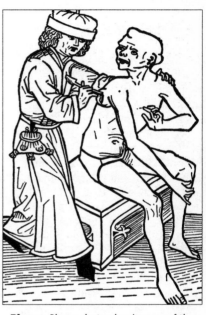

Plague *Plague doctor, lancing one of the boils characteristic of the disease.*

Black Hand Gang

Secret terrorist organization active in Serbia from 1912. In June 1914, seven members of the Serbian nationalist gang planned to assassinate Archduke **Franz Ferdinand** at Sarajevo in Bosnia. The eldest member of the gang was Nedjelko Cabrinovic (1895–1981) aged nineteen, the youngest was only fifteen. Cabrinovic attempted to kill the archduke with a bomb, but missed. Cabrinovic then swallowed poison and threw himself into the river in an attempt to kill himself. However,

Princip only got the chance to shoot the archduke and his wife because he was standing outside a cake shop in a side street. The archduke's car stopped right in front of the shop, when the driver was told that he was going the wrong way.

since the poison only made him violently sick and the river was only two feet deep, his attempt failed. He was dragged from the river by the police and arrested. Gavrilo Princip (1896–1920) aged eighteen, subsequently shot the archduke and his wife as they drove back from the town hall.

The assassination started the chain of events that led to the outbreak of **World War I**.

Blenheim, Battle of

In the War of the **Spanish Succession**, the Battle of Blenheim on 13 August 1704 was a decisive victory for the allied troops under the British Duke of Marlborough (1650–1722) against French and Bavarian armies near the Bavarian village of Blenheim (now in Germany) on the left bank of the River Danube.

Marlborough decided on one of the biggest gambles in military history. He left his base in the Low Countries (the Netherlands) and marched 500 km/311 mi across Europe to **Austria** to join up with **Prince Eugene**, the Austrian commander. The allies attacked the French army near the village of Blenheim, taking the French completely by surprise. The victory was so great that Marlborough was given the palace at Woodstock in Oxfordshire, England, (now Blenheim Palace) as a reward. One of Marlborough's distant descendants, the future British prime minister Winston Churchill (1879–1965), was born at the palace 170 years later.

Marlborough owed his appointment to his wife's (Sarah Churchill) friendship with Queen Anne (1665–1714). Marlborough was dismissed in 1711 when the Queen turned her attentions from Sarah to Abigail Masham.

Although the war was to continue for a further eight years, the Battle of Blenheim marked the turning point at which the power of France was first broken.

> ❝How could God do this to me after all I have done for Him?❞
>
> **Louis XIV**, King of France, attributed remark, on hearing of the defeat of the French at the Battle of Blenheim.

Blücher, Gebhard Leberecht von (1742–1819)

Prussian general and field marshal, popularly known as 'Marshal Forward', who took an active part in the patriotic movement. In the War of German Liberation, he defeated the French as commander-in-chief at

Leipzig in 1813, crossed the Rhine to Paris 1814, and was made prince of Wahlstadt (Silesia).

In 1815 he was defeated by French emperor **Napoleon I** at Ligny but came to the aid of the British Duke of Wellington at **Waterloo**. The arrival of the Prussians on the battlefield at about 5.30 pm on 18 June 1815 was decisive in the final defeat of Napoleon.

❦ What a place to plunder! ❧

Gebhart von Blucher, on viewing London from St Paul's, 1814.

Bolshevik

From Russian *bolshinstvo* 'a majority', the term referred to a member of the 'majority' of the Russian Social Democratic Party who split from the **Mensheviks** in 1903. The Bolsheviks, under the Soviet leader Vladimir **Lenin**, believed that a small committed party was essential if they were to seize power in Russia.

The Bolsheviks were taken by surprise when the **February Revolution** led to the abdication of Tsar **Nicholas II**, but they went on to seize power in October 1917.

In fact there were always more Mensheviks than Bolsheviks. The names reflected the result of a vote taken in 1903 when the Social Democratic Party split into two, but the names stuck.

They changed their name to the Russian Communist Party 1918.

Bonaparte

Corsican family of Italian origin that gave rise to the Napoleonic dynasty of **Napoleon I** and **Napoleon III**. Others were the brothers and sister of Napoleon I.

- **Joseph** (1768–1844) whom Napoleon made king of Naples in 1806 and of Spain in 1808.

- **Lucien** (1775–1840) whose handling of the Council of Five Hundred on 10 November 1799 ensured Napoleon I's future.

- **Louis** (1778–1846), the father of Napoleon III, who was made king of Holland from 1806 to 1810; he was also called (from 1810) the comte de Saint Leu.

- **Caroline** (1782–1839) who married Joachim Murat in 1800; her full name was Maria Annunciata Caroline.

- **Jerome** (1784–1860) who was made king of Westphalia in 1807.

Borodino, Battle of

French victory over Russian forces under the Russian commander Mikhail Kutusov on 7 September 1812 near the village of Borodino, during the French emperor **Napoleon I's** invasion of Russia. This was one of the bloodiest battles of the Napoleonic years: there were 15,000 Russian fatalities and 25,000 wounded; the French lost about 28,000, including 12 generals.

See also: *Beresina.*

Bosnian Crisis

Period of international tension in 1908 when Austria annexed the provinces of Bosnia and Herzegovina, which had been occupied by Austria since 1878.

Austria obtained Russian approval in exchange for conceding Russian access to the Bosporus straits, linking the Black Sea and the Sea of Marmara between Europe and Asia.

The speed of the Austrian action took Russia by surprise, and domestic opposition led to the resignation of Russian foreign minister Izvolsky. Russia also failed to obtain necessary French and British agreements on the straits.

> The annexation led to increased tension between Austria-Hungary and Serbia because the population of Bosnia-Herzegovina was 80% Serbian.

Braganza

The royal house of Portugal whose members reigned from 1640 to 1910; members of another branch of Braganza were emperors of Brazil in the period 1822 to 1889.

Brandt, Willy (1913–1992)

Brandt was a German socialist politician and federal chancellor (prime minister) of West Germany from 1969 to 1974.

- As mayor of West Berlin 1957–66, Brandt became internationally known during the **Berlin Wall** crisis of 1961. He was awarded the Nobel Peace Prize in 1971.

- In the 'grand coalition' of 1966–69, Brandt served as foreign minister and introduced *Ostpolitik*, a policy of reconciliation between East and West Europe, which was continued when he became federal chancellor in 1969. It culminated in the signing of the Basic Treaty with East Germany in 1972.

- He chaired the Brandt Commission in 1977–83, which studied world development issues, and was a member of the European Parliament from 1979–83.

- The Brandt Commission produced the significant report *North–South: A Programme for Survival* (1980), which advocated urgent action by the relatively wealthy, industrialized countries of the northern hemisphere to improve conditions in the poorer southern hemisphere (the developing countries or the Third World).

Braun, Eva (1912–1945)
Mistress of German dictator Adolf **Hitler**, Eva Braun was secretary to Hitler's photographer and personal friend, Heinrich Hoffmann. She became Hitler's mistress in the 1930s and married him in the air-raid shelter of the chancellery in Berlin on 29 April 1945. The next day they committed suicide together.

Breitenfeld, Battle of
Victory of a joint Swedish-Saxon force under King **Gustavus Adolphus** over Imperial forces under Count Tilly (1559–1632) on 17 September 1631 at Breitenfeld during the **Thirty Years' War**. While Gustavus was negotiating alliances with Brandenburg and Saxony, Tilly sacked Magdeburg, which he had promised to relieve. The Swedes were joined by the Saxons and Tilly was driven back. He died from wounds sustained during the battle.
    See also: *Lützen.*

Brest Litovsk, Treaty of
Treaty signed on 3 March 1918 between Russia and the Central European countries of Germany, **Austria-Hungary**, and their allies. Under its terms, Russia agreed to recognize the independence of Georgia, Ukraine, Poland, and the Baltic States, and to pay heavy compensation. Russia lost about 25% of its population. Soviet leader Vladimir **Lenin** was forced to agree to the terms imposed because of the imminent outbreak of civil war in Russia.

> Lenin had to force Trotsky, who was the Bolshevik negotiator at Brest Litovsk, to agree to the terms of the Treaty.

The treaty was annulled under the terms of the November 1918 armistice that ended **World War I** since Russia was one of the winning allies.

Brezhnev, Leonid Ilyich (1906–1982)
Soviet leader who came to power after he and Soviet politician Alexei Kosygin (1904–1980) forced Nikita **Khrushchev** to resign from the premiership in 1964, when Kosygin replaced him and Brezhnev was elected general secretary of the Soviet Communist Party (CPSU). In 1977 he gained the additional title of state president under the new constitution.

- The Brezhnev era witnessed mounting domestic problems, including economic caution and stagnation as well as political corruption.
- The Brezhnev Doctrine stated that the USSR had the right to invade any neighbouring country where socialism (the establishment of a classless

Some Soviet historians believe that Brezhnev suffered an illness (thought to have been a stroke or heart attack) in March–April 1976 that was believed to have affected his thought and speech so severely that he was not able to make decisions.

society with public ownership of the means of production, distribution, and exchange) was threatened. For example, Brezhnev committed US troops to Afghanistan in 1979 to support the Marxist government there.

Brissot, Jacques Pierre (1754–1793)
French revolutionary leader, born in Chartres. He became a member of the Legislative Assembly during the French Revolution and later of the National Convention, but his party of moderate republicans, the **Girondins**, or Brissotins, was ousted when French Jacobin leader Maximilien **Robespierre** and the **Jacobins** executed King Louis XVI and seized power.

Brownshirts
The SA (*Sturmabteilung*) or Storm Troopers constituted the private army of the German Nazi party, founded in 1919 and led by German dictator Adolf **Hitler**. They derived their name from the colour of their uniform.

Bukharin, Nikolai Ivanovich (1888–1938)
Soviet politician and theorist, he was the chief **Bolshevik** thinker after Soviet theorist and leader Vladimir **Lenin**. Bukharin was executed in 1938 on a charge of treason on the orders of Soviet leader Joseph **Stalin.** However, political and national opinion later restored his reputation and Bukharin was officially rehabilitated in 1988.

Bukharin was the architect of the **New Economic Policy**, but was forced out of power by Stalin in 1928. In 1938 he was imprisoned and tried for treason in one of Stalin's **Show Trials**. He pleaded guilty to treason, but defended his moderate policies and denied criminal charges. Nevertheless, he was executed, as were all other former members of Lenin's central committee, except the Russian revolutionary Leon **Trotsky**, who was murdered.

❝ We might have a two-party system, but one of the two parties would be in office and the other in prison. ❞

Nikolai Ivanovich Bukharin, attributed remark.

Bulganin, Nikolai Aleksandrovich (1895–1975)

Soviet politician and military leader Bulganin's career began in 1918 when he joined the **Cheka**, the Soviet secret police. He helped to organize Moscow's defences in World War II, became a marshal of the USSR in 1947, and was minister of defence 1947–49 and 1953–55. On the fall of Georgi **Malenkov**, he became prime minister 1955–58 until ousted by Nikita **Khrushchev.**

Bulganin was allowed to remain as prime minister by Khrushchev from 1957 to 1958 because he was due to visit Britain. Khrushchev thought that it would look bad if he were dismissed before the visit.

Burgundy

An ancient kingdom and later duchy in the Carolingian Empire (founded by Pepin the Short in 751, which controlled France until 987 and Germany until 911), Burgundy was acquired by the Capetian king Robert the Pious in 1002, and until 1361 it was the most important and loyal fiefdom in the realm.

With the death of the last Capetian duke, Philip of Rouvre, in 1361, the duchy went to the Valois king John II (1319–1364). The Valois dukes acquired Hainault in 1428, Brabant and Limburg in 1430, and Luxembourg in 1443. The economically advanced Netherlands brought the duchy great wealth, and it was here that the new Burgundy had its centre, rather than in its ancient southern territories.

In the 15th century this wealthy region was the glittering capital of European court culture. The duchy was incorporated into France on the death of Burgundy duke Charles the Bold (1433–1477).

See also: *Capet, Hugh.*

Calvin, John also known as Cauvin or Chauvin (1509–1564)

Born in Noyon, in the northern French region of Picardy (Picardie), Calvin studied theology and then law, and in about 1533 became prominent in Paris as an evangelical preacher. In 1534 he was forced to leave Paris and moved to Basel (Basle) in Switzerland, where he studied Hebrew. In 1536 he accepted an invitation to Geneva, Switzerland, to assist in the religious reform movement there (the **Reformation**), but was expelled in 1538 because of the drastic changes he introduced.

He returned to Geneva in 1541 and set up the Calvinist Church, which had very strict rules. All aspects of life in the city were controlled by the church, including:

- shop prices;
- street cleaning;
- hotels and inns;
- people's names.

John Calvin *Founder of the Calvinist Church*

Members of the church patrolled the streets enforcing the rules, and people who broke the rules could be fined and whipped. One boy who attacked his parents was beheaded.

Cambrai, League of

An alliance formed at Cambrai in northern France in December 1508 by European powers hostile to Venice. The stated aim of the Holy Roman Emperor Maximilian I (1459–1519), Louis XII (1462–1515) of France, and **Ferdinand II** of Aragon was to fight the Ottoman Turks, but in practice their objective was to destroy the Venetian Empire. The alliance was joined by Pope Julius II (1443–1513) and the dukes of Mantua and Ferrara, all of whom had territorial disputes with Venice. After some initial successes, beginning with the Battle of Agnadello in 1509, the League began to collapse in 1510, owing to the defection of the pope and Ferdinand. By 1517 Venice had won back virtually all the territory it had lost.

Canossa

Meeting between the Holy Roman Emperor Henry IV and Pope Gregory VII in 1077, where the emperor was forced to do penance by the tyrannical pope. Henry had attempted to have Gregory deposed in 1076 for his strict ecclesiastical policies, including the denial of lay rights to make clerical appointments. Henry was forced to wait in the snow for four days, dressed as a penitent, before receiving pardon.

Henry was forced to crawl to meet Gregory on his knees.

Cape St Vincent, Battle of

During the French Revolutionary Wars, the battle that saw British victory over a Spanish fleet on 14 February 1797 off Cape St Vincent on the Portuguese coast; the British victory wrecked French plans to invade England. The two British commanders were both honoured for this crucial victory: John Jervis (1735–1823) became Lord St Vincent and Horatio Nelson (1759–1805) gained his knighthood.

Nelson broke one of the most important rules of naval warfare during the battle. He left the line and put his ship in the middle of the Spanish fleet, which was separated into two sections.

Capet, Hugh (938–996)

King of France from 987, when he claimed the throne on the death of Louis V (967–987) and founded the Capetian dynasty. His direct descendants ruled France until 1328, when the House of Valois succeeded to the throne, but all kings until 1830 were descended from him.

In the 10th and 11th centuries the Capetians ruled only the area around Paris and found themselves constantly at war with neighbouring rulers. For example, William of Normandy (1027–1087) tried to seize possession of the Vexin, the area due west of Paris and was killed fighting there in 1087. In the 12th century the Capetians were threatened by the ambitions of

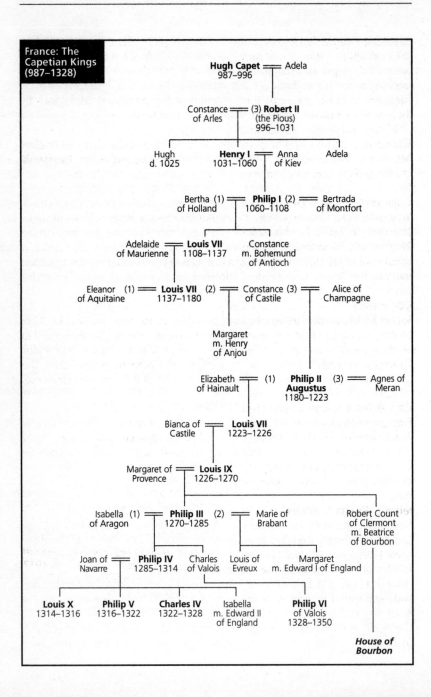

France: The Capetian Kings (987–1328)

Hugh Capet 987–996 ═ Adela

Constance of Arles ═ (3) **Robert II** (the Pious) 996–1031

Hugh d. 1025 — **Henry I** 1031–1060 ═ Anna of Kiev — Adela

Bertha (1) of Holland ═ **Philip I** 1060–1108 (2) ═ Bertrada of Montfort

Adelaide of Maurienne ═ **Louis VII** 1108–1137 — Constance m. Bohemund of Antioch

Eleanor (1) of Aquitaine ═ **Louis VII** 1137–1180 (2) ═ Constance of Castile (3) ═ Alice of Champagne

Margaret m. Henry of Anjou

Elizabeth of Hainault ═ (1) **Philip II Augustus** 1180–1223 (3) ═ Agnes of Meran

Bianca of Castile ═ **Louis VII** 1223–1226

Margaret of Provence ═ **Louis IX** 1226–1270

Isabella (1) of Aragon ═ **Philip III** 1270–1285 (2) ═ Marie of Brabant — Robert Count of Clermont m. Beatrice of Bourbon

Joan of Navarre ═ **Philip IV** 1285–1314 — Charles of Valois — Louis of Evreux — Margaret m. Edward I of England

Louis X 1314–1316 — **Philip V** 1316–1322 — **Charles IV** 1322–1328 — Isabella m. Edward II of England — **Philip VI** of Valois 1328–1350

House of Bourbon

English king Henry II (1133–1189) who already controlled Anjou in France and who had set his sights on an Angevin (Anjou) Empire to include the whole of France.

When Louis XVI was arrested in 1791, he was known as Louis Capet by the Republicans.

By the end of the 12th century France was unified by **Philip II**, only to fall apart again after the English began the Hundred Years' War in 1337 and the dukes of **Burgundy** challenged for control of France.

Caporetto, Battle of
In **World War I**, joint German-Austrian victory over the Italian army in October 1917. The battle took place at Caporetto (Kobarid), a village on the River Isonzo in northwest Slovenia. The German commander, Gen Karl von Bülow (1849–1929), broke through Italian lines on the Isonzo, forcing their retreat.

Carbonari
Secret revolutionary society in southern Italy in the first half of the 19th century that supported constitutional government. The movement spread to northern Italy but support fell after the formation of Italian nationalist Giuseppe Mazzini's 'Young Italy' nationalist movement (Giovane Italia). The Carbonari helped pave the way for the unification of Italy, the Risorgimento.

Catherine (II) the Great (1729–1796)
Empress of Russia from 1762, she was the daughter of the German prince of Anhalt-Zerbst. In 1745, Catherine married the Russian grand duke Peter (1728–1762). Catherine dominated her husband, who, six months after he became Tsar Peter III in 1762, was murdered in a coup. Catherine then ruled alone. During her reign Russia extended its boundaries to include territory gained from wars with the Turks from 1768 to 1774 and 1787 to 1792, and from the **partitions of Poland** 1772, 1793, and 1795, and established control over the Black Sea.

Catherine was notorious for her love affairs, but was also known for her correspondence with French writer François-Marie Voltaire (1694–1778) and for founding the first girls' school in Russia in the Smolni Convent. In 1917 the convent became the headquarters of the **Bolsheviks**.

> ❝I shall be an autocrat: that's my trade. And the good Lord will forgive me: that's his.❞
>
> **Catherine (II) the Great**, attributed remark.

Catherine de' Medici (1519–1589)

French queen, wife of Henry II, whom she married in 1533, Catherine was the daughter of Lorenzo de' **Medici**, Duke of Urbino; and mother of Francis II (1544–1560), Charles IX (1550–1574), and Henry III (1551–1589). At first outshone by Henry's mistress Diane de Poitiers (1490–1566), she became regent 1560–63 for Charles IX and remained in power until his death in 1574.

During the religious wars of 1562–69, she first supported the Protestant Huguenots against the Roman Catholic Guises to ensure her own position as ruler; she later opposed them, and has been traditionally implicated in the **Massacre of St Bartholomew** of 1572.

See also: *Coligny.*

Cavour, Camillo Benso di, Count (1810–1861)

Italian nationalist politician and a leading figure in the Italian unification, Cavour was prime minister of **Piedmont** 1852–59 and 1860–61.

As prime minister, he gained French and British sympathy for Italian unity by sending Piedmontese troops to fight in the Crimean War. In 1858 he had a secret meeting with French emperor **Napoleon III** at Plombières and won French support in the war of 1859 against Austria, which resulted in the union of Lombardy with Piedmont. The central Italian states subsequently joined the kingdom of Italy, although Savoy and Nice were given to France.

> Cavour was the inventor of *realpolitik*. He sent Piedmontese troops to fight in the Crimea for the express purpose of gaining French support in his efforts to drive the Austrians out of northern Italy.

With Cavour's approval, Italian soldier Giuseppe **Garibaldi** overthrew the Neapolitan monarchy. However, Cavour occupied part of the **Papal States**, which, with Naples and Sicily, were annexed to Italy to prevent Garibaldi from marching on Rome.

See also: *Mazzini; Pius IX.*

> 𝒢 Rome must be the capital of Italy because without
> Rome Italy cannot be constituted. 𝟇
>
> **Count Camillo di Cavour**, speech given in Turin, 25 March 1861.

Ceaușescu, Nicolae (1918–89)

Romanian politician and leader of the Romanian Communist Party (RCP), in power 1965–89. Ceaușescu pursued a policy of independence from the USSR (Romania had previously been part of Comecon, linking the country economically to the USSR, and the **Warsaw Pact**). He appointed family members, including his wife Elena Ceaușescu (1919–1989), to senior state and party posts, and governed in an increasingly repressive manner. The Ceaușescus were overthrown in a bloody revolutionary coup in December 1989 and executed on Christmas Day that year. After Nicolae Ceaușescu's execution, the full extent of his family's repressive rule and personal extravagances became public.

Central Powers

Originally the signatories of the **Triple Alliance** of 1882: Germany, **Austria-Hungary**, and Italy; the name derived from the geographical position of the Germans and Austrians in Central Europe. During **World War I**, Italy remained neutral before joining the Allies.

Charlemagne, Charles I the Great (742–814)

King of the Franks from 768 and Holy Roman Emperor from 800, Charlemagne by inheritance and extensive conquest had united most of Western Europe by 804, when, after 30 years of war, the Saxons came under his control.

CHARLEMAGNE'S CONQUESTS:

- In 777 Charlemagne crossed the Pyrenees, in 778 he reached the Ebro but had to turn back from Zaragoza.
- The independent duchy of Bavaria was incorporated in the kingdom in 788.
- The Avar people were subdued from 791 to 796.
- From 792 northern Saxony was subdued, and in 804 the whole region came under his rule.
- In 801 the district between the Pyrenees and the Llobregat was organized as the Spanish March.

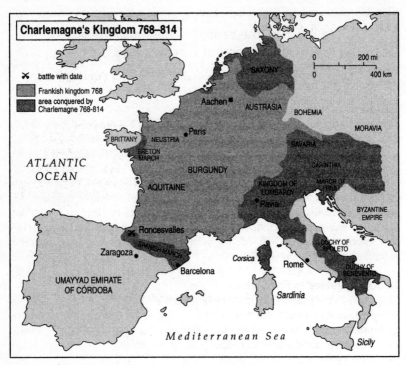

Charlemagne *Map showing the extent of Charlemagne's Kingdom by the end of his reign.*

In Rome, during Mass on Christmas Day 800, Pope Leo III (c. 750–816) crowned Charlemagne emperor. As emperor, Charlemagne had enjoyed diplomatic relations with Byzantium, Baghdad, Mercia, Northumbria, and other regions.

The *Chanson of Roland* describes the rearguard action of his knight Roland against the attacks of the Moors in Spain.

CHARLEMAGNE'S REFORMS:

- Jury courts were introduced and the laws of the Franks revised.
- A new coinage was introduced, weights and measures were reformed, and communications were improved.
- Charlemagne demonstrated a lively interest in theology, systemized the church in his dominions, and organized missionaries and monastic reform.
- He persuaded the Northumbrian scholar Alcuin (c. 737–804) to enter his service in 781 and Charlemagne gathered an elementary academy around him. Although the emperor failed to learn to read, he collected the old heroic sagas, began a Frankish grammar, and promoted religious instruction in the vernacular.
- Charlemagne died on 28 January 814 in Aachen, where he was buried.

Charlemagne *King of the Franks from 768 and Holy Roman Emperor from 800*

Charles X (1757–1836)

King of France from 1824, Charles was a grandson of **Louis XV**, and brother of **Louis XVI** and **Louis XVIII**. Before his accession, he was known as the comte d'Artois. He fled to England at the beginning of the **French Revolution**, and when he came to the throne on the death of Louis XVIII, he attempted to modify the results of the Revolution. A revolt ensued in 1830, and he again fled to England.

Charles V (1500–1558)

Holy Roman Emperor 1519–56, Charles was the son of Philip of Burgundy (1478–1506) and Joanna of Castile (1479–1555). He inherited vast possessions:

Charles V was the uncle of Catherine of Aragon (1485–1536), the first wife of King Henry VIII (1491–1547) of England. When Henry tried to divorce Catherine, Charles took Pope Clement VII (1478–1534) prisoner and forced him to refuse to agree to the divorce, resulting in Henry VIII's break with papal authority.

Charles V *Holy Roman Emperor from 1519 to 1556 and King of Spain from 1516.*

- He acquired the Netherlands from his father in 1506;
- Spain, Naples, Sicily, Sardinia, and the Spanish dominions in North Africa and the Americas on the death of his maternal grandfather, Ferdinand V of Castile (1452–1516);
- The Habsburg dominions in 1519 from his paternal grandfather, **Maximilian I.**

As emperor he was in constant conflict with Francis I (1494–1547) of France, whose alliance with the Ottoman Empire brought Vienna under siege in 1529 and 1532. Charles was also in conflict with the Protestants in Germany until the Treaty of Passau of 1552, which allowed the Lutherans religious liberty.

He abdicated in 1556 and retired to a monastery in Spain.

> ❝I came, I saw, God conquered. ❞
>
> **Charles V**, after defeating the Protestant princes at the Battle of Muhlberg, 23 April 1547.

Charles X (1622–1660)

King of Sweden from 1654, when he succeeded his cousin

Charles was accidentally shot by his own troops in 1660.

Christina. Charles waged war with Poland and Denmark and in 1657 invaded the latter by leading his army over the frozen sea.

Checkpoint Charlie
Western-controlled crossing point for non-Germans between West Berlin and East Berlin, opened in 1961 as the only crossing point along the **Berlin Wall** that divided the Allied and Soviet sectors of the city. Its dismantling in June 1990 was seen as a symbol of the ending of the **Cold War**.

Cheka
Secret police operating in the USSR from 1917–23. It originated from the tsarist Okhrana (the security police under the tsar 1881–1917), and became the OGPU (GPU) from 1923 to 1934, the **NKVD** in 1934 to 1946, the MVD in 1946 to 1953, and the KGB from 1954.

The name was formed from the initials che and ka of the two Russian words meaning 'extraordinary commission', formed for 'the repression of counter-revolutionary activities and of speculation', and extended to cover such matters as espionage and smuggling.

> Under **War Communism** the Cheka murdered at least 50,000 people for hoarding food.

Chemin des Dames
Road in the *département* of Aisne, France, from Craonne to Malmaison across the crest of the Craonne plateau. Its possession was fiercely contested throughout **World War I** and it was the scene of a major battle in April 1917.

Gen Robert Nivelle (1857–1924) decided on an offensive to capture the road, the plateau, and the Aisne valley beyond. After a prolonged and fierce battle the French finally captured the road and plateau by the beginning of November 1917. During the German Spring Offensive of 1918 the French were driven from their position and the road passed back into German hands. Finally, in the Allied advance of September 1918 the road was retaken by Gen Charles Mangin's 10th Army.

Chernenko, Konstantin Ustinovich (1911–1985)
Soviet politician, who was leader of the Communist Party of the Soviet Union (CPSU) and

> Chernenko was taken ill with the incurable lung condition emphysema almost as soon as he became the leader of the Soviet Union. His illness contributed to the inertia in superpower relations (between the USA and Russia) from 1980 to 1985.

president from 1984–85. Chernenko was a protégé of Soviet leader Leonid Brezhnev and from 1978 a member of the Politburo.

When President Yuri Andropov died in February 1984, Chernenko was selected as the CPSU's stopgap leader by cautious party colleagues and was also elected president. From July 1984 he gradually retired from public life because of failing health.

Chetnik
Member of a Serbian nationalist group that operated underground during the German occupation of Yugoslavia in **World War II**. Led by Col Draza Mihailovic (1893–1946), the Chetniks initially received aid from the Allies, but this was later transferred to the communist partisans led by Yugoslav statesman Marshal **Tito**. The term was also popularly applied to Serb militia forces in the 1991–92 Yugoslav civil war.

See also: *Balkans.*

Choiseul, Etienne François, duc de (1719–1785)
French politician, who was originally a protégé of Madame de Pompadour (1721–1764), the mistress of **Louis XV**. He became minister for foreign affairs in 1758, and held this and other offices until 1770. He banished the Roman Catholic Jesuits, and was a supporter of the 18th-century European social and scientific movement, the Enlightenment, through the works of French philosophers Denis Diderot (1767–1837) and François-Marie Voltaire (1694–1778).

Christina (1626–1689)
Queen of Sweden 1632–54, she succeeded her father **Gustavus Adolphus** at the age of six and assumed power in 1644, but disagreed with the former regent **Oxenstjerna**. Refusing to marry, she eventually nominated her cousin Charles Gustavus (**Charles X**) as her successor. As a secret convert to Roman Catholicism, which was then illegal in Sweden, she abdicated in 1654, and went to live in Rome, twice returning to Sweden and attempting, unsuccessfully, to claim the throne.

Civil War, Spanish
War of 1936–39 brought on by a military revolt led by Spanish general Francisco **Franco** against the Republican government. Franco's Falangists (nationalists, who were supported by **Fascist** Italy and **Nazi** Germany) seized power in the south and northwest, but were suppressed in areas such as Madrid and Barcelona by the workers' militia. The loyalists (Republicans) were aided by the USSR and the volunteers of the International Brigade, which included several writers, among them the British writer George Orwell (1903–1950).

1937 Bilbao and the Basque country are bombed into submission by the nationalists.

1938 Cataluña is cut off from the main Republican territory.

1939 Barcelona falls in January and Madrid in March, and Franco establishes a dictatorship.

See also: *Falange.*

Clay, Lucius DuBignon (1897–1978)

US commander-in-chief of the US occupation forces in Germany 1947–49. Clay fought the Soviet blockade of **Berlin** in 1948 for 327 days, with an airlift, a term he brought into general use, which involved bringing all supplies into West Berlin by air. He reasoned that ' ... if West Berlin falls, West Germany will be next'.

Colbert, Jean-Baptiste (1619–1683)

French politician, chief minister to Louis XIV, and controller-general (finance minister) from 1665, Colbert reformed the Treasury, promoted French industry and commerce by protecting it against foreign trade, and tried to make France a naval power equal to England or the Netherlands, while favouring a peaceful foreign policy.

Cold War

Ideological, political, and economic tensions during 1945 and 1989 between the USSR and Eastern Europe on the one hand and the USA and Western Europe on the other. The Cold War was a war of propaganda, spying, and economic sanctions. Arms-reduction agreements between the USA and the USSR in the late 1980s, together with a reduction of Soviet influence in Eastern Europe, led to a reassessment of positions, and the 'war' was officially ended in December 1989.

The term 'Cold War' was first used by Bernard Baruch, advisor to US president Harry S Truman (1884–1972).

> ❝ Let us not be deceived – we are today in the midst of a cold war. ❞
>
> **Bernard Baruch**, US financier, speech to South Carolina Legislature, 16 April 1947.

Coligny, Gaspard de (1519–1572)

French admiral, soldier, and a prominent Huguenot (French Protestant), Coligny joined the Protestant cause in about 1557 and helped to lead the Huguenot forces during the **Wars of Religion**. After the Treaty of St Germain of 1570, he became a favourite of the young king Charles IX (1550–1574), but was killed on the first night of the **Massacre of St Bartholomew**.

collectivization

Policy pursued by the Soviet leader Josef **Stalin** in the USSR after 1928. Its aim was to reorganize agriculture by taking land into state ownership or creating collective farms (where the work and the profits are divided between the farmers). This was achieved by brute force during the first and second of Stalin's 'five year plans', with much loss of life among the peasantry.

Resistance to collectivization was so strong, especially among the prosperous peasants or **kulaks**, that productivity remained low on the new farms. Many peasants killed their livestock and destroyed their farm equipment when forced to join the collectives, while the mass deportations of those who refused to give up their private land meant that many experienced farmers were lost to other countries.

10,000,000 people may have died in the famine that followed the introduction of collectivization. The process was more or less complete by 1937, but peasants retained control of their own plots of land. These were reckoned to constitute 70% of the agricultural production of the Soviet Union.

See also: *five-year plans; purges; show trials*.

Cominform

The acronym from letters in the name of the Communist Information Bureau that existed from 1947 to 1956, established to exchange information between European communist parties. The Cominform was a revival of the Communist International or Comintern, which had been formally disbanded in 1943.

The Cominform was made up of nine European communist parties (Soviet, Czechoslovak, Polish, Hungarian, Romanian, Bulgarian, Yugoslav, French, and Italian) who announced their decision to set up an 'Information Bureau' in Belgrade. Yugoslavia was expelled in 1948.

The Cominform was intended to keep before public opinion the fact that communism was an international movement working to a plan. But, in practice, the existence of the Cominform damaged the communist cause far more than promoted it.

Committee of Public Safety

In the French Revolution, a body appointed by the members of the National Convention in 1793 to supervise the actions of the government. However, the Committee of Public Safety took virtually dictatorial control over the country, and began the **Reign of Terror**. Its principal spokesman was the French Jacobin leader Maximilien **Robespierre**.

Using propaganda to control public opinion, the Committee created a war machine based on conscription, the direction of labour, price controls and the requisitioning of food and scarce materials.

Confederation of the Rhine
Union of German states established under French protection after the abolition of the **Holy Roman Empire** in 1806. A French puppet confederation, it was designed to allow French emperor **Napoleon I** to dominate the German states. The union lasted until 1813.

Napoleon adopted the title of Protector of the Confederation of the Rhine.

Congress System
A series of international meetings that developed from the Congress of Vienna 1814–15 at the end of the Napoleonic Wars, held in Aachen, Germany, in 1818, Troppau, Austria, in 1820, and Verona, Italy, in 1822. Klemens **Metternich**, the Austrian chancellor, tried to use the congresses as a weapon against liberal and national movements inside Europe. This brought them to an end as a way of settling international disputes, although congresses continued to meet throughout the 19th century.

The British foreign secretary Lord Castlereagh (1769–1822) attended the first two congresses, but refused to attend the last two because he believed that they were going to use force against countries in western Europe.

See also: *Holy Alliance.*

Constance, Council of
Council held by the Roman Catholic Church 1414–17 in Constance, Germany. It elected Pope Martin V, thus ending the Great Schism of 1378–1417 when there were rival popes in Rome and Avignon.

Between 1378 and 1417 there were two popes. The Avignon popes built a palace for themselves, which is still remembered in the name of the French wine, Châteauneuf du Pape.

Continental System
An attempt to starve Britain into submission by preventing trade with Continental Europe from 1806 to 1813, initiated by the French emperor

Napoleon I. Apart from its function as economic warfare, the system also reinforced the French economy at the expense of other European states. The system failed owing to British naval superiority.
See also: *Napoleonic Wars; Tilsit.*

The Continental System had the effect of doubling the price of bread in Britain from 1805 to 1811.

Corday, Charlotte (Marie-Anne Charlotte Corday d'Armont) (1768–1793)

A member of the French **Girondin** party (right-wing republicans during the **French Revolution**), who murdered the **Montagnard** leader Jean Paul

Charlotte Corday forced her way into Marat's house claiming that she had urgent busines with Citizen Marat.

Marat. After the overthrow of the Girondins by the extreme left-wing Jacobins in May 1793, Corday stabbed Marat to death with a bread knife as he sat in his bath in July of the same year. She was guillotined.

❝I have done my task, let others do theirs.❞

Charlotte Corday, on being interrogated for the murder of Marat, July 1793.

Corfu Incident

International crisis from 27 August to 27 September 1923. In 1923 an international commission was in the process of determining the frontier between Greece and Albania. On 27 August 1923, the chief of the commission, Italian general Tellini was found murdered (together with four of his staff) near the Albanian border, but on Greek territory. The Italian government under Benito **Mussolini** sent an ultimatum to the Greek government demanding compensation, which was rejected. On 31 August Mussolini ordered the Italian

The Corfu Incident created the impression that there was one law for small countries and another for large countries. Italy, a permanent member of the Council of the League, had been allowed to get away with aggression against another member of the League of Nations.

bombardment and occupation of the Greek island of Corfu. The Greeks appealed to the **League of Nations** and, under pressure from Britain and France, Mussolini withdrew from Corfu on 27 September 1923. Greece had to accept most of the Italian demands, including the payment of a large indemnity.

Council of Europe
Body set up in 1949 to achieve greater unity between European countries, to help economic and social progress, and to uphold the principles of parliamentary democracy and respect for human rights.

In addition to its concern for human rights, the council is active in the fields of mass media, social welfare, health, population trends, migration, social equality, crime, education, culture, youth affairs, sport, and the environment. It cooperates with the United Nations (UN) and other international organizations, and has particularly close relations with the European Union (EU).

Counter-Reformation
Measures initiated by the Catholic Church at the Council of **Trent** (1545–63) to counter the spread of the religious Reformation and Protestantism. The measures taken by the Council included the reaffirmation of traditional doctrine and the reorganization of the Catholic Church; the repression of heresy through increased use of the **Inquisition** and censorship, and the use of new clerical orders – the Jesuits in particular – as missionaries to 'reconvert the lost souls'.

Crécy, Battle of
First major battle of the **Hundred Years' War**, fought on 26 August 1346. Philip VI of France (1293–1350) was defeated by Edward III (1312–1377) of England at the village of Crécy-en-Ponthieu, now in the Somme *département* of France. The battle became a series of charges by the French knights, but the English archers played a crucial role in the French defeat. After the battle Edward was able to take Calais.

Edward's grandfather, Edward I (1239–1307) had learnt of the value of the longbow in his wars against the Welsh. This particular weapon was used over and over again against French knights during the Hundred Years War. It had a much quicker rate of fire than the French crossbow and a shaft could pierce plate armour.

Crimean War
War during the period 1853 to 1856 between Russia and the allied powers of England, France, Turkey, and Sardinia, arising from

When asked by his son what was the meaning of Crimea, Richard Cobden, the English politician said 'crime'.

Crimean War *Florence Nightingale nursing injured troops on the battlefield.*

British and French mistrust of Russia's ambitions in the **Balkans**. The war began with an allied Anglo-French expedition to the Crimea, a peninsula in the Ukraine region of Russia, to attack the Russian Black Sea port of **Sevastopol**. The Battles of the River Alma, **Balaclava** (including the Charge of the Light Brigade), and **Inkerman**, all in 1854, led to a siege which, owing to military mismanagement, lasted for a year until September 1855. The war ended with the **Treaty of Paris** in 1856. The scandal surrounding French and British losses through disease led to the introduction of proper military nursing services, organized by Florence Nightingale.

1853 Russia invades the Balkans and sinks the Turkish fleet at the Battle of Sinope on 30 November.

1854 Britain and France declares war on Russia, invades the Crimea, and lay siege to Sevastopol (September 1854 to September 1855) through the Battles of the Alma on 20 September, Balaclava on 25 October (including the Charge of the Light Brigade), and Inkerman on 5 November.

1855 Sardinia declares war on Russia.

1856 The Treaty of Paris in February ends the war.

❛ The angel of death has been abroad throughout the land; you may almost hear the beating of his wings. ❜

John Bright, English radical, speech in the House of Commons, February 1855, appealing for an end to the Crimean War.

Crusades, the

Series of wars undertaken between 1096 and 1291 by European rulers striving to recover Palestine (the Holy Land) from the Muslim Arabs who had seized the region in 636 AD. Crusaders went to war because of religious zeal, the desire for land, and the trading ambitions of the major Italian cities. The Crusades had varying degrees of success in their aims and effects.

Muslims regarded the Crusades as Frankish Invasions.

1099 The First Crusade retakes Jerusalem and sets up four Christian states in the Middle East.

1148 The Second Crusade is defeated at Damascus.

1187 Jerusalem is recaptured by the Egyptian sultan Saladin (1138–1193).

1189 The Third Crusade is led by Holy Roman Emperor Frederick Barbarossa (1123–1190), Philip II of France and **Richard I** (1157–1199) of England. Acre is recovered, but Jerusalem stays in Muslim hands.

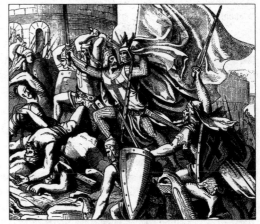

The Crusades *Crusaders entering the city of Jerusalem in 1099.*

1204 The Fourth Crusade ends in the sacking of Constantinople in Turkey.

1212 In the Children's Crusade, 30,000 children set off for Jerusalem, but get no further than Marseilles in France, where they are sold into slavery.

1228 The Sixth Crusade recovers Jerusalem, which is lost again in 1243.

Curzon Line
Polish-Soviet frontier proposed after **World War I** at the Versailles Conference in France in 1919, based on the eastward limit of areas with a largely Polish population. The frontier acquired its name after the British foreign secretary Lord Curzon (1859–1925) suggested in 1920 that the Poles, who had invaded the USSR, should retire to this line and wait for a Russo-Polish peace conference. The frontier established in 1945 generally follows the Curzon Line.

Custozza, Battle of
In the **Seven Weeks' War**, the battle that marked the Austrian victory over the Italians on 24 June 1866. Italy had allied with Prussia against Austria at the start of the war and set out to recover Venice. Their advance was halted

by defeat at Custozza, in northern Italy, but the war eventually ended with Austria having to cede Venice to the Italians.

Czechoslovakia

Chronology

8th century The area is part of **Charlemagne's** Holy Roman Empire

9th century Known as the Kingdom of Greater Moravia, the region centres around the eastern part of what is now the Czech Republic, founded by the Slavic prince Sviatopluk; Christianity is adopted.

995 An independent state of Bohemia in the northwest, centres around Prague, and becomes a kingdom in 12th century.

1355 King Charles IV of Bohemia becomes Holy Roman Emperor.

early 15th century The nationalistic Hussite religion, opposed to German and papal influence, is founded in Bohemia by John Huss.

1526 Bohemia comes under the control of the Austrian Catholic **Habsburgs.**

1618 A Hussite revolt precipitates the Thirty Years' War.

1867 Dual **Austro-Hungarian** monarchy is created..

1918 The Austro-Hungarian Empire is dismembered; the Czechs join the Slovaks in forming Czechoslovakia as an independent democratic nation, with Tomas **Masaryk** as president.

1938 Under the **Munich Agreement**, Czechoslovakia is forced to surrender the Sudeten German districts in the north to Germany .

1939 The remainder of Czechoslovakia is annexed by Germany, Bohemia-Moravia being administered as a 'protectorate'; President Eduard **Beneš** sets up a government-in-exile in London; there are liquidation campaigns against intelligentsia.

1945 The area is liberated by Soviet and US troops; a communist-dominated government of national unity is formed under **Beneš** 2 million Sudeten Germans are expelled.

1948 Beneš was ousted; the communists assumes full control under a Soviet-style single-party constitution.

1950s Political opponents are purged; industries are nationalized.

1968 The **'Prague Spring'** political liberalization programme, instituted by the Communist Party leader Alexander **Dubček**, is crushed by invading **Warsaw Pact** forces to restore the 'orthodox line.'

1969 A new federal constitution is established, creating a separate Czech Socialist Republic.

1987 The reformist Miloš Jakeš replaces Gustáv Husák (1919–1931) as communist leader, and introduces a *prestvaba* ('restructuring') reform programme based on the Soviet leader Mikhail Gorbachev's *perestroika* model.

1989 The Communist Party is stripped of its powers. A new 'grand coalition' government is formed; Václav Havel is appointed state president. Amnesty is granted to 22,000 prisoners.

1999 The Czech Republic becomes a full member of NATO.

Daladier, Edouard (1884–1970)

French politician and prime minister in 1933, 1934, and from 1938 to 1940, who signed the **Munich Agreement** in 1938, the unsuccessful attempt to halt German aggression in Europe. After declaring war on Germany in September 1939, Daladier's government failed to aid Poland and, at home, was responsible for the imprisonment of pacifists and communists. After his government resigned in March 1940, Daladier was arrested by the right-wing Vichy government authorities (who collaborated with the Germans), and was tried with Léon Blum (1872–1950) at Riom in 1942. He was then deported to Germany in 1943 (returning in 1945). Daladier was re-elected as a deputy in 1946, retaining this office until 1958.

See also: *Laval; Pétain.*

❝ It is a phoney war. ❞

Edouard Daladier, speech in Chamber of Deputies, Paris, 22 December 1939.

Danton, Georges Jacques (1759–1794)

French revolutionary, who was originally a lawyer. During the early years of the Revolution, Danton was one of the most influential people in Paris.

He organized the uprising on 10 August 1792 that overthrew **Louis XVI** and the monarchy, roused the country to expel the Prussian invaders, and in April 1793 formed the revolutionary tribunal and the **Committee of Public Safety**, of which he was the leader until July of that year.

Danton was the most popular figure in the revolutionary government. He had actually retired from public life, when he was arrested and charged with conspiring to overthrow the government.

Thereafter he lost power to the **Jacobins**, and, when he attempted to recover it, was arrested and guillotined.

See also: *Robespierre.*

Dardanelles campaign

In **World War I**, an unsuccessful Allied naval operation in 1915 against the Turkish-held Dardanelles, a narrow channel between Asiatic and European Turkey, forming a passage between the Mediterranean and the Sea of Marmora and thence to the Black Sea. After a series of unsuccessful naval attacks from January to March 1915, the idea of a purely naval attack was abandoned, and instead planning began for a military action against the Gallipoli peninsula in northwest Turkey. The only real impact of the naval attack had been to alert the Turkish army so that they had time to reinforce and fortify the area before the Gallipoli landings.

The site of the landings at Anzac Cove was actually about one and a half miles away from the correct landings. The Allied soldiers were faced with a sheer cliff, instead of gently sloping hills.

The Gallipoli Landings took place on 25 and 26 April, but failed to have any effect on the Turkish positions. Troops were mistakenly landed at the wrong places and were then forced to climb steep cliffs, which were overlooked by the Turkish positions. Further landings took place in August, also without success. The whole force was evacuated in December 1915.

Darlan, Jean Louis Xavier François (1881–1942)

French admiral and politician, Darlan entered the navy in 1899, and was appointed admiral and commander-in-chief in 1939. He commanded the French navy from 1939 to 1940, took part in the evacuation of Dunkirk during **World War II**, and entered the cabinet under Vichy general Henri **Pétain** as naval minister. In 1941 he was appointed vice premier, and adopted a strongly pro-German

Darlan was shot as part of an Allied plot to seize control of the French territories in North Africa.

stance in the hope of obtaining better conditions for the French people, with little success. When Pierre Laval replaced Pétain in 1942, Darlan was dropped from the cabinet and sent to North Africa, where he was assassinated by the Allies on 24 December.

Dawes Plan

A loan of $200 million that enabled Germany to pay enormous war debts after **World War I**. The loan temporarily reduced tensions in Europe but was superseded by the Young Plan (which reduced the total reparations bill) in 1929. Charles Dawes (1865–1951), who instigated the loan plan, was made

US vice-president in 1924, under Calvin Coolidge (1872–1933), received the Nobel Peace Prize in 1925, and was ambassador to the UK from 1929 to 1932.

D-day

The day of the Allied invasion of Normandy on 6 June 1944, under the command of US general Dwight Eisenhower (1890–1969), to commence Operation Overlord, the liberation of Western Europe from German occupation. The Anglo–US invasion fleet landed on the Normandy beaches

There were only three days in June when it would be possible to launch D-day, – 4, 5, and 6 June. On the first two days the weather was too rough. If the landings had not taken place on 6 June, they would have had to have been postponed for another month.

between the Orne River and St Marcouf. Artificial harbours known as 'Mulberries' were constructed and towed across the Channel so that equipment and armaments could be unloaded on to the beaches.

> ❝ There's one thing you men can say when it's all over and you're home once more. You can thank God that twenty years from now when you're sitting by the fireside with your grandson on your knee, and he asks you what you did in the war, you won't have to shift him to the other knee, cough and say, "I shovelled shit in Louisiana". ❞
>
> **George Patton**, US general, speech to US 5th Army prior to D-day landings, 6 June 1944.

decolonization

Gradual achievement of independence by the former colonies of the European imperial powers, which began after **World War I**. The process of decolonization accelerated after **World War II**, with 43 states achieving independence between 1956 and 1960, 51 between 1961 and 1980, and 23 states from 1981. The movement affected every continent: India and Pakistan achieved independence from Britain in 1947; Algeria from France 1962, and the 'Soviet Empire' broke up between 1989 and 1991.

Defenestration of Prague

An incident in Prague, Bohemia (later Czechoslovakia), in 1618, that sparked off the **Thirty Years' War**. When Ferdinand (1578–1637), archduke of Styria, was elected king of Bohemia in 1617 and chosen to succeed Matthias as emperor, the Bohemian Protestants feared for their religious and civil freedom. On 23 May 1618, invading the Hradschin Palace, they broke up a meeting of the imperial commissioners and threw two Catholic councillors and their secretary out of the window (though the victims survived the fall).

De Gaulle, Charles André Joseph Marie (1890–1970)

French general and first president of the Fifth Republic from 1958 to 1969. De Gaulle organized the Free French troops fighting the Nazis from 1940 to 1944, was head of the provisional French government from 1944 to 1946, and leader of his own Gaullist party. In 1958 the national assembly asked him to form a government during France's economic recovery and to solve the crisis in Algeria. He became president at the end of 1958, having changed the constitution to provide for a presidential system, and served until 1969.

1958 De Gaulle is called to form a government. As prime minister he sets up a constitution which gave greater powers to the president.

1958 De Gaulle takes office as president in December.

1965 He is re-elected president.

1966 He withdraws French forces from the North Atlantic Treaty Organisation (NATO).

1968 De Gaulle orders the crushing of student protests and a general strike across France in May.

1969 He resignes after the defeat of the government in a referendum on constitutional reform. De Gaulle retires to the village of Colombey-les-Deux-Eglises in northeastern France.

> ❦ A great country worthy of the name does not have any friends. ❧
>
> **Charles de Gaulle**, French general and first president of the Fifth Republic, *Time*, 28 May 1965.

De Witt, Cornelius (1623–1672)

Dutch burgomaster, the brother of Jan De Witt, whose republican policy he supported. After the French invasion of 1672, Cornelius was arrested on a false charge of conspiring to poison Prince William of **Orange**. He was murdered by the crowd on his release from prison.

De Witt, Jan (1625–1672)

Dutch statesman and republican who opposed the dynastic claims of the

House of **Orange** and sought to abolish the office of **Stadtholder**. He negotiated the Treaty of Breda in 1667, ending the Second Anglo – Dutch War, and a triple alliance between Holland, Britain, and Sweden in 1668. When Louis XIV of France invaded the United Provinces of the Netherlands in 1672, the people appointed the Prince of Orange commander of the Dutch forces and De Witt resigned. He was murdered by an angry crowd when he went to meet his brother, Cornelius, on his release from prison.

Directory

The five-man ruling executive in France from 1795 to 1799, which was established by the constitution of 1795. It failed to deal with the political and social tensions in the country and became increasingly unpopular after military defeats. It was overthrown by a military coup on 9 November 1799 that brought French emperor **Napoleon I** to power.

Members of the executive, known as the 'five majesties', included Paul-Jean **Barras** and the Abbé Sieyès (1748–1836).

Dollfuss, Engelbert (1892–1934)

Austrian Christian Socialist politician. He was appointed chancellor in 1932, and in 1933 suppressed parliament and ruled by decree. In February 1934 he forcibly crushed a protest by socialist workers. The Nazis attempted a coup on 25 July and Dollfuss was murdered.

> Dollfuss was almost certainly murdered by accident when Nazis broke into the Chancellery.

See also: *Anschluss.*

> ❝I have only desired peace. We have never attacked anybody. We have always fought to defend ourselves. May God forgive them.❞
>
> **Engelbert Dollfuss**, last words at his assassination, 1934.

Drang nach Osten

The desire of Germany for territorial expansion in the east, which was revived by 19th century nationalists, and became one of the aims of Kaiser Wilhelm II. Germany tried to put it into effect in the two world wars. The term includes both the conquest in Eastern Europe and the extension of German influence towards the Persian Gulf.

The Dreikaiserbund or Three Emperor's League
League formed by the emperors of Germany and **Austria-Hungary** and the tsar of Russia in 1872. It did not have exact, binding clauses, but the powers agreed to crush any subversive movements and to defend the monarchy. The three great powers of Central and Eastern Europe were now linked in a loose agreement, which was intended to maintain the status quo. The League effectively broke up in 1879.

Dreyfus, Alfred (1859–1935)
French army officer who was a victim of a miscarriage of justice, anti-Semitism, and military cover-up. Dreyfus was employed in the War Ministry and in 1894 he was accused of betraying military secrets to Germany, subsequently court-martialled, and sent to the penal colony on Devil's Island, French Guiana. When his innocence was discovered in 1896 the military establishment tried to conceal it, and the implications of the Dreyfus affair were avidly discussed in the press until the officer was exonerated in 1906.

French society became divided into Dreyfusards and anti-Dreyfusards. The French writer Emile Zola (1840–1902) authored the famous pamphlet *J'Accuse*, attacking the treatment of Dreyfus.

Dual Alliance
Treaty signed by Germany and **Austria-Hungary** in 1879. It became the most important part of Prince Otto von **Bismarck's** attempts to give security to German interests against Russia. If either power were attacked by Russia, the other would declare war immediately

Dual Entente
Alliance between France and Russia signed in 1894, which was intended to be a counterweight to the **Triple Alliance**. Both powers agreed to defend the other if attacked by Germany and to mobilize their forces immediately in response to any threat from the powers of the Triple Alliance. The Dual Entente created the situation which **Bismarck** had tried for so long to avoid, namely, the possibility of a war on two fronts, with Germany caught between the armies of France and Russia.

Dual Monarchy
Another title for the **Austro-Hungarian** Empire established in 1867. The ruler was king of Hungary and emperor of Austria.

Dubček, Alexander (1921–1992)

Czechoslovak politician who was first secretary of the Communist Party from 1967 to 1969 and chair of the federal assembly from 1989 to 1992. He launched the liberalization campaign known as the **Prague Spring** that was opposed by the USSR and led to the Soviet invasion of Czechoslovakia in 1968. Dubček was arrested by Soviet troops and expelled from the party in 1970. In 1989 he gave speeches at pro-democracy rallies, and after the fall of the hard-line regime, he was elected speaker of the National Assembly in Prague, a position to which he was re-elected in 1990. He was fatally injured in a car crash in September 1992.

> ❧ Socialism with a Human Face. ❧
>
> **Alexander Dubček**, motto on the Prague Spring, attributed.

Duma

In Russia, before 1917, an elected assembly that met four times following the short-lived 1905 revolution. The Duma was largely powerless, but increasingly criticized the tsar's government. After the abdication of Tsar Nicholas II, members of the Duma formed the Provisional Government.

Dzerzhinski, Feliks Edmundovich (1877–1926)

Polish-born Russian revolutionary, who founded the **Cheka**, the forerunner of the KGB (the Russian secret police). He was responsible for enforcing the policy of War Communism and organized the Red Terror in 1918, in which 50,000 Russians were killed.

Dzerzhinski was chosen by Soviet leader Vladimir Lenin to head the Cheka because, as a Pole, Lenin believed that Dzerzhinski would have no sympathy for his Russian victims.

Eastern Front

The battlefront between Russia and Germany during **World War I** and **World War II**.

Eastern Question

The name given to the international and diplomatic problems caused by the weakness and eventual collapse of the Ottoman Empire during the 18th and 19th centuries. Most of the disputes arose over the future of the Empire's possessions in the **Balkans**, into which both Russia and Austria-Hungary wanted to expand. The European naval and Mediterranean powers were also anxious to control the Bosporus between Europe and Asia in order to prohibit the Russians from having access rights.

> The British prime minister Lord Palmerston (1783–1865) claimed to be one of the few people to understand the Eastern Question.

REASONS THE CRISIS OCCURED

- the Russo-Turkish wars in the 18th century;
- the Greek War of Independence in the 1820s;
- a series of disputes over Egypt and the Balkans.

East Prussia

Former easternmost province of Prussia, between the Vistula and Neman rivers. In 1919 the creation of the Polish Corridor separated it from the rest of Germany, and in 1945 the province was divided between the USSR and Poland.

Ebert, Friedrich (1871–1925)

German socialist politician, the first president of the German Republic, from February 1919 until his death. Always a moderate, Ebert did much to

hold together the Weimar system in its early years.
See also: *Weimar Republic.*

Egmont, Lamoral, Graaf von (1522–1568)
Flemish nobleman born in Hainault who, as a servant of the Spanish crown, defeated the French first at St Quentin in 1557 and then at Gravelines in 1558, and became Stadtholder (chief magistrate) of Flanders and Artois. From 1561 he opposed **Philip II's** religious policy in the Netherlands of persecuting Protestants, but in 1567 the Duke of Alva (1508–1582) was sent to crush the resistance, and Egmont was beheaded.

Eichmann, (Karl) Adolf (1906–1962)
Austrian Nazi who, as an SS official during German dictator Adolf **Hitler's** regime 1933–1945, was responsible for atrocities, including genocide, against Jews and others. Eichmann managed to escape at the fall of Germany in 1945, but was discovered in Argentina in 1960, abducted by Israeli agents, tried in Israel in 1961 for war crimes, and executed.

Einsatzgruppen
German extermination squads operating during **World War II** set up after the invasion of the USSR in 1941. They were ordered to exterminate Jews, communists, and other 'non-Aryan elements'.

The technique used by the squads was brutal: Jews were simply rounded up and shot, although a few experimental gas trucks were used. The squads are estimated to have executed some 2 million victims between 1941 and 1944.

Elector
Any of originally seven (later ten) princes of the Holy Roman Empire who had the right to elect the emperor. The electors were the archbishops of Mainz, Trier, and Cologne, the court palatine of the Rhine, the duke of Saxony, the margrave of Brandenburg, and the king of Bohemia.

Elizabeth (1596–1662)
The 'Winter Queen', wife of **Frederick V**, Elector Palatine, Elizabeth was the daughter of James I of England and Anne of Denmark. From 1603 until her marriage in 1613 she was brought up in England. Her husband's acceptance of the throne of Bohemia in 1619 precipitated the **Thirty Years' War**.

Both Bohemia and the Palatinate were lost during the Thirty Years' War and the royal family fled to Holland where they lived in extreme poverty, dogged by misfortunes.

Entente Cordiale

The name given to the 'friendly agreement' signed by Britain and France in 1904. It was not a treaty as such, but a settling of long-standing sources of friction. Britain recognized French influence in Morocco and the French recognized British influence in Egypt. Territorial disputes in Canada, Africa, and Indo-China were also settled. More significant, however, was the fact that the Entente led subsequently to discussions on naval issues.

The Entente was made possible by visits to Paris by the English king Edward VII.

The two navies agreed to divide responsibility for European waters. In 1912 the British navy withdrew its forces from the Mediterranean and the French navy withdrew its forces from the Channel.

Erzberger, Matthias (1875–1921)

German politician who was a member of the Armistice delegation in November 1918 at the end of **World War I**. Erzberger supported acceptance of the terms of the Treaty of **Versailles,** signed in June 1919, despite fierce opposition from the German contingent. He was appointed finance minister and vice premier in 1919, but resigned in 1921. He was assassinated in August 1921.

Erzberger was assassinated because of his connection with the Armistice.

Eugene, François, Prince of Savoy (1663–1736)

French-born general who commanded the Imperial army in Italy against the French in the **War of the Spanish Succession**. In 1703 Eugene became president of the Council of War, took over command of the Imperial army, and assisted the English duke of Marlborough (1650–1722) in his victory at the Battle of **Blenheim**, Italy, in 1704. After being checked by the French general Louis Vendôme and twice wounded, Eugene finally defeated the French and drove them out of Italy. He shared with Marlborough the victories of Oudenarde and Malplaquet. After the retirement of Britain and Holland from the struggle, Eugene was unable to withstand the enemy on the Rhine and was defeated by French marshal Claude Villars (1653–1734) in 1712.

European Defence Community

International Western European army planned after **World War II** and designed to counterbalance the military superiority of the USSR in Eastern

Europe. Although a treaty was signed 1952, a thaw in East-West relations reduced the need for this force and negotiations were instead directed to the formation of the Western European Union (WEU) in 1955.

European Economic Community (EEC) or Common Market

Original name for the organization formed in 1957 by the Treaty of Rome (effective from January 1958) consisting of Belgium, France, West Germany, Italy, Luxembourg, and the Netherlands. It later expanded to become the European Community (EC) to also include Denmark, the UK, the Republic of Ireland, Portugal, Spain, and Greece. It was renamed the **European Union** (EU) in 1993.

European Union (EU)

Political and economic alliance evolving from the European Economic Community established by the Treaty of Rome in March 1957 (later the European Community or EC). It was renamed the European Union in 1993.

There were six member countries at first: France, West Germany, Italy, Belgium, the Netherlands, and Luxembourg. These countries had been members of the European Coal and Steel Community. The EEC came into effect on 1 January 1958. At the same time the European Atomic Community was set up. Delegates from the six countries met in the European Economic Assembly in March 1958, under the presidency of Robert Schuman.

At first the EEC, or the Common Market as it became known, was a strictly economic body. It encouraged trade between the members and set tariffs on imports from outside. The Treaty of Rome, however, contained clauses that allowed for political union at some future date.

Falange
Former Spanish Fascist Party, founded in 1933 by José Antonio Primo de Rivera (1903–1936), son of military ruler Miguel Primo de Rivera. It was closely modelled in programme and organization on the Italian Fascists and on the Nazis. In 1937, when Gen Francicso **Franco** assumed leadership, it was declared the only legal party, and altered its name to Traditionalist Spanish Phalanx.

Falk, Paul Ludwig Adalbert 1827–1900
Prussian statesman who was Prince Otto von **Bismarck's** education minister. Falk gave the state direct control over ecclesiastical matters, particularly education, which led to the struggle with the Catholic Church known as the **Kulturkampf**.

Farnese
Italian family originating in upper Lazio who held the duchy of Parma, which endured from 1545 to 1731. Among the family's most famous members were:
- Alessandro Farnese (1468–1549), who became Pope Paul III in 1534 and granted the duchy to his illegitimate son Pier Luigi (1503–1547);
- Elizabeth (1692–1766), niece of the last Farnese duke, who married Philip V of Spain and was an important influence in the politics of Europe.

fascism
Political ideology that believes that the rights of individuals are less important than the power of the state.

Fascism was created by the economic and political crisis in Italy in the years after World War I. Units called *fasci di combattimento* (combat groups), from the Latin 'fasces', were originally established to oppose communism (which emphasized social classlessness and shared ownership of the means of production). The Fascist Party, the *Partitio Nazionale Fascista*, controlled Italy from 1922 to 1943. Fascism attacked working-class movements and provided scapegoats such as Jews, foreigners, or blacks; it also prepared the citizenry for the economic and psychological mobilization of war.

The Fascist movement in Italy was led by Benito **Mussolini**. The symbol of Fascism (*Fascismo*) was the fasces and the *Fascista* salute was the outstretched arm reminiscent of ancient Rome. The military organization of the National Fascista Party was on pseudo-Roman lines and used Roman names like *legion, consul, centurion, triarii,* and *senior.*

Fascism in Italy grew out of the failure of the Italian forces during **World War I** and the disappointments of the **Treaty of Versailles**, when the Allies refused to honour their promises made at the **Treaty of London**.

In 1922, after a great meeting at Naples and after the **March on Rome**, Mussolini was summoned by the king to form the first Fascist cabinet.

Fashoda Incident
Dispute in 1898 in the town of Fashoda (now Kodok) situated on the White Nile in southeastern Sudan, in which a clash between French and British expeditionary forces nearly led the two countries into war.

Originally a disagreement over local territorial claims, the clash between the French forces under Col Jean Baptiste Marchand (1863–1934) and British forces under Lord Kitchener (1850–1916) came close to precipitating a full-scale war.

A political solution was found, marking a turning point in Anglo-French relations that led ultimately to the ***Entente Cordiale*** of 1904.

February Revolution
The first of the two political uprisings of the Russian Revolution in 1917, which led to the overthrow of the tsar and the end of the Romanov dynasty established in 1603.

The immediate cause of the revolution was the incompetence of the tsar's government during **World War I**. But inflation and shortages of food in the capital Petrograd provided the flash point.

- By January 1917 there was increasing unrest in Petrograd: food prices had risen 400% since the beginning of the war and the population had increased by 50%.
- On 22 February 1917 the temperature during a bitter winter rose by 20 degrees Celsius. This encouraged people to venture on to the streets and demonstrate.
- The International Women's Day was held on 23 February 1917; there were parades and demonstrations. This led to strikes.
- By 25 February 1917 half the workers in Petrograd were on strike.
- Rodzianko (1860–1927), the chair of the Duma (assembly), relayed the

seriousness of the situation to the tsar, urging the formation of a new government. However, believing that Rodzianko was motivated by self interest, the tsar decided to act on the conflicting story of his wife, the tsarina, who reported only minor disturbances.

When Nicholas attempted to return to Petrograd on 1 March, his train was sent to Pskov, where he was forced to abdicate. He unsuccessfully tried to pass the throne to his son, but finally agreed to nominate his brother as his successor.

- On 27 and 28 February troops were sent to stop the unrest, but the garrison of Petrograd supported the strikers.
- On 1 March the tsar attempted to return to Petrograd, but it was too late. He was forced to abdicate on 2 March in favour of his brother, Michael (who in turn abdicated on 3 March).

Ferdinand V, also known as Ferdinand II of Aragon (1452–1516)

King of Castile from 1474 and king of Aragon from 1479. He married **Isabella of Castile** in 1469 and they were therefore able to create a united kingdom of Spain for the first time. He became Ferdinand II of Naples from 1504.

feudalism

A system that was the main form of social organization in medieval Europe, based primarily on rights to the land.

In return for military service the monarch allowed powerful barons to hold land, and often also to administer justice and levy taxes. They in turn passed on such rights to sub-tenants, again in return for military service.

At the bottom of the system were the serfs, who worked on their lord's manor lands in return for being allowed to cultivate a portion of the land for themselves. The serfs could not be sold as if they were slaves, but

The term feudalism was first used in the 19th century.

they could not leave the estate to live or work elsewhere without their lord's permission. The system declined from the 13th century, partly because of the growth of a money economy, with commerce, trade, and industry, and partly because of the many peasants' revolts during the period 1350 to1550.

Serfdom ended in England in the 16th century, but lasted in France until 1789 and in the rest of Western Europe until the early 19th century. In Russia the system continued until 1861.

Field of the Cloth of Gold

Site between Guînes and Ardres near Calais, France, where a meeting took place between Henry VIII (1491–1547) of England and Francis I (1494–1547) of France in June 1520. The event was remarkable for the lavish clothes worn and the tent pavilions erected there. Francis hoped to gain England's support in opposing the Holy Roman Emperor, **Charles V**, but failed.

The Field of the Cloth of Gold ruined Henry VIII. He had been left £1,300,000 by his father, but by 1520 he had spent it all.

fifth column

Group within a country secretly aiding an enemy attacking from without. The term originated in 1936 during the **Spanish Civil War**, when supporters of Gen Francisco Franco boasted that they were attacking Madrid with four columns and that they had a 'fifth column' inside the city.

final solution

Term used by the Nazis to describe the extermination of Jews (and other racial groups and opponents of the regime) before and during **World War II** as part of the Holocaust.

The term came from a statement in May 1941 by SS commander Heinrich **Himmler** to Rudolf **Hoess**, commandant of **Auschwitz** extermination camp, their führer Adolf Hitler had given orders 'for the final solution of the Jewish question'. Extermination squads (**Einsatzgruppen**) were formed and extermination camps such as Auschwitz, Sobibor, Treblinka, and Maidanek were established in Poland. Jews were shipped to the camps from all parts of German-occupied Europe to be gassed or shot. The most reliable estimates suggest that about 5.75 million Jews, and a further million gypsies, communists, Soviet prisoners, incurable invalids, homosexuals, and other *Untermenschen* (those considered by the Nazis to be 'subhuman') were murdered.

First World War

Another name for **World War I**, 1914–18.

five-year plan

Long-term strategic plan for the development of a country's economy, which was from 1928 the basis of economic planning in the USSR. The strategies aimed particularly to develop heavy and light industry in a primarily agricultural country.

Soviet leader Josef **Stalin** believed that the Soviet Union was 100 years behind the West and wanted to modernize the country as quickly as possible. All factories were set targets for each year and for the end of the plans, but these were often impossible

Stalin halted the First Five-Year Plan after just over four years in an effort to make workers work harder.

because the plans were devised in Moscow and took no account of local conditions. Even so, the Soviet Union had become the world's second-largest industrial power by 1941.

Flanders
Region and county of the Low Countries that in the 8th and 9th centuries extended from Calais to the Schelde. During the 10th and 11th, the county resisted Norman encroachment, expanded its territory, and became a leading centre of the wool industry. In 1194, **Philip II** married the niece of Count Philip of Alsace (1143–1191), and so began a period of active French involvement in the county.

The last count, Louis de Male, died 1384, and the county was inherited by his son-in-law, Philip the Bold of Burgundy (1342–1404), to become part of the Burgundian domains.

Flanders underwent a decline under Austrian rule from the 17th to the 19th centuries. Fierce battles were fought in the region during **World War I**, such as the Battle of Ypres. In **World War II** the Battle of Flanders began with the German breakthrough on 10 May 1940 and ended with the British amphibious retreat from Dunkirk from 27 May to 4 June.

Foch, Ferdinand (1851–1929)
Marshal of France during **World War I**, largely responsible for the Allied victory at the first Battle of the Marne in September 1914. Foch commanded on the northwestern front from October 1914 to September 1916. He was appointed commander-in-chief of the Allied armies in the spring of 1918, and launched the Allied counter-offensive in July that brought about the negotiation of an armistice to end the war.

> ❝ My centre is giving way, my right is in retreat; situation excellent. I am attacking. ❞
>
> **Ferdinand Foch**, attributed remark, quoted in Aston, *Biography of Foch*.

Fouché, Joseph, Duke of Otranto (1759–1820)
French politician who was elected to the National Convention (the post-Revolutionary legislature), and who organized the conspiracy that

overthrew the **Jacobin** leader Maximilien **Robespierre**. Emperor **Napoleon I** employed him as police minister.

❝ It is worse than a crime; it is a blunder. ❞

Joseph, Duke of Otranto Fouché, referring to the political murder of the duc d'Enghien by Napoleon, on 21 March 1804, (attributed also to Doulay de la Meurthe and French diplomat Charles Maurice de Talleyrand).

Fouquet, Nicolas (1615–1680)

French politician and a rival to **Louis XIV's** minister Jean-Baptiste **Colbert**, Fouquet became *procureur général* of the Paris parliament in 1650 and superintendent of finance in 1651. He was responsible for raising funds for the long war against Spain, a post he held until he was arrested and imprisoned for embezzlement (at the instigation of Colbert, who succeeded him in 1665).

Fourth Republic

The French constitutional regime that was established between 1944 and 1946 and lasted until 4 October 1958: from liberation after Nazi occupation during **World War II** to the introduction of a new constitution by Gen Charles de Gaulle.

France

Chronology

751–68	Pepin the Short usurps the Frankish throne, reunifies the kingdom, and founds the Carolingian dynasty.
768–814 Charlemagne	conquers much of Western Europe and creates the Holy Roman Empire
843	The Treaty of Verdun divides the Holy Roman Empire into three parts, with the western portion corresponding to modern France.
987	The Frankish crown passes to the House of **Capet**.
1180–1223 Philip II	doubles the royal domain and tightens control over the nobles; the power of the Capets gradually extends with the support of the church and towns.
1337	The start of the Hundred Years' War: Edward III of England claims the throne; the English win victories at Crécy in 1346 and Agincourt in 1415.
1429	Joan of Arc raises the siege of Orléans; the Hundred Years' War ends with Charles VII expelling the English in 1453.
1483	France annexes Burgundy and Brittany after Louis XI restores royal power.
16th–17th centuries	The French kings fight the **Habsburgs** (of the Holy Roman Empire and Spain) for supremacy in western Europe.

1562–98	Civil wars between nobles are fought under religious slogans, such as the **Wars of Religion.**
1589–1610	**Henry IV**, the first king of the Bourbon dynasty, establishes peace, religious tolerance, and absolute monarchy.
1634–48	The French ministers Cardinal **Richelieu** and Jules Mazarin secure Alsace by intervening in the Thirty Years' War, making France the leading power in Europe.
1701–14	The War of the **Spanish Succession**: England, Austria, and their allies check the expansionism of France under **Louis XIV**.
1756–63	During the **Seven Years' War** France loses most of its colonies in India and Canada to British control.
1789	The **French Revolution** abolishes absolute monarchy and feudalism.
1799	**Napoleon I** seizes power in a coup; he crowns himself emperor in 1804; France conquers much of Europe.
1814	France is defeated; the Bourbon monarchy is restored; comes back by Napoleon, who is defeated at **Waterloo** in 1815.
1830	The liberal revolution deposes **Charles X** in favour of his cousin **Louis Philippe**, the 'Citizen King'.
1848	The Revolution establishes the Second Republic; **Louis Napoleon**, nephew of Napoleon I, is elected president..
1852	Louis Napoleon proclaims the Second Empire, taking the title **Napoleon III.**
1870–71	The Franco-Prussian War: France loses Alsace-Lorraine; the Second Empire is abolished; the Paris **Commune** is crushed; the Third Republic is founded.
1914–18	France resists German invasion in World War I; the region of **Alsace-Lorraine** is recovered in 1919.
1939	France enters World War II.
1940	Germany invades and occupies northern France; Marshal **Pétain** forms the right-wing puppet regime at unoccupied **Vichy**; active resistance is maintained by the French resistance group **Maquis** and the **Free French** group in the UK; the Germans occupy all France by 1942.
1944	The Allies liberate France; a provisional government was formed by Gen Charles **de Gaulle**, leader of the Free French.
1946	The **Fourth Republic** is proclaimed.
1949	France becames a member of NATO; the country withdraws from military command structure in 1966.
1957	France is a founder member of the European Economic Community (EEC).
1958	The Algerian crisis causes the collapse of the Fourth Republic; de Gaulle takes power, becoming president of the Fifth Republic in 1959.
1962	Algeria achieves independence from France.
1968	Revolutionary students riot in Paris; there is a general strike throughout France.
1981	François **Mitterrand** is elected the Fifth Republic's first socialist president.
1995	Conservative Jacques Chirac elected president.
1997	General election called by President Chirac. Victory for the socialists; Lionel Jospin appointed prime minister.

Franco, Francisco (Paulino Hermenegildo Teódulo Bahamonde) (1892–1975)

Spanish general who led the insurgent nationalists to victory in the **Spanish Civil War** 1936–39, supported by Fascist Italy and Nazi Germany, and established a dictatorship in Spain. In 1942 Franco reinstated a *Cortes* (Spanish parliament), which in 1947 passed an act by which Franco became head of state for life.

On the outbreak of **World War II**, in spite of Spain's official attitude of 'strictest neutrality', his pro-**Axis** sympathies led him to send aid, later withdrawn, to the German side.

At home, he curbed the growing power of the *Falange Española* (the Fascist party), and in later years slightly liberalized his regime. In 1969 he nominated Juan Carlos as his successor and future king of Spain. He relinquished the premiership in 1973, but remained head of state until his death.

Franco-Prussian War

War from 1870 to 1871 ensuing when the Prussian chancellor Otto von **Bismarck** put forward a German candidate for the vacant Spanish throne with the deliberate, and successful, intention of provoking the French emperor Napoleon III into declaring war. The Prussians

> Bismarck provoked France into declaring war on Prussia by altering the Ems Telegram (as Bismarck's famous telegram became known). This gave the impression that Napoleon III had been insulted by the Prussian government.

defeated the French at Sedan, then besieged Paris. The Treaty of Frankfurt in May 1871 gave Alsace-Lorraine, plus a large French indemnity, to Prussia. The war established Prussia, at the head of a newly established German empire, as Europe's leading military power.

Frankfurt Parliament

An assembly of liberal politicians and intellectuals that met for a few months in 1848 in the aftermath of the revolutions that overthrew the monarchies in most of the German states. They discussed a constitution for a united Germany, but the restoration of the old order and the suppression of the revolutions ended the parliament.

Franz Ferdinand or Francis Ferdinand (1863–1914)

Archduke of Austria and heir to his uncle, Emperor Franz Joseph, from 1884. During a visit to Sarajevo in Bosnia on 28 June 1914, Franz Ferdinand and his wife were assassinated by a Serbian nationalist, a member of the

Black Hand Gang. Austria used the episode to make unreasonable demands on Serbia that ultimately led to **World War I**.

> *Sophie, don't die, live for the children.*
>
> **Franz Ferdinand**, last words to his wife, on his assassination at Sarajevo, 1914.

Franz Joseph or Francis Joseph (1830–1916)

Emperor of **Austria-Hungary** from 1848, when his uncle Ferdinand I abdicated. After the suppression of the 1848 revolution, Franz Joseph tried to establish an absolute monarchy but had to grant Austria a parliamentary constitution in 1861 and grant Hungary equality with Austria in 1867. He was defeated in the Italian War of 1859 and the Prussian War of 1866. In 1914 he made the assassination of his heir and nephew Franz Ferdinand the excuse for attacking Serbia, thus bringing about the outbreak of **World War I**.

Franz Ferdinand lost favour with the Habsburg royal house because of his marriage to Sophie, which was deemed unsuitable. He was only allowed to attend official functions when he was dressed in his field marshal's uniform. Nevertheless, he and his wife were given a royal funeral so that the murders could be used as a pretext for an attack on Serbia.

Franz Joseph lost most of his family in tragic circumstances. His brother Maximilian (1832–1867) was executed in Mexico. His son Rudolf (1858–1889) committed suicide at **Mayerling** in 1889. His wife Elizabeth (1837–1894) was murdered in Geneva in 1894 and his heir **Franz Ferdinand** was shot in Sarajevo, Bosnia, in 1914.

> *You see in me the last monarch of the old school.*
>
> **Franz Joseph**, in conversation with Theodore Roosevelt, 1910.

Frederick V ('The Winter King') (1596–1632)

Elector palatine of the Rhine from 1610 to 1623 and king of Bohemia from 1619 to 1620 (for one winter, hence the name), having been chosen by the Protestant Bohemians as ruler after the deposition of Catholic emperor Ferdinand II. Frederick's appointment was the cause of the **Thirty Years' War** in which Frederick was defeated at the Battle of the White Mountain, near

Prague, in November 1620, by the army of the Catholic League. He fled to Holland.

Frederick V was the son-in-law of James I of England.

Frederick (II) the Great (1712–1786)

King of Prussia from 1740, when he succeeded his father **Frederick William I**. In that year Frederick started the War of the **Austrian Succession** through his attack on Austria. In the peace of 1748 he secured **Silesia**. The struggle was renewed in the **Seven Years' War** in the period 1756 to 1763. Frederick acquired West **Prussia** in the first of the **partitions of Poland** in 1772 and Prussia became Germany's foremost state. He was an efficient and just ruler in the spirit of the Enlightenment (the 18th-century European social and scientific progressive movement) and was also a patron of the arts.

Frederick the Great *King of Prussia from 1740.*

In his domestic policy Frederick encouraged industry and agriculture, reformed the judicial system, fostered education, and established religious toleration. He corresponded with the French writer François-Marie Voltaire, and was a talented musician.

He received a harsh military education from his father, and in 1730 was threatened with death for attempting to run away. In the **Seven Years' War**, in spite of assistance from Britain, Frederick had a hard task holding his own against the Austrians and their Russian allies. The skill he displayed in doing so proved him to be one of the great soldiers of history.

Frederick was an accomplished musician and on one occasion suspended a council meeting to hear German composer Johann Bach (1685–1750) play the organ. *The Brandenburg Concertos* were dedicated to him by Bach, along with the *Musical Offering*.

Frederick III (1831–1888)

King of Prussia and emperor of Germany in 1888. The son of William I, Frederick married the eldest daughter (Victoria) of Queen Victoria of Great Britain in 1858 and, as a liberal, frequently opposed the German chancellor, Otto von **Bismarck.** Frederick died three months after his accession.

Frederick died in agony of cancer of the throat.

Frederick William I (1688–1740)

King of Prussia from 1713, who first developed Prussia's military might and commerce.

Frederick William I terrorized his son **Frederick the Great**, murdered his flute teacher, and imprisoned Frederick for eleven months. He was determined to turn his son into a soldier.

Frederick William IV (1795–1861)

King of Prussia from 1840. He upheld the principle of the divine right of kings, but was forced to grant a constitution in 1850 after the Prussian revolution of 1848. He suffered two strokes in 1857 and became mentally debilitated. His brother Wilhelm (later emperor) took over his duties.

In 1848 Frederick William refused to accept the crown of a united Germany, which he was offered by the **Frankfurt Parliament**. He said he would not pick it up from the gutter.

> 6 Henceforth Prussia merges into Germany. 9
>
> **Frederick William IV**, proclamation in response to nationalistic
> revolutionary pressure, Berlin, 21 March 1848.

Free French

In **World War II**, a movement in the UK originated by French general **Charles de Gaulle** in June 1940, consisting of French soldiers who continued to fight against the **Axis** after the Franco-German armistice. They took the name 'Fighting France' in 1942 and served in many campaigns. Their emblem was the Cross of Lorraine, a cross with two bars.

French Revolution

The period covering 1789 to 1799 that saw the end of the monarchy in France. The revolution began as an attempt to create a constitutional monarchy. A Legislative Assembly was set up, which at first was peaceful. But the most influential force became the Paris mob, which forced the king to return to Paris from Versailles and then

French Revolution *Contemporary engraving of the September Massacres of 1972.*

organized massacres in September 1792. The First Republic was set up and the National Convention established. **Louis XVI** was put on trial and executed in January 1793. The Convention soon became dominated by the **Jacobins**. They began the **Reign of Terror** in 1793, which led to the deaths of tens of thousands of royalists.

In August 1794 the Thermidorean Reaction led to the overthrow of Maximilien **Robespierre**, the Jacobin leader, and in 1795 the **Directory** was set up. The collapse of the Directory in 1799 enabled **Napoleon I** to seize power in November and establish the Consulate.

❝I survived.❞

Emmanuel-Joseph Sieyès, French statesman, on being asked what he had done during the French Revolution.

French revolutionary calendar

The calendar adopted at the time of the French Revolution from 1789, initially known as the 1st Year of Liberty. When the monarchy was abolished on 21 September 1792, the 4th year became the 1st Year of the Republic. This calendar was formally adopted in October 1793 but its usage

The calendar named each month after the usual weather conditions, so August became **Thermidor** (hot) and November became Brumaire (misty).

was backdated to 22 September 1793, which became 1 Vendémiaire. The calendar was discarded from 1 January 1806.

Friedland, Battle of
French victory on 14 June 1807 during the **Napoleonic Wars** over the combined Prussian and Russian armies at Friedland (now Pravdinsk, Russia). Ten days later, Tsar **Alexander I** and **Napoleon I** met on a raft in the middle of the Neman River and signed the **Treaty of Tilsit**.

Fronde
French revolts during the period 1648 to 1653 against the administration of the chief minister Jules Mazarin (1602–1661) during **Louis XIV's** minority reign. During 1648 to 1649 the Paris parliament attempted to limit the royal power; its leaders were arrested, Paris revolted, and the rising was suppressed by the royal army under Louis II Condé (1621–1686). In 1650 Condé led a new revolt of the nobility, but this had been suppressed by 1653. The defeat of the Fronde enabled Louis to establish an absolutist monarchy in the later 17th century.

Führer or Fuehrer
Title adopted by Adolf **Hitler** as leader of the **Nazi** Party, and as dictatorial leader of Germany from August 1934.

G

Gabelle

Term that originally referred to a tax on various items but came to be used exclusively for a tax on salt, first levied by Philip the Fair (1268–1314) in 1286. It was a major source of complaint in the years leading up to the **French Revolution** and was abolished in 1790.

Garibaldi, Giuseppe (1807–1882)

Italian soldier who played a central role in the unification of Italy by conquering Sicily and Naples in 1860. From 1834 he was a member of the nationalist Giuseppe **Mazzini's** 'Young Italy' society and was forced into exile until 1848 and again from 1849–54. He fought against Austria from 1848 to 1849.

In 1860, at the head of his 1,000 redshirts, Garibaldi won Sicily and Naples for the new kingdom of Italy. He served in the Austrian War of 1866 and fought for France in the **Franco-Prussian** War from 1870 to 1871.

See also: *Cavour.*

Garibaldi *Italian nationalist leader and head of the band of 'redshirts' who won Sicily and Naples during the unification of Italy.*

Garibaldi's crossing from Sicily to Naples was aided by the presence of British warships sent by the prime minister Lord Palmerston (1784–1865). The red attire of Garibaldi's redshirts convinced onlookers that they were British infantry.

Geneva Convention
International agreement of 1864 regulating the treatment of those wounded in war, and later extended to cover the types of weapons allowed, the treatment of prisoners and the sick, and the protection of civilians in wartime. The rules were revised at conventions held in 1906, 1929, and 1949, and by the 1977 Additional Protocols.

German Spring Offensive
Germany's Final Offensive on the Western Front during **World War I**. By early 1918, German forces outnumbered the Allies on the Western Front. Germany staged three separate offensives, which culminated in the Second **Battle of the Marne**, fought between 15 July and 6 August. It marked the turning point of World War I. After winning the battle the Allies advanced steadily, and, by September, Germany had lost all the territory it had gained during the spring.
See also: *Ludendorff.*

Girondin or Girondist or Brissotin
Member of the moderate republican party in the **French Revolution**, so called because a number of its leaders came from the Gironde region of southwestern France. The Girondins controlled the legislative assembly from late 1791 to early 1793, but were ousted by the extremist **Jacobins** in the spring of that year. Many Girondin leaders were executed during the **Reign of Terror**.

Prominent Girondins included leader Jacques-Pierre Brissot (hence their alternative name) and Charles Dumouriez. The faction drew its support from businessmen, merchants, and government officials. Their fall from popularity began with their refusal to join the more radical revolutionaries in overthrowing the monarchy.
See also: *guillotine; Robespierre.*

Goebbels, (Paul) Joseph (1897–1945)
German Nazi leader who was first a journalist and then joined the **Nazi Party** in 1924, which had been under **Hitler's** leadership for just three years. He was given control of the party's propaganda machine in 1929. Goebbels' commitment to Nazism was total, and as minister of propaganda from 1933 his organizational abilities and oratorical skills were major factors in spreading the party line throughout Germany and abroad.

Under Goebbels, the whole spectrum of German culture and education was centralized under Nazi control. He also championed Nazi-like movements abroad to wage a psychological 'war of nerves' against Hitler's intended victims. When the city of Berlin was captured by the Allies in

1945 at the end of **World War II**, Goebbels committed suicide.
See also: *Reichstag Fire.*

Goering, Hermann Wilhelm (1893–1946)

German Nazi leader who became a renowned fighter pilot in **World War I** and a German field marshal from 1938. He joined the **Nazi** Party in 1922, under the future dictator Adolf **Hitler**, and was elected to the Reichstag (assembly) in 1928, becoming its president in 1932. As part of Hitler's inner circle, he was appointed minister of the interior for Prussia in 1933. This position gave him full control of the police and security forces; he organized the Gestapo (secret police) and built the first concentration camps. He then handed control for the Gestapo and other security forces, including the camps, to the SS (the elitist paramiliary group). Goering subsequently transferred his energies to developing the Luftwaffe (German airforce), and was appointed commissioner for aviation from 1933. In addition, he supervised the four-year economic plan between 1935 and 1939 to prepare the country for war.

The Luftwaffe's failure to break the British air defences was a serious blow to his reputation from which Goering never really recovered. He built up a vast economic empire in occupied Europe, but by the end of the war he had lost favour and was expelled from the party in 1945. Tried at **Nuremberg** between 1945 and 1946, he was found guilty of gross atrocities of war and sentenced to death by hanging. However, he poisoned himself before he could be executed.

> ❝ Guns will make us powerful; butter will only make us fat. ❞
>
> **Hermann Goering**, radio broadcast, 1936.

Gonzaga dynasty

From the 14th century, the ruling family of Mantua in northern Italy.

- Luigi Gonzaga (*c.* 1268–1360) seized power in 1328 and took the title of captain.
- Gianfrancesco Gonzaga (1395–1444) was given the title of Marchese.
- Francesco II Gonzaga (1466–1519) married Isabella d'Este linking the family with the rulers of Ferrara
- Federico II Gonzaga became duke of Mantua in 1530.

Grand Design
In the early 17th century, a plan attributed by the French minister Maximilien de Béthune, duc de Sully (1560–1641) to **Henry IV** of France (who was assassinated before he could carry it out) for a great Protestant union against the Holy Roman Empire; the term was also applied to French president **de Gaulle's** vision of his country's place in a united 20th-century Europe.

Great Patriotic War
The Soviet name for war between the USSR and Germany which began in 1941 during **World War II**.

When Germany invaded the USSR in June 1941, the Soviet troops retreated, carrying out a scorched earth policy (literally destroying all of Russia's commodities in their wake). Strategic industries were then relocated to areas beyond the Ural Mountains. Soviet leader Josef **Stalin** remained in Moscow and the Soviet forces, inspired to fight on by his patriotic speeches, launched a counter-offensive. The Allies endeavoured to provide the USSR with vital supplies through Murmansk and Archangel, despite German attempts to blockade the ports. In 1942 the Germans failed to take **Leningrad** (St Petersburg) and Moscow, and launched attacks towards the River Volga and on oil wells at Baku.

Stalin chose the name the Great Patriotic War in an attempt to persuade the Soviet peoples to fight for him. In a Soviet history of the Second World War, eight of the ten most important events in the war took place during the Great Patriotic War. The Germans lost 90% of their battle casualties on the Eastern Front.

In August 1942 the Germans attacked **Stalingrad** (Volograd) but were held off by the Russians, and a large German contingent was forced to surrender there in January 1943. The Russian Red Army, under the command of Marshal Georgi **Zhukov**, gradually forced the Germans back and by February 1945 the Russians had reached the German border. In April 1945 the Russians, who had made tremendous sacrifices (20 million dead and millions more wounded), entered the German capital of Berlin. In May 1945 the war ended.

See also: *Barbarossa; Kursk.*

Greece

Chronology
1204   Crusaders partition the Byzantine Empire; Athens, Achaea, and Thessaloniki come under Frankish rulers.

late 14th century–1461 Ottoman Turks conquer mainland Greece and capture Constantinople in 1453.
1685 Venetians capture the Peloponnese; it is regained by the Turks in 1715.
1821 Peloponnese brigands revolt against the Turks; the War of Independence ensues.
1827 Battle of **Navarino**: Britain, France, and Russia intervene to destroy the Turkish fleet; Count Ioannis Kapodistrias is elected president of Greece.
1829 The Treaty of Adrianople: under Russian pressure, Greece achieves independence.
1832 Otto of Bavaria is elected as king of Greece.
1843 A coup forces King Otto to grant a constitution.
1862 Mutiny and rebellion lead King Otto to abdicate.
1863 George of Denmark becomes king of the Hellenes.
1864 Britain transfer the Ionian islands to Greece.
1881 Following the Treaty of Berlin in 1878, Greece is allowed to annex Thessaly and part of Epirus.
1912–13 **Balkan Wars**: Greece annexed a large area of Epirus and Macedonia.
1917–18 Greek forces fight on the Allied side in World War I.
1924 A republic is declared amid great political instability.
1935 A Greek monarchy is restored with George II as king.
1940 Greece successfully repels an Italian invasion.
1941–44 The German occupation of Greece; rival monarchist and communist resistance groups operates from 1942.
1946–49 Civil war: the communists are defeated by monarchists helped by military aid from Britain and the USA.
1952 Greece becomes a member of NATO.
1967 The 'Greek Colonels' seizes power under George Papadopoulos (born 1919); political activity is banned; King Constantine II is exiled.
1973 A republic is proclaimed, with Papadopoulos as president.

Grotius, Hugo or Huig de Groot (1583–1645)

Dutch jurist and politician, whose book *De Jure Belli et Pacis/On the Law of War and Peace* (1625) is the foundation of international law.

Grotius held that the rules governing human and international relations are founded on human nature, which is rational and social and that these rules constitute a natural law binding on citizens and rulers.

> ❝ Not to know something is a great part of wisdom. ❞
>
> **Hugo Grotius**, *Docta Ignorantia*.

Guderian, Heinz Wilhelm (1888–1954)

German general in **World War II**, who created the *Panzer* (German 'armour') divisions that formed the ground spearhead of Adolf **Hitler's** *Blitzkrieg* attack strategy, achieving a significant breakthrough at Sedan in Ardennes, France, in 1940, and leading the advance to Moscow in 1941.

Guderian's initial advance on Moscow was rapid, but the elements of a bitter winter and a determined Soviet resistance led him to make a partial withdrawal. As a result, Hitler dismissed him from his post. He was reinstated as inspector general of armoured troops in 1943 and became Chief of Staff after the **July Plot** against Hitler in 1944, but was again dismissed by Hitler in March 1945.

Guillotine

Beheading device consisting of a metal blade that descends between two posts. It was common in the Middle Ages and an improved design was introduced in France in 1791 by a physician, Joseph Ignace Guillotin (1738–1814). It was subsequently used for executions during the French Revolution. The guillotine is still in use in some countries.

Joseph Guillotin named his invention Madame Guillotine after his wife.

Guillotine *The guillotine gained notoriety as an instrument of execution during the Reign of Terror of the French Revolution.*

Guizot, François Pierre Guillaume (1787–1874)

French politician and historian, professor of modern history at the Sorbonne (the University of Paris) from 1812 to 1830. He wrote histories of French and European culture and became prime minister of France in 1847. His resistance to all reforms was a factor leading to the revolution of 1848.

❝ The spirit of revolution ... of insurrection is a spirit
radically opposed to liberty. ❞

François Guizot, speech in Paris, 29 December 1830.

Gulag
Russian term for the system of prisons and labour camps used to silence
dissidents and opponents of the Soviet regime. They were mostly situated in
Siberia or inside the Arctic Circle.

In the Stalin era (1928–1953), millions of prisoners died from the harsh
conditions of these remote camps.

See also: *purges.*

Gustavus Adolphus or Gustavus II or Gustaf II (1594–1632)
King of Sweden from 1611, when he succeeded his father Charles IX. He
waged successful wars with Denmark, Russia, and Poland, and in the **Thirty
Years' War**, and became a champion of the Protestant cause. Landing in
Germany in 1630, he defeated the German general Albrecht **Wallenstein** at
Lützen, southwest of Leipzig on 6 November 1632, but was killed in the
ensuing battle. He was known as the 'Lion of the North'.

See also: *Breitenfeld.*

Habsburg or Hapsburg

European royal family, former imperial house of **Austria-Hungary**, founded by Rudolf I (1218–1291), who became king of Germany in 1273 and began the family's control of Austria and Styria. The family acquired a series of lands and titles, including that of Holy Roman Emperor which they held during 1273–91, 1298–1308, 1438–1740, and 1745–1806. The Habsburgs reached the height of their power under the emperor **Charles V** (1519–1556) who divided his lands, creating an Austrian Habsburg line (which ruled until 1918) and a Spanish line (which ruled to 1700).

The name comes from the family castle in Aargau, Switzerland.

See also: *Charlemagne; Franz Joseph; Holy Roman Empire.*

Hague Convention

Agreement relating to the rights and duties of belligerents (countries engaged in war) in wartime at a conference that that took place in The Hague in the Netherlands between June and October 1907. The principles agreed on by the delegates of the convention included a provision for the humane treatment of prisoners of war and the outlawing of the use of poisons as weapons of war. Some of the principles are also incorporated in the **Geneva Convention** (1864, revised 1906, 1929, and 1949, and by the 1977 Additional Protocols), which, largely because of the latter's more limited aims, have been implemented more successfully.

Henlein, Konrad (1898–1945)

Sudeten-German leader of the Sudeten **Nazi** Party in Czechoslovakia, and closely allied with German dictator Adolf Hitler's Nazis. He was partly responsible for the destabilization of the Czechoslovak state in 1938, which led to the **Munich Agreement** in the same year and the handing over of the Sudetenland to Germany.

See also: *Nuremberg trials.*

Henry IV (1553–1610)

King of Navarre and King of France from 1589, Henry was the son of Antoine de Bourbon and Jeanne, Queen of Navarre, he was brought up as a Protestant and from 1576 led the Huguenots (French Protestants) in their religious campaigns. On his accession he settled the religious question by

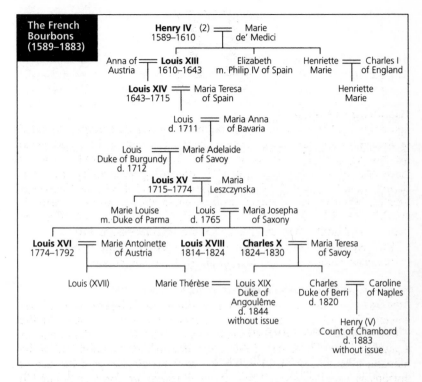

The French Bourbons (1589–1883)

Henry IV (2) ══ Marie
1589–1610   de' Medici

Anna of ══ Louis XIII   Elizabeth   Henriette ══ Charles I
Austria   1610–1643   m. Philip IV of Spain   Marie   of England

Louis XIV ══ Maria Teresa
1643–1715   of Spain

Henriette
Marie

Louis ══ Maria Anna
d. 1711   of Bavaria

Louis ══ Marie Adelaide
Duke of Burgundy   of Savoy
d. 1712

Louis XV ══ Maria
1715–1774   Leszczynska

Marie Louise   Louis ══ Maria Josepha
m. Duke of Parma   d. 1765   of Saxony

Louis XVI ══ Marie Antoinette   Louis XVIII   Charles X ══ Maria Teresa
1774–1792   of Austria   1814–1824   1824–1830   of Savoy

Louis (XVII)   Marie Thérèse ══ Louis XIX   Charles ══ Caroline
Duke of   Duke of Berri   of Naples
Angoulême   d. 1820
d. 1844
without issue

Henry (V)
Count of Chambord
d. 1883
without issue

adopting Catholicism while tolerating Protestantism. He restored peace and strong government to France and brought back prosperity by measures for the promotion of industry and agriculture and the improvement of communications. He was assassinated by a Catholic extremist.

See also: *Wars of Religion.*

❝ Paris is well worth a mass. ❞

Henry IV, attributed remark on his conversion to Catholicism.

Henry the Navigator (1394–1460)
Portuguese prince, the fourth son of John I, Henry is credited with setting up an observatory and a school for navigators in 1419 which applied classical and Arab principles to produce ships capable of long sea voyages. Under Henry's patronage Portuguese sailors explored and colonized Madeira, the Cape Verde Islands, and the Azores, all off the northwest coast of Africa, and continued their voyages along the west coast of Africa almost

to Sierra Leone. These expeditions led to the navigation of the sea route to India.

Herzl, Theodor (1860–1904)

Hungarian-born Austrian writer and founder of political Zionism, the Jewish movement for a Jewish homeland in Palestine, in response to anti-Semitism (persecution of the Jews). Herzl was convinced by the **Dreyfus** case in 1894 that the only solution to the problem of anti-Semitism was the resettlement of the Jews in a state of their own. His book *Jewish State* (1896) launched the political Zionist movement, and he became the first president of the World Zionist Organisation in 1897.

He was born in Budapest, Hungary, and became a successful playwright and journalist, mainly in Vienna, Austria.

❝ Don't forget that your people need young, healthy strength and that you are the heir to the name Herzl. ❞

Theodor Herzl, last words, to his son, 1904.

Heydrich, Reinhard Tristan Eugen (1904–1942)

German Nazi and head of the *Sicherheitsdienst* (SD), the party's security service, who was Heinrich **Himmler's** deputy in the SS (*Schutzstaffel*) elitist paramilitary corp. Heydrich was the main organizer of the **final solution**, the **Nazi** policy of genocide used against Jews and others. 'Protector' of Bohemia and Moravia from 1941, he was ambushed and killed the following year by three members of the Czechoslovak forces in Britain, who had landed by parachute. Reprisals by the Nazis followed, including the execution of several hundred prisoners and the notorious massacre in the Czechoslovakian town of Lidice in 1942.

> Heydrich's fanaticism was feared by many of the Nazi leaders, who also regarded his insistence on travelling in an open car without a bodyguard as madness. Many were secretly overjoyed at the news of his death.

Heydrich is believed to have had Jewish ancestry, although this was not widely known at the time and seems, if anything, only to have made him a more fanatical Nazi.

Himmler, Heinrich (1900–1945)

German Nazi leader, who was head of the SS (*Schutzstaffel*) paramilitary elite corps from 1929 and of the police and the Gestapo secret police from 1936, and supervisor of the Nazi policy of extermination of the Jews in Eastern Europe. During **World War II** he replaced Hermann **Goering** as Hitler's second-in-command.

Born in Munich, he joined the **Nazi** Party in 1925 and became chief of the Bavarian police in 1933. His accumulation of offices meant he had command of all German police forces by 1936, making him one of the most powerful people in Germany. He was appointed minister of the interior in 1943 in an attempt to stamp out defeatism and, in the wake of the **July Plot** in 1944, he became commander-in-chief of the home forces. In April 1945 he made a proposal to the Allies that Germany should surrender to the USA and Britain but not to the USSR, which was rejected. He was arrested at the end of the war in May 1945 and committed suicide at the **Nuremberg trials** at which several Nazis were tried for war crimes.

> 𝟲 We shall never be rough and heartless when it is not necessary. 𝟵
>
> **Heinrich Himmler**, speech, 4 October 1943.

Hindenburg, Paul Ludwig Hans Anton von Beneckendorf und Hindenburg (1847–1934)

German field marshal and right-wing politician, who was supreme commander during **World War I**. With Erich von **Ludendorff**, Hindenburg practically directed Germany's policy until the end of the war. He was president of Germany from 1925 to 1934.

Born in Poznan of a Prussian Junker (aristocratic landowner) family, he was commissioned (given rank in the army) in 1866, served in the Austro-Prussian and Franco-German wars, and retired in 1911. Given the command in East Prussia in August 1914, he received the credit for the defeat

Hindenburg despised Hitler, who had been a corporal in the war. He opposed his persecution of the Jews because he knew that many Jews had fought and died for Germany during World War I.

> 𝟲 The German army was stabbed in the back. 𝟵
>
> **Paul von Hindenburg**, quoting an English general, in a statement read to a Reichstag Committee of Inquiry, 18 November 1919.

of the Russians at **Tannenberg** and was promoted to supreme commander and field marshal. Re-elected president in 1932, he was persuaded to invite Nazi leader Adolf **Hitler** to become chancellor in January 1933.

Hitler, Adolf (1889–1945)

German **Nazi** dictator, born in Braunau-am-Inn in Austria. He spent his early years in poverty in Vienna and later in Munich, Germany. After serving as a volunteer in the German army during **World War I**, Hitler was employed as a spy by the military authorities in Munich and in 1919 was sent to join the German Workers' Party. By 1921 he had become leader of the latter and renamed it the National Socialist German Workers' Party (NSDAP, Nazi Party for short), providing it with a programme that mixed nationalism with anti-Semitism (persecution of the Jews). After an unsuccessful uprising of the party in Munich 1923, the **Beer-Hall Putsch**, he served nine months in prison, during which he wrote his political testament, *Mein Kampf*.

The Nazi Party did not achieve national importance until the elections of 1930. Although Field Marshal **Hindenburg** defeated Hitler in the presidential elections in 1932, the Nazis formed the largest group in the Reichstag (parliament). As the result of an intrigue directed by Chancellor Franz **von Papen**, Hitler became chancellor in a Nazi-Nationalist coalition on 30 January 1933. The opposition was rapidly suppressed, the Nationalists removed from the government, and the Nazis were declared the only legal party. In 1934 Hitler succeeded Hindenburg as head of state. Meanwhile, Hitler's aggressive drive to war began; Germany left the **League of Nations**, conscription was reintroduced, and in 1936 the Rhineland was reoccupied.

Hitler and Italian dictator **Mussolini**, who were already both involved in the Spanish Civil War, formed an alliance (the Axis) in 1936 (joined by Japan in 1940). When Germany invaded Poland in September 1939 Britain and France declared war on Germany and **World War II** ensued. Hitler narrowly escaped death on 20 July 1944 from a bomb explosion instigated by high-ranking officers (the **July Plot**), while attending a staff meeting. On 29 April 1945, when the German capital Berlin was largely in Soviet hands, he married his mistress Eva **Braun** in their bunker under the chancellery building. The following day he committed suicide with her. Germany surrendered to the Allies in May 1945.

See also: *Nazi state; final solution; Holocaust.*

> ❝I go the way that Providence dictates with the assurance of a sleepwalker.❞
>
> **Adolf Hitler**, speech in Munich, March 1936.

Hoare-Laval Pact

Plan for a peaceful settlement to the Italian invasion of **Abyssinia** in October 1935, which was devised by Samuel Hoare (1880–1959), the British foreign secretary, and Pierre **Laval**, the French premier, at the request of the **League of Nations**. Realizing that none of the European countries were willing to go to war over Abyssinia, Hoare and Laval suggested that Abyssinia should be divided, with parts going to Italy. Public outcry in Britain was so great that the pact had to be disowned and Hoare was forced to resign.

Hoess, Rudolf Franz (1900–1947)

German commandant of the **Auschwitz** extermination camp from 1940 to 1943 when more than 2.5 million people were exterminated there as part of the **Nazi** policy of anti-Semitism (persecution of the Jews and other minorities). Hoess considered the recommended method of gassing by carbon monoxide as inefficient, and so introduced the cyanide gas Zyklon B that increased the execution rate to 6,000 people per day. In late 1943 he was appointed chief inspector of all German concentration camps and committed himself to improving the 'efficiency' of their extermination centres. Arrested by the Allied military police in 1946, he was handed over to the Polish authorities, who tried him for war atrocities and executed him in 1947.

At his trial Hoess showed no remorse for his actions. His main concern appeared to be that people might think him inefficient.

See also: *Holocaust; final solution.*

Hohenzollern

German family, originating in Württemberg, the main branch of which held the titles of Elector of Brandenburg from 1415, king of Prussia from 1701, and German emperor from 1871. The last emperor, **William II**, was dethroned in 1918 after the disastrous course of **World War I**. Another branch of the family were kings of Romania who ruled from 1881 to 1947.

Holocaust, the

The annihilation of an estimated 16 million people by Adolf **Hitler's Nazi** regime between 1933 and 1945, principally in the numerous extermination and concentration camps, most notably **Auschwitz** (Oswiecim), Sobibor, Treblinka, and Maidanek in Poland, and Belsen, Buchenwald, and Dachau in Germany. Of the victims, around 6 million were Jews (over 67% of European Jews); around 10 million were Ukrainian, Polish, and Russian civilians and prisoners of war, gypsies, socialists, homosexuals, and others

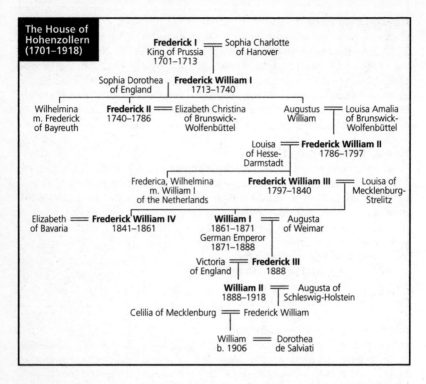

The House of Hohenzollern (1701–1918)

Frederick I — Sophia Charlotte
King of Prussia — of Hanover
1701–1713

Sophia Dorothea | Frederick William I
of England — 1713–1740

Wilhelmina — Frederick II === Elizabeth Christina — Augustus === Louisa Amalia
m. Frederick — 1740–1786 — of Brunswick- — William — of Brunswick-
of Bayreuth — Wolfenbüttel — Wolfenbüttel

Louisa === Frederick William II
of Hesse- — 1786–1797
Darmstadt

Frederica, Wilhelmina — Frederick William III === Louisa of
m. William I — 1797–1840 — Mecklenburg-
of the Netherlands — Strelitz

Elizabeth === Frederick William IV — William I === Augusta
of Bavaria — 1841–1861 — 1861–1871 — of Weimar
German Emperor
1871–1888

Victoria === Frederick III
of England | 1888

William II === Augusta of
1888–1918 | Schleswig-Holstein

Celilia of Mecklenburg === Frederick William

William === Dorothea
b. 1906 — de Salviati

(labelled 'defectives') who were also imprisoned and/or exterminated. Victims were variously starved, tortured, experimented on, or forced to work until their death from exhaustion. Millions were executed in gas chambers, shot, or hanged. It was euphemistically termed the **final solution** (of the Jewish question). The precise death toll will never be known.

> ❝ This is for the dead. This is not charity from the Swiss. My father deposited the money. This is my money. ❞
>
> **Estelle Sapir**, holocaust survivor, on finally receiving some of the money deposited with Crédit Suisse by her father Joseph, who died in the Maideneck concentration camp in 1943, *Daily Telegraph*, 14 August 1998.

Holy Alliance

'Christian Union of Charity, Peace, and Love' set up by **Alexander I** of Russia in 1815 and signed by every crowned head in Europe, except for

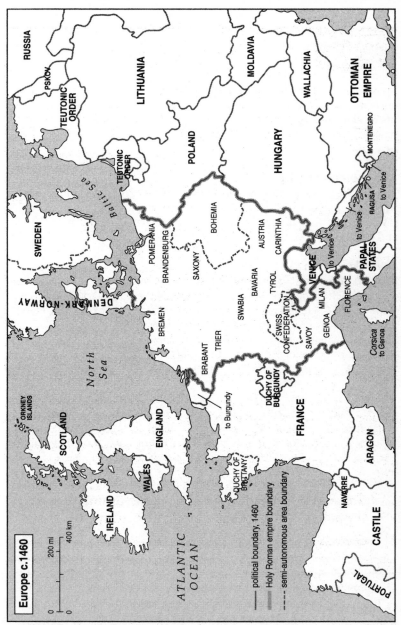

Holy Roman Empire *Map of Europe c. 1460 showing the boundaries of the Holy Roman Empire.*

George IV of Britain (the prince regent, 1762–1830), the sultan of Turkey, and the Pope. The alliance became associated with Russian attempts to preserve autocratic monarchies at any price, and used as an excuse to meddle in the internal affairs of other states.

Lord Castlereagh, the British foreign secretary, prevented the prince regent from signing it. He described it as a 'piece of sublime mysticism and nonsense'.

Holy Roman Empire
The empire of **Charlemagne** and his successors, and the German Empire from 962 to 1806, both being regarded as the Christian (hence 'holy') revival of the Roman Empire. At its height it comprised much of Western and Central Europe. (See map p. 85)

Honecker, Erich (1912–1994)
German communist politician who was in power in East Germany from 1973 to 1989. Honecker was elected chair of the council of state (head of state) in 1976. He governed in an outwardly austere and efficient manner and, while favouring an East-West détente, was a loyal ally of the USSR. In 1989, following a wave of pro-democracy demonstrations, he was replaced as leader of the Socialist Unity Party (SED) and as head of state by Egon Krenz (1937–), and expelled from the Communist Party. He died in exile in Chile.

Horn, Philip de Montmorency, Count of Horn (c. 1518–1568)
Flemish politician who held high offices under the Holy Roman Emperor **Charles V** and his son **Philip II**. From 1563 Horn was one of the leaders of the opposition to the rule of Cardinal Granvella (1517–1586) and to the introduction of the **Inquisition** (set up by the Roman Catholic Church in 1233 to suppress dissenters). In 1567 Horn was arrested, together with another champion of religious toleration, Lamoral Graf von **Egmont**, and both were beheaded in Brussels.

Hoxha, Enver (1908–1985)
Albanian communist politician who was the country's leader from 1954. Hoxha founded the Albanian Communist Party in 1941, and headed the liberation movement from 1939 to 1944. He was prime minister from 1944 to 1954, also handling foreign affairs during the years 1946 to 1953, and from 1954 he was first secretary of the Albanian Party of Labour. His principles were based on those of Soviet leader Joseph **Stalin,** but remained

independent of both Chinese and Soviet communism. Under his rule Albania became an isolated and secretive country, with almost no contact with the outside world, and had the poorest economy in Europe.

Hungary, Republic of

Chronology

1001	St Stephen founds the Hungarian kingdom to replace tribal organization and converts Hungarians to Christianity.
12th century	Hungary becomes a major power when King Béla III wins temporary supremacy over the Balkans.
1456	The Battle of Belgrade: János Hunyadi defeats the Ottoman Turks and saves Hungary from invasion.
1526	The Battle of Mohács: Turks under Suleiman the Magnificent decisively defeat the Hungarians.
16th century	The Partition of Hungary between Turkey, Austria, and the semi-autonomous Transylvania.
1699	The Treaty of Karlowitz: Austrians expel the Turks from Hungary, which was reunified under Habsburg rule.
1780–90	**Joseph II's** attempts to impose uniform administration throughout the Austrian Empire provokes nationalist reaction among the Hungarian nobility.
early 19th century	The 'National Revival' movement led by Count Stephen Széchenyi and Lajos **Kossuth** begins.
1848	The Hungarian Revolution: the nationalists proclaim self-government; the Croat minority resists Hungarian rule.
1849	Kossuth repudiates the **Habsburg** monarchy; the Austrians crush the revolution with the help of Russian support.
1867	Austria concedes equality to Hungary within the dual monarchy of **Austria-Hungary**.
1918	Austria-Hungary collapses in military defeat; Count Mihály Károlyi proclaims a Hungarian Republic.
1919	The Communists take power under Béla Kun; the Romanians invade; Admiral Miklós Horthy overthrows Béla Kun.
1920	The Treaty of Trianon: Hungary loses 72% of its territory to Czechoslovakia, Romania, and Yugoslavia; Horthy restores the Kingdom of Hungary with himself as regent.
1941	Hungary declares war on the USSR in alliance with Germany.
1944	Germany occupies Hungary and instals a Nazi regime.
1945	The USSR 'liberates' Hungary.
1947	A peace treaty restores the 1920 frontiers.
1949	Hungary becomes a Soviet-style dictatorship; Rákosi pursues the Stalinist policies of collectivization and police terror.
1956	The **Hungarian Uprising** erupts.
1989	The communist dictatorship is dismantled.
1997	Hungary is invited to join NATO and begins negotiations for membership of the European Union.
1999	Hungary becomes a full member of NATO.

Hundred Days, The

In European history, the period from 20 March to 28 June 1815 that marked the French emperor **Napoleon I's** escape from imprisonment on the Mediterranean island of Elba, to his departure from Paris after losing the Battle of **Waterloo** on 18 June.

Napoleon's return posed a considerable problem for his marshals. Should they support him, or stay loyal to the restored King Louis XVIII? One of them solved the problem by committing suicide.

hyperinflation

Rapid and uncontrolled inflation, or increases in prices, usually associated with political and/or social instability, for example as witnessed in Germany in the 1920s. After the invasion of the Ruhr by French and Belgian forces in January 1923, the **Weimar** Government began to print large amounts of money to pay the striking German miners in the occupied area. This led to massive increases in prices. By September 1923, the sum of £1 was equal to 2,300,000,000 marks. People with savings or who lived on pensions were ruined.

At the peak of hyperinflation, people drove around in open-topped cars with bundles of banknotes piled up with no fear of being robbed. One man left a bag of money outside a shop and returned to find that the money had been tipped out and that the bag had been stolen.

Inkerman, Battle of

In the **Crimean War**, the British and French victory of 5 November 1854 over the Russians attacking the Inkerman Ridge, which was occupied by the British army besieging the Black Sea port of **Sevastopol**.

A serious attack was launched on 5 November under cover of fog, which enabled the Russians to reach the British lines without being seen. The Russians outnumbered the British at their point of attack, and were able to seize the hilltop and bring up artillery. However, mist prevented them from opening effective fire, and a rapid counterattack by the British 2nd Division recaptured the hilltop and drove off the Russians.

At the Battle of Inkerman the phrase the 'Thin Red Line' was coined to describe the British infantry holding back the Russians.

The fighting lasted about seven hours, during which time the British lost about 2,400 troops, the French about 1,000, and the Russians an estimated 11,000.

Innocent III (c. 1161–1216)

Pope from 1198, Innocent asserted papal power over kings and princes, in particular over the succession of Holy Roman Emperors.

- He adjudicated between the rival claimants for the Holy Roman Empire and deposed Otto IV (c. 1178–1218).

- He excommunicated King John of England (1167–1216) and put the country under the Interdict (ecclesiastical punishment banning Roman Catholic activities).

- He promoted the Spiritual Movement, which led to the founding of the Franciscan and Dominican Friars.

In 1215 Innocent held the Fourth Lateran Council, which declared;

- the Church as 'one and universal';
- the sacraments as the only way of achieving salvation;
- rules to govern the elections of bishops, education, and monasteries.

> ❝ Greediness closed Paradise; it beheaded John the Baptist. ❞
>
> **Innocent III,** *De Contemptu Mundi.*

Inquisition

Tribunal of the Roman Catholic Church established in 1233 to suppress heresy, originally by excommunication. The Inquisition operated in France, Italy, Spain, and the Holy Roman Empire, and was especially active after the Reformation (16th-century religious and social movement); it was later extended to the Americas. Its trials were conducted in secret, under torture, and penalties ranged from fines, flogging, and imprisonment, to death by burning.

Inquisition *A witness giving testimony at an inquisition trial.*

During the course of the Spanish Inquisition, until its abolition in 1834, some 60,000 cases were apparently tried. The Roman Inquisition was established in 1542 to combat the growth of religious Protestantism. However, it is unclear how thorough or effective the Inquisition ever was.

International Brigade

International volunteer forces of about 40,000 men on the Republican side in the **Spanish Civil War** from 1936 to 1939.
See also: *Franco; Popular Front.*

The British writer George Orwell and the American writer Ernest Hemingway were among the volunteers.

Iron Curtain

In Europe after **World War II**, the symbolic boundary between the capitalist West and the communist East during the so-called **Cold War** (1945–1990), a period of severe political tension between the two sides. The term was popularized by the UK prime minister Winston Churchill (1879–1965) in his speech at Fulton, Missouri, USA, in March 1946.

An English traveller to Bolshevik Russia, Ethel Snowden (1881–1951), used the term with reference to the Soviet border in 1920. The Nazi minister Paul **Goebbels** used it a few months before Churchill in 1945 to describe the divide between Soviet-dominated and other nations that would follow German capitulation.

> ❝ From Stettin in the Baltic to Trieste in the Adriatic, an iron curtain has descended across the Continent. ❞
>
> **Winston Churchill**, British Conservative prime minister, speech at Westminster College, Fulton, Missouri 5 March 1946.

Isabella I of Castille (1451–1504)

Queen of Castille from 1474, in 1469 Isabella had married **Ferdinand of Aragon** and from 1479 they were jointly king and queen and credited with uniting Spain for the first time. During their reign Granada was recaptured and the Italian navigator Christopher Columbus (1451–1506) set sail for the Americas.

Italy

Chronology

756	The **Papal States** are created in central Italy.
800	**Charlemagne** unites Italy and Germany in the Holy Roman Empire.
14th century	The beginnings of the **Renaissance** in northern Italy.
15th century	Most of Italy was ruled by five rival states: the city-states of Milan, Florence, and Venice; the **Papal States**; and the Kingdom of **Naples**.
1529–59	The Spanish **Habsburgs** secure dominance in Italy.
17th century	Italy is effectively part of the Spanish Empire; there is economic and cultural decline.
1713	The Treaty of **Utrecht** gives political control of most of Italy to the Austrian Habsburgs.
1796–1814	France conquers Italy, setting up satellite states and introducing principles of the **French Revolution**.
1815	The old regimes are largely restored; Italy is divided between Austria, the Papal States, Naples, Sardinia, and the four duchies.

Map showing the Italian states as they were in c. 1460

1831   Giuseppe **Mazzini** founds the **'Young Italy'** movement with the aim of creating a unified republic.

1848–49   Revolutions occur throughout Italy; they are reversed everywhere except in Sardinia, which becomes a centre of nationalism under the leadership of Count Camillo di **Cavour**.

1859   France and Sardinia forcibly expel the Austrians from Lombardy.

1860	Sardinia annexes the duchies and the **Papal States** (except Rome); Giuseppe **Garibaldi** overthrows the Neapolitan monarchy.
1861	Victor **Emmanuel II** of Sardinia is proclaimed King of Italy in Turin.
1866	Italy gains Venetia after the defeat of Austria by Prussia.
1870	Italian forces occupy Rome in defiance of the Pope, completing the unification of Italy.
1882	Italy joins Germany and Austria-Hungary in the Triple Alliance.
1896	An attempt to conquer **Abyssinia** (Ethiopia) is defeated at the Battle of Aduwa.
1912	The annexation of Libya and Dodecanese after the Italo-Turkish War.
1915	Italy enters **World War I** on the side of the Allies.
1919	Peace treaties award Trentino, South Tyrol, and Trieste to Italy.
1922	Italian dictator Benito **Mussolini** establishs his Fascist dictatorship following a period of strikes and agrarian revolts.
1935–36	Conquest of **Abyssinia** (Ethiopia)
1939	Albania is invaded.
1940	Italy enters **World War II** as an ally of Germany.
1943	The Allies invade southern Italy; Mussolini is removed from power; the Germans occupy northern and central Italy.
1945	The Allies complete liberation.
1946	The Monarchy is replaced by a republic.
1957	Italy becomes a founder member of the European Economic Community (EEC).

Ivan (IV) the Terrible (1530–1584)

Grand Duke of Muscovy from 1533 and tsar from 1544. He was crowned as first tsar of Russia in 1547.

- He conquered Kazan in 1552, Astrakhan in 1556, and Siberia in 1581.

- He reformed the legal code and local administration in 1555 and established trade relations with England.

- In his last years he alternated between debauchery and religious austerities, executing thousands including, in rage, his own son.

> ❝ Did I ascend the throne by robbery or armed bloodshed? I was born to rule by the grace of God … I grew up upon the throne. ❞
>
> **Ivan IV**, letter to Prince Kurbsky, September 1577.

Jacobin

Member of an extremist republican club of the **French Revolution** founded in Paris in 1789. Helped by the revolutionary speeches of Georges Jacques **Danton**, they proclaimed France a republic, had the king executed, and overthrew the moderate **Girondins** in 1793. Through the **Committee of Public Safety**, they began the **Reign of Terror**, led by **Robespierre**. After his execution in 1794, the club was abandoned and the name 'Jacobin' passed into general use for any left-wing extremist.

> The Jacobins were so called because they used a former Jacobin (Dominican) friary as their headquarters in Paris.

Jacquerie

French peasant uprising in 1358, caused by the ravages of the English army and the French nobility during the Hundred Years' War, which reduced the rural population to destitution.

> The word derives from the nickname for French peasants, *Jacques Bonhomme*.

Jena, Battle of (also known as the Battle of Äuerstadt)

In the **Napoleonic Wars**, comprehensive French victory over the combined Prussian and Saxon armies on 4 October 1806 at Jena, Germany. Prussian and Saxon losses amounted to some 40,000 troops and 200 guns, while French casualties were 14,000. The Prussian forces were so weakened that they were unable to prevent French emperor **Napoleon I** marching on Berlin. This disaster led to the complete overhaul and re-organization of the Prussian Army, which laid the foundations for its subsequent military prowess.

jingoism

A term denoting fierce patriotism. The expression originated in 1878 when the British prime minister Benjamin Disraeli (1804–1881) developed a pro-Turkish policy, which nearly involved the UK in war with Russia. His supporters' war song included the line 'We don't want to fight, but by jingo if we do ...'.

> ❝ We don't want to fight, but, by jingo if we do, /
> We've got the ships, we've got the men, we've got
> the money too. ❞
>
> **G W Hunt**, English writer, music hall song.

John III or John Sobieski (1624–1696)
King of Poland from 1674, John Sobieski became commander-in-chief of the army in 1668 after victories over the Cossacks (warrior-peasants of the tsarist cavalry) and the plundering Turkish Tatars (or Tartars). A victory over the Turks in 1673 helped to get him elected to the Polish throne, and he saved Vienna, Austria, from the besieging Turks in 1683.

John of Austria, Don (1547–1578)
Spanish soldier and the illegitimate son of the Holy Roman Emperor **Charles V**, John defeated the Turks at the Battle of **Lepanto** in 1571.

John captured Tunis in Tunisia in 1573 but quickly lost it. He was appointed governor general of the Netherlands in 1576 but discovered that real power in the country lay in the hands of William of **Orange**. John withdrew in 1577 and then attacked and defeated the Netherlands patriot army at Gemblours on 31 January 1578 with the support of reinforcements from **Philip II** of Spain (in his efforts to regain the Netherlands). Lack of money prevented John from going any further. He died of fever.

> ❝ An attractive and glamorous hero ... he was out
> to compensate for his illegitimacy by winning a
> throne. ❞
>
> **E N Williams**, English historian, on John of Austria, *Penguin Dictionary of English and European History* 1485–1789.

Joseph II (1741–1790)
Holy Roman Emperor from 1765, Joseph ruled jointly with his mother **Maria Theresa** until her death in 1780.

The reforms he carried out after her death provoked revolts from those who lost privileges. The main features of Joseph's reign were:

- the decrease in the power of the nobility and an attempt to end serfdom (peasants tied to the land);
- reduced power of the church, which lost control of education; 700 monasteries were closed;
- religious tolerance for all groups, including Jews, the end of press and theatre censorship.

Joseph's autocratic manner made him many enemies and most of his reforms were reversed after his death.

> ❝ Here lies Joseph, who failed in everything he undertook. ❞
>
> **Joseph II**, attributed suggestion for his own epitaph, when reflecting upon disappointment of his hopes for reform.

Joyce, William (1906–1946)
Born in New York, son of a naturalized Irish-born American, Joyce pursued fascist activity in the UK as a 'British subject'. During **World War II** from 1939 to 1945 he made propaganda broadcasts from Germany to the UK, his upper-class accent earning him the nickname Lord Haw Haw. He was hanged for treason.

> ❝ Germany calling! Germany calling! ❞
>
> **William Joyce**, habitual introduction to propaganda broadcasts by Joyce to Britain during World War II.

Julius II (1443–1513)
Born Giuliano della Rovere, he was Pope from 1503 to 1513, as well as a politician who strove to make the Papal States the leading power in Italy. He formed international alliances first against Venice and then against France.

Julius began the building of St Peter's Church in Rome in 1506 and was a patron of the artists Michelangelo and Raphael.

> ❝ Nay, give me a sword, for I am no scholar. ❞
>
> **Julius II**, to Michelangelo who, while carving a statue at Bologna to commemorate Julius' capture of the city, asked the Pope what he should place in his hand, 1506.

July Plot or July Conspiracy

An unsuccessful attempt to assassinate the **Nazi** dictator Adolf **Hitler** and overthrow his regime on 20 July 1944. Col von Stauffenberg planted a bomb under the conference table at Hitler's headquarters at Rastenburg, East Prussia, during a staff meeting. Believing that Hitler had been killed, Stauffenberg flew to Berlin to join Field Marshal von Witzleben and Gen von Beck to proclaim a government headed by resistance leader and former lord mayor of Leipzig, Carl Goerdeler.

Hitler escaped serious injury because someone moved the briefcase containing the bomb. It had been placed on the inside of a leg of a large wooden table, but it was moved to the outside of the leg. This protected Hitler from the full force of the blast.

However, Hitler was only slightly injured, although five senior officers had been killed. Reprisals were savage: the conspirators and their sympathizers were given the choice of committing suicide or being hanged. At least 250 officers died this way, including Field Marshal Erwin Rommel, and some 10,000 people were sent to concentration camps.

July Revolution

Revolution of 27 to 29 July 1830 in France that overthrew the restored Bourbon monarchy of **Charles X** and replaced it with the constitutional monarchy of **Louis Philippe**, whose rule during the period 1830 to 1848 is sometimes referred to as the 'July Monarchy.'

Junker

Member of the landed aristocracy in Prussia; favoured by **Frederick the Great** and Chancellor Otto von **Bismarck**, they controlled land, industry, trade, and the army. From the 15th century until the 1930s they were the source of most of the Prussian civil service and officer corps.

Kaiser

Title formerly used by the Holy Roman Emperors, Austrian emperors 1806–1918, and German emperors 1871–1918.

The word, like the Russian 'tsar', is derived from the Latin *Caesar*.

Kamenev, Lev Borisovich (1883–1936)

Russian leader of the **Bolshevik** movement after 1917 who, with Soviet leader Joseph **Stalin** and Soviet politician Grigory **Zinoviev**, formed a ruling triumvirate in the USSR after Soviet leader **Lenin's** death in 1924. Kamenev's links with the Trotskyists (followers of the principles of Leon **Trotsky**) led to his dismissal by Stalin from office and from the Communist Party in 1926. Arrested in 1934 after Sergei **Kirov's** assassination, Kamenev was secretly tried and sentenced, then retried, condemned, and shot in 1936 for allegedly plotting to murder Stalin.

Lev Kamenev was Trotsky's son-in-law.

Kerensky, Alexandr Feodorovich (1881–1970)

Russian revolutionary politician, prime minister of the second provisional government before its collapse in November 1917, during the Russian Revolution. Kerensky was overthrown by the **Bolshevik** revolution and fled to France in 1918 and to the USA in 1940.

Kerensky's father, Feydor Kerensky, was **Lenin's** schoolteacher.

Khair ed-Din (*c.* 1465–1546)

Turkish corsair and admiral of the Ottoman fleet. Known as Barbarossa (Italian for 'Redbeard'), he harassed European shipping and settlements in the Mediterranean, capturing Algiers from the Spanish in 1519, and gradually took control of all the North African states. He later won several victories against the fleet of Emperor **Charles V**. His campaigns severely weakened Spain's influence in the Mediterranean.

Khrushchev, Nikita Sergeyevich (1894–1971)

Soviet politician, secretary general of the Soviet Communist Party from 1953 to 1964, and premier from 1958 to 1964. He emerged as leader from the interim committee that ruled after Soviet leader Joseph **Stalin's** death and was the first official to denounce Stalin (in a secret session of the party in 1956). Khrushchev's de-Stalinization programme gave rise to revolts in Poland and Hungary in 1956. Because of problems with the domestic economy and in foreign affairs (a breach with China in 1960 and conflict with the USA in the Cuban missile crisis of 1962), he was ousted by the Soviet politicians Leonid **Brezhnev** and Alexei Kosygin.

Khrushchev was an outspoken critic of modern art during his lifetime. In his will he asked a sculptor, whose work he had ridiculed to design his memorial.

Many victims of Stalin's **purges** of the 1930s were either released or posthumously rehabilitated. However, when Hungary revolted in October 1956 against Soviet domination, there was immediate Soviet intervention. In 1958 Khrushchev succeeded Nikolai **Bulganin** as chair of the council of ministers (prime minister). His policy of competition with the capitalist West was successful in the Soviet space programme, which launched the world's first satellite (*Sputnik*). Because of the Cuban crisis and the personal feud with Chinese rule Mao Zedong that led to the Sino-Soviet split, he was compelled to resign in 1964, although by 1965 his reputation was to some extent officially restored. In April 1989 his 'secret speech' against Stalin in February 1956 was officially published for the first time.

> ❝ Comrades! We must abolish the cult of the individual decisively, once and for all. ❞
>
> **Nikita Khrushchev**, speech to the secret session of 20th Congress of the Communist Party, 25 February 1956.

Kirov, Sergei Mironovich (1886–1934)

Russian Bolshevik leader who joined the Bolshevik Party (former name until 1918 of the Communist Party) in 1904 and played a prominent part in the civil war from 1918 to 1920. Kirov was one of Soviet leader Joseph **Stalin's** closest associates, and became first

At a meeting of the Communist Party in 1934, Kirov won more votes than all other members, including Stalin.

secretary of the Leningrad Communist Party. His assassination, possibly engineered by Stalin, led to the political trials held during the next four years as part of Stalin's **purges**.

Kornilov, Lavr Georgyevich (1870–1918)
Russian general, commander-in-chief of the army who in August 1917 launched an attempted coup, backed by officers, against the revolutionary prime minister, Alexandr **Kerensky**. The coup failed, but severely weakened the provisional government, clearing the way for the **Bolsheviks** to seize power. Kornilov was captured and executed by the Bolsheviks in 1918.

Kossuth, Lajos (1802–1894)
Hungarian nationalist and leader of the revolution of 1848, who proclaimed Hungary's independence of **Habsburg** rule and became governor of a Hungarian republic in 1849. When Hungary was defeated by Austria and Russia, Kossuth fled first to Turkey and then to exile in Britain and Italy.

In 1850 Kossuth visited Britain and was received by the foreign secretary Lord Palmerston (1784–1865). This offended Queen Victoria (1819–1901), because Kossuth had rebelled against the Habsburgs.

❦ Despotism and oppression never yet were beaten except by heroic resistance. ❧

Lajos Kossuth, speech on landing in the USA, Staten Island, 5 December 1851.

Kristallnacht
'Night of (broken) glass' on 9 to 10 November 1938 when the Nazi *Sturm Abteilung* (SA) in Germany and Austria mounted a concerted attack on Jews, their synagogues, homes, and shops. It followed the assassination of a German embassy official in Paris, France, by a Polish-Jewish youth. Subsequent measures included German legislation against Jews owning businesses or property, and restrictions on their going to school or leaving Germany. It was part of the **Holocaust**.

During the Kristallnacht 91 Jews were killed and more than 200,000 Jewish men were arrested and sent to concentration camps, but almost all were released within days. The damage to property was estimated at 25 million marks.

The incident led to a rush by Jews for visas to other countries, but restrictive immigration policies throughout the world, and obstructive Nazi regulations at home, made it impossible for most of them to leave.

After Kristallnacht Jews were banned from employing any German woman under the age of 45. This was a move that was intended to arouse hatred amongst ordinary Germans.

Kronstadt uprising

Revolt in February 1921 by sailors of the Russian Baltic Fleet at their headquarters in Kronstadt, outside Petrograd (now St Petersburg). On the orders of the leading **Bolshevik**, Leon **Trotsky**, Red Army troops, dressed in white camouflage, crossed the ice to the naval base and captured it on 18 March. The leaders were subsequently shot.

The sailors at Kronstadt had always been loyal supporters of the Bolsheviks. It was their revolt which forced Lenin to change his policies.

The revolt was a warning to Soviet leader Vladimir **Lenin** that his policy of **War Communism** could not continue. In 1921 he introduced the **New Economic Policy**.

Kruger Telegram

Message sent by Kaiser **William II** of Germany to President Kruger of the Transvaal on 3 January 1896 congratulating him on defeating the Jameson Raid of 1895 (a campaign to overthrow the government by British colonial administrator Leander Starr Jameson (1853–1917)). The text of the telegram provoked indignation in Britain and elsewhere, and represented a worsening of Anglo-German relations, in spite of a German government retraction.

Krupp

German steel-making armaments firm, founded in 1811 by Friedrich Krupp (1787–1826) and developed by his son Alfred Krupp (1812–1887) by pioneering the Bessemer steel-making process (the first cheap method of making steel, invented by Henry Bessemer in England in 1856). The company developed the long-distance artillery used in **World War I**, and supported German dictator Adolf **Hitler's** regime in their preparation for **World War II**, after which the head of the firm, Alfred Krupp (1907–1967), was imprisoned.

kulak

Russian term for a peasant who could afford to hire labour and often acted as the village moneylender. The kulaks resisted the Soviet government's policy of collectivization, and in 1930 they were 'liquidated as a class', with up to 10 million being either killed or deported to Siberia.

> The word kulak meant 'tight fist' in Russian and referred to the fact that kulaks were often the village bankers.

Kulturkampf

German word for a policy introduced by Chancellor Otto **Bismarck** in Germany 1873 that attempted to reduce the power of the Catholic Church in Germany.

The **Falk** Laws gave the German government control over the education of the Catholic clergy and of appointments within the Church. The Laws proved unpopular and Bismarck was eventually forced to withdraw them.

Kursk, Battle of

In **World War II**, the name of an unsuccessful German offensive against a Soviet salient (projection into enemy-held territory) in July 1943. The Battle of Kursk was the greatest tank battle in history and proved to be a turning point in the **Eastern Front** campaign. With nearly 6,000 tanks and 2 million troops involved the battle was hard fought, reaching its climax with the pitched battle on 12 July between 700 German and 850 Soviet tanks.

See also: *Stalingrad.*

Lateran Treaties

Series of agreements that marked the reconciliation of the Italian state with the papacy in 1929. They were hailed as a propaganda victory for the **fascist** regime. The treaties involved:

- recognition of the sovereignty of the Vatican City State;
- the payment of an indemnity for papal possessions lost during unification in 1870;
- the Control of education in the hands of the Catholic Church;
- salaries of Catholic clergy to be paid by the Italian government;
- agreement on the role of the Catholic Church within the Italian state in the form of a concordat between Pope **Pius XI** and the dictator **Mussolini**.

See also: *Pius IX; Papal States.*

Laval, Pierre (1883–1945)

French extreme-right wing politician, who served as prime minister and foreign secretary from 1931to 1932 and from 1935 to 1936.

Laval negotiated the **Hoare-Laval Pact** in 1935, providing concessions to Italy in **Abyssinia** (Ethiopia). In July 1940 he was instrumental in securing the voting of full powers to prime minister Henri **Pétain** and served as his vice premier until December 1940. At German dictator Adolf **Hitler's** insistence Laval was reinstated as head of government from April 1942, reducing Pétain to the role of figurehead. As head of the Vichy government and foreign minister from 1942 to 1944, Laval was responsible for the deportation of Jews and for requisitioning French labour to Germany.

He fled the country in 1944 but was captured in Austria, tried for treason in France in October 1945, and was executed by firing squad, after trying to poison himself.

League of Nations

International organization formed after **World War I** to solve international disputes by arbitration. Established in Geneva, Switzerland, in 1920, the League included representatives from states throughout the world, but was severely weakened by the US decision not to become a member, and had no power to enforce its decisions. It was dissolved in 1946.

The League of Nations consisted of:

- a Council that met three times a year with nine members, five of which were permanent;
- an Assembly that met once a year and could only vote unanimously;
- a secretary general and a secretariat to carry out decisions;
- the International Labour Organisation (ILO) formed 1920, based in Geneva and concerned primarily with working conditions and social welfare;
- the High Commission for Refugees created to assist refugees, primarily from the USSR and Eastern Europe.
- the Permanent Court of Justice created in The Hague 1921 and, based on ideas for some form of international court put forward at The Hague congress 1907; it survived and is now known as the International Court of Justice.

The League was successful in settling a series of minor disputes in the 1920s, but was unable to deal with the dictators in the 1930s.

Lebensraum
German 'living space', a theory adopted by German dictator Adolf **Hitler** for the expansion of Germany into Eastern Europe, and in the 1930s used by the Nazis to justify their annexation of neighbouring states on the grounds that Germany was overpopulated.

Lenin, Vladimir Ilyich (1870–1924)
Adopted name of Vladimir Ilyich Ulyanov, who was the leader of the **Bolsheviks**, and ruler of Russia from 1917 to 1924.

Active in the 1905 Revolution, which failed, Lenin was forced to leave Russia, and settled in Switzerland in 1914. After the renewed outbreak of revolution in Russia from February to March 1917, Lenin was

Lenin *Lenin speaking at the first Russian Soviet Congress in 1917.*

smuggled back into Russia in April by the Germans. They believed that he would take up his revolutionary activities and remove Russia from the war, allowing Germany to concentrate the war effort on the Western Front. On arriving in Russia, Lenin established himself at the head of the Bolsheviks, against the provisional government of **Kerensky**. After the **Kornilov** Revolt, the Bolsheviks seized power in October 1917; a Bolshevik government was formed, and peace negotiations with Germany were begun, leading to the signing of the Treaty of **Brest Litovsk** on 3 March 1918.

From the overthrow of the provisional government in November 1917 until his death, Lenin effectively controlled the USSR, although an assassination attempt in 1918 injured his health. He founded the Third (Communist) International in 1919. With communism proving inadequate to put the country on its feet, he introduced the private enterprise **NEP** New Economic Policy in 1921.

> 6 It is true that liberty is precious – so precious that
> it must be rationed. 9
>
> **Vladimir Lenin**, quoted in S and B Webb, *Soviet Communism*.

Leningrad, Siege of

In **World War II**, the German siege of the Soviet city of Leningrad in Russia (now St Petersburg) from 1 September 1941 to 27 January 1944. The city constituted about 20% of the population. Leningrad was awarded the title of 'Hero City' for withstanding the siege.

The German army reached Leningrad in the initial stages of the invasion of the USSR (Operation **Barbarossa**) and were prepared to take it by force. However, **Hitler** ordered his troops to besiege the city in order to achieve a bloodless occupation. Within a week, all

Some 600,000 inhabitants of the city are reckoned to have died during the 900 days of the siege, either from disease, starvation, or enemy action.

land communication was cut off and the city was subjected to air and artillery bombardment. Before the year was out, starvation was resulting in 300 deaths a day, although this was partially eased when Lake Ladoga froze and a truck route was established to bring in food over the ice. Meanwhile the population laboured in munitions factories, dug defences, and served in the front line.

Lepanto, Battle of

Sea battle on 7 October 1571 between the Ottoman Empire and 'Holy League' forces from Spain, Venice, Genoa, and the Papal States, jointly commanded by the Spanish soldier **Don John of Austria**. The battle took place in the Mediterranean Gulf of Corinth, off Lepanto (the Greek port of Naupaktos), then in Turkish possession. It was not decisive, but the combined western fleets halted Turkish expansion and broke Muslim sea power.

Liberty, equality, fraternity (*liberté, égalité, fraternité*)

Motto of the French republic from 1793, it was changed during 1940 and 1944 under the **Vichy** government to a new motto, 'work, family, fatherland'.

Liebknecht, Karl (1871–1919)

German socialist who was a founder of the German Communist Party, originally known as the Spartacus League (the Spartacists). Liebknecht led an unsuccessful revolt with Rosa **Luxemburg** in Berlin in 1919 and both were murdered by army officers.

See also: *Spartacists.*

❝We are fighting for the gates of heaven.❞

Karl Liebknecht, said during the abortive German revolution of 1918–1919. Quoted in Albert Camus, *The Rebel*, ch. 3.

Locarno, Pacts of

Series of diplomatic documents initialled in Locarno, Switzerland , on 16 October 1925 and formally signed in London, UK, on 1 December 1925. The Pacts settled the question of French security, and the signatories – Britain, France, Belgium, Italy, and Germany – guaranteed Germany's existing frontiers with

> The most important point of the Locarno Pacts was that they guaranteed that France and Belgium could not invade Germany.

France and Belgium. Following the signing of the pact, Germany was admitted to the League of Nations.

London, Treaty of

Secret treaty signed on 26 April 1915 between Britain, France, Russia, and Italy. It promised Italy territorial gains (at the expense of **Austria-Hungary**) on condition that it entered **World War I** on the side of the **Triple Entente** (Britain, France, and Russia). Italy's intervention did not achieve the rapid victories expected, and the terms of the treaty (revealed by Russia in 1918) angered the USA.

Britain and France refused to honour the treaty and, in the post-war peace treaties, Italy received far less territory than promised.

Italy was allied to Germany and Austria-Hungary in 1914, but the Italian government waited to see which side was likely to win the war before committing itself. It signed the treaty in an effort to gain international recognition for Italy and to acquire an empire in the Balkans.

Louis XIV (1638–1715)

King of France from 1643, when he succeeded his father Louis XIII (1602–1643), Louis became known as the Sun King; his mother was **Anne of Austria**. Until 1661 France was ruled by the chief minister, Jules Mazarin (1602–1661), but later Louis took absolute power, summed up in his saying *L'Etat c'est moi* (I am the state). Throughout his reign he was engaged in unsuccessful expansionist wars – 1667–68, 1672–78, 1688–97, and 1701–13 (the War of the **Spanish Succession**) – against various European alliances, always including Britain and the Netherlands. He was a patron of the arts and was responsible for the building of the Palace of Versailles.

His reign was one of prosperity for France: under chief minister Jean Baptiste **Colbert** the finances of the kingdom were reformed, trade was increased, and there was a strong colonial policy. Under his war minister, Louvois (1641–1691), the armies were reorganized, and under his generals, Turenne (1611–1675) and Condé (1621–1686), the French army became the finest fighting machine in Europe.

At home his power was absolute. The courts were entirely under his control, and his principle of embodying the state personally was all but true. He married Maria Theresa (1638–1683) of Spain in 1660, but also had a large number of mistresses, and many illegitimate children. After Maria Theresa's death he married Mme de Maintenon (1635–1719) in 1684. She was greatly influenced by the Jesuits and played a great part in persuading Louis to revoke the Edict of Nantes 1685.

Louis XV (1710–1774)

King of France from 1715, with the Duke of Orléans (1674–1723) as regent until 1723, he was the great-grandson of **Louis XIV**. Louis was indolent and frivolous and left government in the hands of his ministers, the Duke of Bourbon and Cardinal **Fleury**. On the latter's death he attempted to rule alone but became entirely dominated by his mistresses, Madame de

Pompadour (1721–1764) and Madame Du Barry (1741–1793). His foreign policy led to French possessions in Canada and India being lost to England.

> ❦ *Ultima ratio regum* / The last argument of kings ❧.
>
> **Louis XV**, engraved on his cannon (its use as a motto for cannon dates back to 1613).

Louis XVI (1754–1793)

King of France from 1774, he was a grandson of **Louis XV** and married **Marie Antoinette** in 1770. Louis was personally popular, but weak and easily influenced. The monarchy became heavily in debt as a result of the war in America and French finances fell into such confusion that in 1789 the Estates General (parliament) had to be summoned, and the **French Revolution** began. Louis lost his personal popularity in June 1791 when he attempted to flee the country, and in August 1792 the Parisians stormed the Tuileries palace and took the royal family prisoner. Deposed in September 1792, Louis was tried in December, sentenced for treason in January 1793, and guillotined.

Louis XVI *King of France from 1774 until his execution in 1793.*

On 14 July 1789, the day that the Bastille was stormed, Louis wrote in his diary *'rien'* (nothing). He was referring to the day's hunting. His favourite past time was working with his collection of clocks and watches.

> ‘May my blood cement your happiness!’
>
> **Louis XVI**, spoken on the scaffold, 21 January 1793.

Louis XVIII (1755–1824)

King of France 1814–24, he was the younger brother of **Louis XVI**. He assumed the title of king in 1795, having fled into exile in 1791 during the French Revolution, but became king only on the fall of **Napoleon I** in April 1814. Expelled during Napoleon's brief return to France in 1815, he resumed power after Napoleon's final defeat at **Waterloo**, pursuing a policy of calculated liberalism until ultra-royalist pressure became dominant after 1820.

> Louis XVIII is said to have not taken his socks off for 18 months.

> ‘Punctuality is the politeness of kings.’
>
> **Louis XVIII**, attributed remark quoted in *Souvenirs de J Lafitte*, 1844, bk 1, ch. 3.

Louis-Napoleon

Name by which **Napoleon III** was known.

Louis Philippe (1773–1850)

King of France from 1830 to 1848, Louis Philippe was the son of Louis Philippe Joseph, Duke of Orléans; both were known as Philippe Egalité from their support of the 1792 Revolution. Louis Philippe fled into exile during 1793 and 1814, but became king after the 1830 revolution with the backing of the rich bourgeoisie. Corruption discredited his regime, and after his overthrow, he escaped to the UK and died there.

> Louis Philippe was known as the bourgeois king. He was often seen walking around Paris wearing a top hat and carrying an umbrella.

> ‘*La cordiale entente …*/ The friendly understanding that exists between my government and hers.’
>
> **Louis Philippe**, speech, 27 December 1843, referring to an informal understanding reached between Britain and France in 1843. (The more familiar phrase ‘*entente cordiale*’ was first used 1844).

Ludendorff, Erich von (1865–1937)

German general and Chief of Staff to Field Marshal Paul von **Hindenburg** in **World War I**, he was responsible for the Eastern-Front victory at the Battle of **Tannenberg** in 1914. After Hindenburg's appointment as chief of general staff and his own as quartermaster general in 1916, Ludendorff was also politically influential and the two were largely responsible for the conduct of the war from then.

Ludendorff planned the **German Spring Offensive** of 1918 but the collapse of the Hindenburg Line under British attack in September and the collapse of Bulgaria shortly afterwards caused him to lose confidence and he called for peace negotiations. When talks were opened he changed his mind, refused to cooperate, and was dismissed by the Kaiser (king) on 26 October 1918.

After the war he propagated the myth of the 'stab in the back', according to which the army had been betrayed by the politicians in 1918. He took part in the Nazi rising in Munich in 1923 and sat in the Reichstag (parliament) as a right-wing Nationalist.

> 6 The Army had been fought to a standstill and was utterly worn out. 9
>
> **Erich von Ludendorff**, on the Battle of the Somme.

Luther, Martin (1483–1546)

German Christian church reformer and a founder of **Protestantism**. As a priest at the University of Wittenberg, Luther attacked the sale for financial gain of indulgences within the Roman Catholic Church (remissions of punishment for sin after forgiveness has been granted).

Luther was enraged when Johann Tetzel (c. 1465–1519) visited Wittenberg in 1517 to sell indulgences as a means of raising funds for the rebuilding of St Peter's Basilica in Rome. In response, on 31 October 1517, Luther nailed on the church door in Wittenberg a statement of 95 theses concerning indulgences, and the following year he was summoned to Rome to defend his action. His reply was to attack the papal system even more strongly, and in Wittenberg 1520 he publicly burned the papal bull (edict) that had been launched against him.

The Holy Roman Emperor **Charles V** summoned Luther to the Diet (meeting of dignitaries of the **Holy Roman Empire**) of Worms in Germany, in 1521, where he refused to retract his objections. Originally intending reform, Luther's protest led to a schism within the Roman Catholic Church with the emergence of a new Protestant Church after the Augsberg

Confession in 1530 (a statement of the Protestant faith). Luther is regarded as the instigator of the Protestant revolution, and Lutheranism is now the predominant religion of many north European countries, including Germany, Sweden, and Denmark.

> ❝ My conscience is taken captive by God's word, I cannot and will not recant anything. ... Here I stand. I can do no other. God help me. Amen. ❞
>
> **Martin Luther**, speech at the Diet of Worms, 18 April 1521.

Lützen, Battle of
In the **Thirty Years' War**, the Swedish victory of 16 November 1632 over an Imperial army under Albrecht von **Wallenstein**. The Swedish army, about 19,000 troops, was led by King **Gustavus Adolphus** who was killed in the battle.

Luxemburg, Rosa (1870–1919)
Polish-born German communist, who helped found the Polish Social Democratic Party in the 1890s, the forerunner of the Polish Communist Party. She was a leader of the left wing of the German Social Democratic Party from 1898 where she collaborated with Karl **Liebknecht** in founding the Spartacus League in 1918 (the **Spartacists**-socialist radicals). She was murdered, together with Liebknecht, in January 1919, by the Frei Corps who crushed the Spartacist uprising.

> ❝ Freedom is always and exclusively freedom for the one who thinks differently. ❞
>
> **Rosa Luxemburg**, The Russian Revolution.

Machiavelli, Niccolò (1469–1527)

Italian politician and author, whose name is synonymous with cunning and cynical statecraft. In his chief political writings, *Il principe/The Prince* (1513) and *Discorsi/Discourses* (1531), he discussed ways in which rulers can advance the interests of their states (and themselves) through an often amoral and opportunistic manipulation of other people.

The Prince, based on his observations of Cesare Borgia, is a guide for the future prince of a unified Italian state (which did not occur until the Risorgimento in the 19th century). In *L'Arte della guerra/The Art of War* (1520), Machiavelli outlined the provision of an army for the prince, and in *Historie fiorentine/History of Florence* he analysed the historical development of Florence until 1492.

See also: *Medici; Renaissance.*

❝ One of the most powerful safeguards a prince can have against conspiracies is to avoid being hated by the populace. ❞

Niccolò Machiavelli, *The Prince*, (1513).

Maginot, André (1877–1932)

French soldier who was the originator of the fortifications that became known as the Maginot Line. He had been an infantryman at Verdun in **World War I**. In 1922 and 1929, he was minister of war. The Maginot Line was completed after his death in 1934.

The Maginot line proved to be a complete waste of time. It finished at the Belgian border and did not cover the wooded area of the Ardennes through which the German army attacked in 1940.

Malenkov, Georgi Maximilianovich (1902–1988)

Soviet prime minister from 1953 to 1955, who was Soviet leader Josef **Stalin's** designated successor but who was abruptly ousted as Communist Party secretary within two weeks of Stalin's death by Nikita **Khrushchev**, and forced out as prime minister in 1955 by Nikolai **Bulganin**.

Malenkov subsequently occupied minor party posts. He was expelled from the Central Committee in 1957 and from the Communist Party in 1961.

After being dismissed by Khrushchev, Malenkov was sent to be the manager of a hydroelectric plant in Kazakhstan. This was typical of Khrushchev's attitude to the purges.

Maquis

French resistance movement that fought against the German occupation during **World War II**.

The word '*maquis*' meant scrub of brush.

Marat, Jean Paul (1743–1793)

Swiss-born French Revolutionary leader, physician, and journalist, Marat was imprisoned several times for his revolutionary principles. He was elected to the National Convention in 1792. He was the leader of the radical **Montagnard** faction and carried on a long struggle with the right-wing **Girondins**, which resulted in their overthrow in May 1793. In July of that year, he was murdered in his bath by Charlotte **Corday**, a Girondin supporter.

While hiding in the Paris sewers from royalists he contracted a painful skin disease, which was only relieved by long periods of immersion in a bath. This where Charlotte Corday found him.

March on Rome, the

Means by which Fascist leader Benito **Mussolini** came to power in Italy in 1922. A protracted crisis in government and the threat of civil war enabled him to demand the formation of a Fascist government to restore order. On 29 October 1922, King **Victor Emmanuel III** invited Mussolini to come to Rome to take power. The 'march' was a propaganda myth: Mussolini travelled overnight by train from Milan to Rome, where he formed a government the following day on 30 October. Some 25,000 Fascist Blackshirts were also transported to the city, where they marched in a ceremonial parade on 31 October.

Marengo, Battle of

During the Napoleonic Wars, the battle that saw the defeat of the Austrians on 14 June 1800 by the French army under French emperor **Napoleon I**, as part of his Italian campaign, near the village of Marengo in Piedmont, Italy. It was one of Napoleon's greatest victories and resulted in the Austrians ceding northern Italy to France.

Maria Theresa (1717–1780)

Empress of Austria from 1740 when she succeeded her father, the Holy Roman Emperor Charles VI. Her claim to the throne was challenged and she became embroiled in conflict, first in the War of the **Austrian Succession** from 1740 to 1748, then in the **Seven Years' War** from 1756 to 1763; she remained in possession of Austria but lost **Silesia**.

After 1763 she pursued a consistently peaceful policy, concentrating on internal reforms; although her methods were despotic, she fostered education, codified the laws, and abolished torture. She also expelled the Jesuits. In these measures she was assisted by her son, **Joseph II**, who became emperor 1765, and succeeded her in the **Habsburg** domains.

> Maria Theresa was the victim of Salic Law, which said that a women could not succeed to the Habsburg crown.

❝ I want to meet my God awake. ❞

Maria Theresa, refusing to take a drug when dying, 1780.

Marie Antoinette (1755–1793)

Queen of France from 1774, she was the fourth daughter of Empress **Maria Theresa** of Austria and the Holy Roman Emperor Francis I (1708–1765). She married **Louis XVI** of France in 1770. Marie

Marie Antoinette's most famous remark 'Let them eat cake' is actually a mistranslation of what was supposed to be a helpful, if somewhat naïve remark, 'Why don't they eat brioche?' Brioche is a soft, cake-like bread.

Marie Antoinette *The Queen of France before her execution by guillotine in 1793.*

Antoinette's devotion to the interests of Austria and her reputation for extravagance made her unpopular, and dislike of her contributed to the **French Revolution** of 1789. She was tried for treason in October 1793 and guillotined.

> 𝕔 Courage! I have shown it for years. Do you think I shall lose it at the moment when my sufferings are to end? 𝕕
>
> **Marie Antoinette**, remark as she was taken to the guillotine, October 1793.

Marie de' Medici (1573–1642)
Queen of France, wife of **Henry IV** from 1600, and regent (after his murder) for their son Louis XIII (1601–1643). Marie left control of the government to her favourites, the Concinis, until Louis XIII seized power and executed them in 1617. She was banished but, after she led a revolt in 1619, Cardinal **Richelieu** brought about her reconciliation with her son. When she attempted to oust her son again in 1630, she was exiled.

Marie Louise (1791–1847)
Second wife of **Napoleon I** from 1810 (after his divorce from Josephine), and mother of Napoleon II, Marie Louise was the daughter of Francis II (1768–1835) of Austria. On Napoleon's fall she returned with their son to Austria, where she was granted the duchy of Parma in 1815.

Marignano, Battle of
During the Italian Wars, the battle that marked a French victory over the Swiss on 13 and 14 September 1515 at Marignano, a village close to the Swiss-Italian border. The French lost about 6,000 troops but gained the Duchy of Milan.

Market Garden, Operation
In **World War II**, the codename for the unsuccessful operation by British and US forces to cross the Meuse, Waal, and Neder-Rijn rivers in Holland in September 1944.

The intention was for British airborne forces to capture vital bridges at Arnhem to open the way for an armoured thrust from the south. When the airborne operation failed, the armoured force was unable to reach Arnhem and the whole operation collapsed.

Marne, Battles of the
In **World War I** the First Battle of the Marne, in September 1914, halted the

German advance during the **Schlieffen Plan**. The German armies that had circled through Belgium were attacked along the River Marne and forced to retreat to the Aisne. This not only halted the Schlieffen Plan but also led to the beginning of **trench warfare**.

The Second Battle of the Marne, from 15 July to 4 August 1918, was the final thrust of the **German Spring Offensive** of 1918. German general Erich von **Ludendorff** threw 35 divisions across the Marne, planning to encircle Reims. The French were prepared for the attack, with four armies under good generals, together with a strong US force, and although the Germans initially gained ground they were eventually halted and turned back.

The Allied counterattack, which was launched on 18 July, is sometimes referred to as the Third Battle of the Marne and it forced the Germans back to a line running from Reims to Soissons.

Marshall Plan

Programme of US economic aid to Europe, which was set up at the end of **World War II**, totalling $13,000 billion between 1948 and 1952. Officially known as the European Recovery Programme, it was announced by US secretary of state George C Marshall (1880–1959) in a speech at Harvard in June 1947, but it was in fact the work of a state department group led by Dean Acheson (1893–1971). The possible danger of a communist takeover in post-war Europe was the main reason for the aid effort.

See also: *Truman Doctrine.*

Marx, Karl Heinrich (1818–1883)

German philosopher, economist, and social theorist whose account of change through conflict is known as historical, or dialectical, materialism.

In 1844 Marx began his lifelong collaboration with German philosopher Friedrich Engels (1820–

Karl Marx *Frontispiece of 'The Communist Manifesto' published in 1948, which Marx wrote with Friedrich Engels.*

1895), with whom he developed the Marxist philosophy. This was first put forward in *The Communist Manifesto* (1847–48). In the wake of the 1848 revolution, Marx was expelled from Prussia 1849. He then settled in London, where he wrote his monumental work *Das Kapital/ Capital* (1867).

Many of Marx's ideas were based on his observations of the effects of industrialization in the north of England.

> 6 Religion is the sigh of the oppressed creature, the sentiment of the heartless world, and the soul of soulless conditions. It is the opium of the people. 9
>
> **Karl Marx**, quoted in Ernst Fischer, *Marx in His Own Words*.

Masaryk, Jan Garrigue (1886–1948)
Czechoslovak politician, son of Tomás Masaryk, who was foreign minister from 1940 when the Czechoslovak government was exiled in London during **World War II**. Masaryk returned home in 1945, retaining his post, but as a result of political pressure by the communists committed suicide.

Masurian Lakes, Battles of
In **World War I**, a battle lasting from 5 to 15 September 1914 in which German forces defeated the Russians between the Masurian Lakes and Königsberg, East Prussia (now Kaliningrad, Russia). This ended the Russian advance into Germany, which had upset the **Schlieffen Plan**.
    See also: *Tannenberg*.

The Russian commanders contributed to their own downfall by sending wireless messages to each other without bothering to put them into code. As a result the Germans knew exactly what the Russians were planning.

Matteotti, Giacomo (1885–1924)
Italian socialist politician, who was an outspoken opponent of the Fascist regime, after Benito **Mussolini** gained power in 1922. Matteotti was murdered in June 1924 by a gang of five Fascists, but not on the orders of Mussolini.

Matteotti disappeared on 12 June 1924 and his body was found nearly two months later in a shallow grave outside Rome. He had a rasp sticking into his chest. Mussolini was paralysed with guilt because of the murder and was virtually inactive for six months.

Maximilian I (1459–1519)

German king from 1486 and Holy Roman Emperor from 1493. He was the son of the emperor Frederick III (1415–93). Through a combination of dynastic marriages and diplomacy backed up by military threats, Maximilian was able to build up the Habsburg inheritance.

- He married Mary of Burgundy in 1477, and after her death in 1482 held onto Burgundian lands.

- He arranged the marriage of his son, Philip the Handsome (1478–1506), to Joanna (1479–1555), the daughter of **Ferdinand** and **Isabella**, and undertook long wars with Italy and Hungary in attempts to extend **Habsburg** power.

- The eventual beneficiary of these arrangements was Maximilian's grandson, **Charles V**.

Mayerling

Site near Vienna of the hunting lodge of Crown Prince Rudolph of Austria, where he and his mistress were found shot dead in 1889. He had been forbidden to marry her by his father **Franz Joseph**.

Mazzini, Giuseppe (1805–1872)

Italian nationalist who was a member of the revolutionary society, the **Carbonari**, and founded in exile the nationalist movement Giovane Italia (**Young Italy**) in 1831. Mazzini returned to Italy on the outbreak of the 1848 revolution and headed a republican government in Rome. However, he was forced into exile again on its overthrow in 1849. Mazzini acted as a focus for the movement for Italian unity.

> ❝ Nations are the citizens of humanity, as individuals are the citizens of the nation. ❞
>
> **Giuseppe Mazzini**, *Duties of Man.*

Medici family

Noble family that ruled the Italian city-state of Florence from the 15th to the 18th centuries. The Medici arrived in Florence in the 13th century and made their fortune in banking.

- The first family member to control the city, from 1434 to 1464, was Cosimo de' Medici ('the Elder') (1389–1464)

- Lorenzo ('the Magnificent') (1449–1492), who ruled from 1469 to 1492, made Florence the foremost city-state in Renaissance Italy. He and his grandfather Cosimo de' Medici were famed as patrons of the arts and humanist thought.

- Four Medici were elected pope, and others married into the royal families of Europe, such as the French queens **Catherine de' Medici** and **Marie de' Medici**.

Mein Kampf

Book dictated by the Nazi leader Adolf **Hitler** to his deputy Rudolf Hess (1894–1987) during 1923 and 1924, while they were imprisoned in the Bavarian fortress of Landsberg for attempting the 1923 Munich **beer-hall putsch**. The title is German for 'my struggle'. Part autobiography, part political philosophy, the book presents Hitler's ideas of German expansion, anti-communism, and anti-Semitism (persecution of the Jews), and formed the blueprint for the racist ideology of **National Socialism**. It was published in two volumes, in 1925 and 1927.

Menshevik

Russian *menshinstvo* 'minority', meaning a member of the minority of the Russian Social Democratic Party, which split from the **Bolsheviks** (precursors of the Communists) in 1903. The Mensheviks believed in a large, loosely organized party and the idea that before socialist revolution could occur in Russia, capitalist society had to develop further. During the **Russian Revolution** they had limited power and set up a government in Georgia, but were suppressed in 1922.

> The Mensheviks were always more numerous than the Bolsheviks, but had been the minority in the argument that split the Social Democrat Party in 1903.

Messines, Battle of

In **World War I**, the scene of a successful British attack between 7 and 15 June 1917 on a German-held Belgian village and ridge in West Flanders, southeast of **Ypres**. The village was occupied by the Germans in November 1914,

> 6 Gentlemen, we may not make history tomorrow, but we shall certainly change the geography. 9

Hubert Plumer, British World War I general, remark to his staff before the Battle of Messines, 1917.

enabling them to hold a dominant position overlooking the British lines. A significant factor in the battle was the scale of mining operations by the British; some 20 mines were excavated and charged with 600 tons of explosive. However, only 18 mines were exploded and the other two were then forgotten about. One exploded in 1956, but the other is still undiscovered.

Metternich, Klemens Wenzel Nepomuk Lothar, Prince von Metternich (1773–1859)

Austrian politician who was the leading figure in European diplomacy after the fall of French emperor **Napoleon I**. As foreign minister from 1809 to 1848 (as well as chancellor from 1821), Metternich tried to maintain the balance of power in Europe, supporting monarchy and repressing liberalism.

At the Congress of **Vienna** in 1815, Metternich advocated cooperation by the great powers to suppress democratic movements. The revolution of 1848 forced him to flee to the UK; he returned in 1851 as a power behind the scenes.

Metternich *Austrian politician and diplomat and one of the leading European figures following the fall of Napoleon.*

Metternich made one of the classic blunders of all time in 1848. On 21 February he made a speech in which he stated that revolution in France was impossible. The Paris Revolution of 1848 began the following day, on February 22.

❝ For great evils drastic remedies are necessary and whoever has to treat them should use the instrument which cuts the best. ❞

Prince von Metternich, reporting as ambassador in Paris, to the Austrian Foreign Minister, 24 September 1808.

Mirabeau, Honoré Gabriel Riqueti, comte de (1749–1791)

French politician and leader of the National Assembly in the **French Revolution** who wanted to establish a parliamentary monarchy on the English model. From May 1790 he secretly acted as political adviser to the king.

Mirabeau's eloquence won him the leadership of the National Assembly; nevertheless, he was out of sympathy with the majority of the deputies, whom he regarded as mere theoreticians.

> ❝ To administer is to govern; to govern is to reign. ❞
>
> **Honoré Gabriel Riqueti**, Comte de Mirabeau, memorandum, 3 July 1790.

Missolonghi, Battle of

During the Greek War of Independence from 1820 to 1830, the scene of a Turkish victory over the Greeks on 22 April 1826, at the town of Missolonghi, Greece. The capture of the town finally moved Britain, France, and Russia to come to the aid of the Greeks.

Lord Byron, the English poet, died at Missolonghi, having volunteered to fight for the Greeks.

Mitterand, François (1916–1996)

French socialist politician, who after a successful ministerial career under the Fourth Republic, holding posts in 11 governments from 1947 to 1958, joined the new Socialist Party (PS) in 1971, establishing it as the most popular party in France. He then won two successive terms as president from 1981 to 1988 and 1988 and 1995.

Mitterand's ambitious programme of social, economic, and institutional reforms was hampered by deteriorating economic conditions after 1983. When the socialists lost their majority in March 1986, he was compelled to work with the Gaullist Jacques Chirac as prime minister, and grew in popularity, defeating Chirac's bid for the presidency in May 1988. In 1993 he entered a second term of 'cohabitation' with the conservative prime minister Edouard Balladur. Towards the end of his presidency his failing health weakened his hold on power. Whereas he was able to enhance his reputation when 'cohabiting' with Chirac, the successful elements of Balladur's premiership contrasted with Mitterand's waning popularity and weakened influence.

> ❝A man loses contact with reality if he is not
> surrounded by his books.❞
>
> **François Mitterrand**, on why he remained in his former home, using the
> Elysée Palace only for official functions, *Times*, 10 May 1982.

Molotov-Ribbentrop Pact also known as the Nazi–Soviet Pact or the Berlin-Moscow Axis

Non-aggression treaty signed by Germany and the USSR on 23 August 1939. Under the terms of the treaty both countries agreed to remain neutral and to refrain from acts of aggression against each other if either went to war.

- On the face of it the Pact was a simple non-aggression pact between the two countries. They both agreed not to attack the other. But Hitler and Stalin had been bitter enemies and the agreement astounded politicians throughout Europe.
- In fact there were a number of secret clauses that were not revealed to the public.
- The Soviet Union agreed not to interfere when Germany attacked Poland and also would allow Hitler a free hand in Western Europe.
- In return, Germany would allow the Soviet Union to occupy eastern Poland and would not interfere if Stalin occupied the Baltic States and Finland.
- It was, therefore, a cold-blooded and calculated agreement to interfere in the lives of helpless and innocent people.

On 1 September 1939 Nazi dictator Adolf **Hitler** invaded Poland. The pact ended when Hitler invaded Russia on 22 June 1941.

Molotov, Vyacheslav Mikhailovich (1890–1986)

Assumed name of Vyacheslav Mikhailovich Skriabin, Soviet communist politician. He was chair of the Council of People's Commissars (prime minister) from 1930 to 1941 and foreign minister from 1939 to 1949 and

> ❝To Soviet patriots the homeland and communism
> become fused in one inseparable whole.❞
>
> **Vyacheslav Molotov**, speech to the Supreme Soviet, 6 November 1939.

Chamberlain claimed that the Agreement would guarantee 'peace in our me', and returned in triumph to Britain. This was seen as appeasement in ction.

However, the agreement did not prevent Hitler from seizing the remain- er of western Czechoslovakia in March 1939.

> ❝We have seen today a gallant, civilized, and democratic people betrayed and handed over to a ruthless despotism.❞
>
> **Clement Attlee**, British Labour politician, speech in the House of Commons during the Munich debate, October 1938.

Mussolini, Benito Amilcare Andrea (1883–1945)

Founder of the Fascist Movement (**Fascism**) in 1919 and prime minis- er from 1922 who became known as *Il Duce* ('the leader'); he was Italian dictator from 1925 to 1943.

Mussolini's great claim to fame in Italy was that he made the trains run on time.

October 1922 Mussolini comes to power after the March on Rome as prime minister at the head of a coalition government.

1925 He assumes dictatorial powers.

1926 All opposition parties are banned.

During the years that follow, the political, legal, and education systems were remodelled on Fascist lines.

From 1930 Mussolini's domestic policies began to fail and he pursued a high-profile foreign policy intended to distract public attention.

1935-36 He invades Abyssinia.

1936-39 He intervenes in the Spanish Civil War in support of Spanish dictator Francisco Franco.

1939 Mussolini conquers Albania.

June 1940 Italy enters World War II supporting German dictator Adolf Hitler.

Forced by military and domestic setbacks to resign in 1943, Mussolini stablished a breakaway government in northern Italy during 1944 and 945. In April 1945 he and his mistress, Clara Petacci, were captured by artisans at Lake Como while heading for the Swiss border, and shot. Their odies were taken to Milan and hung upside down in a public square.

---

from 1953 to 1956. He negotiated the 1939 non-aggression treaty with Germany (the **Nazi-Soviet** pact), and, after the German invasion in 1941, the Soviet partnership with the Allies. His post-war stance prolonged the **Cold War** and in 1957 he was expelled from the government for Stalinist (based on the principles of Soviet leader Joseph **Stalin**) activities.

Molotov was the longest-surviving member in the top ranks of the Soviet Communist Party. He was a member of the **Bolshevik** Party (precursor to the Communist Party) before the revolution, participated in the events of 1917, survived the **purges** of the 1930s, was one of the candidates to replace Stalin in 1953, and was still a leading figure several years afterwards. In 1957 he was appointed ambassador to Outer Mongolia.

Moltke, Helmuth Johannes Ludwig von (1848–1916)

German general (nephew of Count von Moltke (1800–1891), the Prussian general), chief of the German general staff from 1906 to 1914. His use of Gen Alfred von **Schlieffen's** plan for a rapid victory on two fronts failed and he was relieved of command after the defeat at the **Marne**.

Despite warnings from other staff officers, Moltke made several modifications to the **Schlieffen Plan** that severely diluted its effect. Once operations had begun he failed to keep in contact with the various formations, delayed decisions, shifted troops from one flank to another, withdrew others to reinforce the Eastern Front, and in general showed himself to be incapable of discharging the duties of his office.

monasticism

Way of life based on the belief that mankind needs constant prayer in order to receive salvation. A series of monastic orders was set up in the Middle Ages. Monks were expected to give up so-

monasticism *A monk working on an illuminated manuscript in a monastic library.*

called worldly pleasures and devote their lives to God. Monks usually attended seven church services a day.

- **525** The Benedictines, founded by St Benedict, lived in poverty, obedience, and chastity.
- **910** The Cluniacs followed the rule of Benedict, but grew very wealthy and powerful. They were less strict in observing their observance of strict monastic life.

In the eleventh century there was a revival of monasticism.

- **1084** The Carthusians lived in almost unbroken silence and had one vegetarian meal a day
- **1098** The Cistercians became the most important of orders and built monasteries in remote areas. They became skilled sheep farmers.

Monnet, Jean (1888–1979)

French national and international economic strategist. He established his economic planning machine in France in 1946 and set in motion the process of European economic and political integration through his authorship of the 1950 Schuman Plan (commissioned by French prime minister Robert **Schuman**).

- Monnet chaired the 1951 Paris Conference where six states – France, Belgium, Germany, Holland, Luxemburg, and Italy – agreed to establish the European Coal and Steel Community (ECSC). He was appointed president of its High Authority from 1952 to 1955.
- Monnet's idea for a European Atomic Energy Community was taken up by the Belgian foreign minister Paul-Henri Spaak (1899–1972) and adopted at the June 1955 Messina Conference of 'the Six', along with a more ambitious scheme for a Common Market (European Economic Community). The treaties founding these two communities were signed in Rome in March 1957.

Mons, Battle of

During **World War I**, the German victory over the British Expeditionary Force in August 1914, which was brought about when a planned attack on the German armies invading Belgium fell apart when French troops did not arrive, leaving the British to extricate themselves as best they could.

The retreat from Mons was regarded as a victory by the BEF and played an important part in the defeat of the **Schlieffen Plan**. It is the only 'defeat' to be included on the battle standards of British regiments.

Montagnard

Member of a group in the legislative assembly and National Convention convened after the **French Revolution**. They supported the more extreme aims of the revolution, and were destroyed as a political force after the fall of **Robespierre** in 1794. Their leader was Jean Paul **Marat**.

The Montagnards got th[e] because they sat in the top se[ats] left of the chamber. This also beginnings of the terms left a[nd] The most extreme member[s] National Convention always sa[t] left and the most moderate sa[t] right.

Moor

Any of the northwestern African Muslims, of mixed Arab and Berber who conquered Spain and ruled its southern part from 711 to 1492 they were forced to renounce their faith and became Christian (the then known as *Moriscos*).

Moroccan Crises

Two periods of international tension in 1905 and 1911 following Ge[rman] objections to French expansion in Morocco, northwest Africa. Ger[many] intended to break up the Anglo-French *Entente Cordiale* of 1904, bu[t the] crises served to reinforce the entente and further isolate Germany. Th[e] crisis erupted when **Kaiser Wilhelm II** made a speech at the port of Ta[ngier] following which Germany was invited to an international conference Sultan of Morocco. The dispute was settled at the **Algeciras Conferen[ce]** second crisis brought Europe to the brink of war and is known as the **[Agadir] Incident**.

Munich Agreement

Pact signed on 29 September 1938 by the leaders of the UK Chamberlain, France (Edouard **Daladier**), Germany (Adolf **Hitler**), (Benito **Mussolini**), under which Czechoslovakia was compelled [to surren]der its Sudeten-German districts (the **Sudetenland**) to Germ[any]

Sudetenland contained most of Czechoslovakia's iron ores and coal and also its military defences.

Hitler had demanded self-government for the Sudeten Germans on 12 September, but changed his demand to union with Germany on 22 September.

When Chamberlain returne[d] after the conference, he a[ppeared on] the balcony of Buckingham the king and queen. The prime minister to do this Churchill after the Second

Nagy, Imre (1895–1958)

Hungarian politician, prime minister from 1953 to 1955 and in 1956. He led the Hungarian revolt against Soviet domination in 1956, for which he was executed in 1958.

1953 After Soviet leader Josef Stalin's death, Nagy becomes prime minister and introduces such liberal measures as encouraging the production of consumer goods; he is dismissed in 1955 by hard-line Stalinist premier Matyas Rákosi.

October 1956 Nagy is reappointed in during the Hungarian uprising and expands liberalization against Soviet wishes – for example, he announced Hungarian withdrawal from the Warsaw Pact.

November 1956 Soviet troops enters Budapest, and Nagy is dismissed.

1958 He is captured by the KGB (the Soviet secret police) and taken to Moscow where he is tried and executed.

In 1989 the Hungarian Supreme Court recognized his leadership of a legitimate government and quashed his conviction for treachery.

Naples, Kingdom of

The southern part of Italy, alternately independent and united with Sicily in the Kingdom of the Two Sicilies.

- Naples was united with Sicily in the period 1140 to 1282, under Norman rule from 1130 to 1194, under Hohenstaufen rule from 1194 to 1266, and under Angevin control from 1268.

- It was separated from Sicily, but continued under Angevin rule until 1435.

- Naples was reunited with Sicily between 1442 and 1503, under the house of Aragon until 1501.

- The kingdom was a Spanish **Habsburg** possession from 1504 to 1707.

- It was under Austrian rule from 1707 to 1735 and under Spanish Bourbon rule from 1735 to 1799.

The Neapolitan Republic was established in 1799 after **Napoleon I** had left Italy for Egypt, but fell after five months to the forces of reaction under

Cardinal Ruffo, with the British admiral Nelson (1759–1805) blockading the city by sea; many prominent citizens were massacred after the capitulation. The Spanish Bourbons were restored 1799, 1802 to 1805, and from 1815 to 1860, when Naples joined the Kingdom of Italy.

Napoleon I (Napoleon Bonaparte) (1769–1821)

Napoleon Bonaparte was emperor of the French from 1804 to 1814 and briefly in 1815. A general from 1796 in the Revolutionary Wars, in 1799 he overthrew the ruling **Directory** and made himself dictator. From 1803 he conquered most of Europe (the **Napoleonic Wars**) and installed his brothers as puppet kings (see **Bonaparte**).

Napoleon Bonaparte *Emperor of France from 1804 to 1814 and, briefly, in 1815.*

1795	He suppresses a royalist uprising in Paris and is given command against the Austrians in Italy defeating them at Lodi, Arcole, and Rivoli during 1796 to 1797.
1798	He invades Egypt, seen as a halfway house to India and Syria, but his fleet is destroyed by the British admiral Nelson at the Battle of the Nile.
1799	Napoleon returns to France and carries out a coup against the government of the **Directory** to establish his own dictatorship, nominally as First Consul.
1800	The Austrians are again defeated at **Marengo** and the coalition against France is shattered, a truce being declared in 1802.
1801	A plebiscite (a vote by the electorate) in the same year makes Napoleon consul for life.
1804	A plebiscite makes him emperor of France.
1803	War is renewed by Britain, aided by Austria and Russia from 1805 and Prussia from 1806.
1805	Napoleon is prevented by the British navy at the Battle of **Trafalgar** from invading Britain; Napoleon drives Austria out of the war by victories at Ulm and **Austerlitz** in 1805, and Prussia by the victory at Jena in 1806.

1807   After the Battles of Eylau and **Friedland**, Napoleon forms an alliance with Russia at **Tilsit** 1807. Napoleon then set up the **Continental System**, which forbids entry of British goods to Europe.

1808   He occupies Portugal and places his brother Joseph on the Spanish throne. Both countries revolts, with British aid, and Austria attempts to re-enter the war but is defeated at Wagram in 1809.

1809   Napoleon had married Josephine de Beauharnais in 1796, but to assert his equality with the Habsburgs, he divorces her to marry the Austrian emperor's daughter.

1812   When Russia failed to adopt the Continental System, Napoleon marched on and occupied Moscow, but his army's retreat in the bitter winter of 1812 encourages Prussia and Austria to declare war again in 1813.

1813   Napoleon is defeated at the Battle of the **Nations** (Leipzig) and is driven from Germany. Despite his brilliant campaign on French soil, the Allies invade Paris and compel him to abdicate in April 1814.

1814   Napoleon is banished to the Mediterranean island of Elba, off the west coast of Italy. But in March 1815 he escapes and takes power for a hundred days, with the aid of Marshal Ney.

1815   Napoleon is finally defeated at Waterloo, Belgium, on 18 June.

1821   Napoleon dies after his abdication and exile in 1815 to the island of St Helena in the Atlantic Ocean. His body is brought back in 1840 and is interred in the Hôtel des Invalides, Paris.

> After Napoleon's death rumours spread that he had been poisoned by the British when traces of arsenic were found in his hair, but this was apparently a natural occurrence.

❝I am the successor not of Louis XVI, but of Charlemagne.❞

Napoleon I, speech, 1813.

Napoleon III (1808–1873)

Born Charles Louis Napoleon Bonaparte, Napoleon III was emperor of the French from 1852 to 1870. He was known as Louis-Napoleon.

The son of Louis Bonaparte and Hortense de Beauharnais, brother and step-daughter respectively of **Napoleon I**, he led two unsuccessful revolts against the French king **Louis Philippe**, at Strasbourg in 1836 and at Boulogne in 1840. After the latter he was imprisoned. He escaped in 1846 disguised as a woman.

1848   He is elected president of the newly established French republic in December.

1851   Louis-Napoleon is declared president for life.

1852   He is proclaimed emperor.

1854   He joins in the **Crimean War** 1854 to 1856.

1859   Louis-Napoleon declares war on Austria in 1859 in support of **Piedmont**–Sardinia, wins the Battle of **Solferino** and annexes Savoy and Nice 1860.

1863–67   He tries to set up an empire in Mexico during 1863 to 1867. In so doing he arouses the mistrust of Europe and isolates France.

1870   He declares war on Prussia but suffers humiliating defeats and is captured at the Battle of **Sedan**. He withdraws to England, where he dies.

At home, Louis-Napoleon's regime was discredited by its notorious corruption; republican and socialist opposition grew, in spite of severe repression, and forced him, after 1860, to make concessions in the direction of parliamentary government.

Napoleon's son by Empress Eugénie, Eugène Louis Jean Joseph Napoleon, Prince Imperial (1856–79), was killed fighting with the British army against the Zulus in Africa.

> ❛ We must not seek to fashion events, but let them happen of their own accord. ❜
>
> **Napoleon III**, to Bismarck at Biarritz, 4 October 1865.

Napoleonic Wars

Series of European wars (1803–1815) fought by **Napoleon I** of France against alliances of Britain, the German states, Spain, Portugal, and Russia, following the **French Revolutionary Wars**. Napoleon aimed to conquer all of Europe.

National Socialism

Official name for the **Nazi** movement in Germany.

Nations, Battle of the

Also known as the Battle of Leipzig, the conflict was a major defeat of **Napoleon I** that took place outside the town of Leipzig, in Saxony, by a coalition of Britain,

Hitler added the two words National Socialist to the German Workers Party in 1921. He wanted to attract right wing Nationalists as well as left wing Socialists.

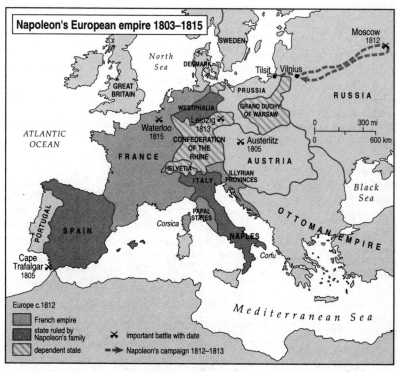

Napoleonic Wars *Map showing the extent of Napoleon's Empire and the locations of important battles.*

Prussia, Russia, Austria, and Sweden from 16 to 18 October 1813. Napoleon offered strong resistance but was greatly outnumbered; his eventual defeat led to a French collapse east of the Rhine.

NATO
See *North Atlantic Treaty Organization.*

Navarino, Battle of
During the Greek War of Independence from 1821 to 1827, the conflict that saw the destruction on 20 October 1827 of a joint Turkish-Egyptian fleet by the combined fleets of the British, French, and Russians under Vice-Admiral

The Battle of Navarino gave its name to the dish Navarin of Lamb.

Edward Codrington (1770–1851). The destruction of their fleet left the Turks highly vulnerable in Greece as they had no protection to their rear and no supply line, and this proved to be the decisive battle of the war. Navarino is the Italian and historic name of Pylos Bay, Greece, on the southwest coast of the Peloponnese.

Nazi

Member of the *Nationalsozialistische Deutsche Arbeiterpartei*, usually abbreviated to the Nazi Party. The party was based on the ideology of Nazism.

Nazism

Ideology based on racism, nationalism, and the supremacy of the state over the individual. The German Nazi Party, the *Nationalsozialistische Deutsche Arbeiterpartei* (National Socialist German Workers' Party), was formed from the German Workers' Party (founded in 1919) and led by Adolf **Hitler** from 1921 to 1945.

The Party's beliefs were set out in *Mein Kampf*/My Struggle that Hitler wrote in 1924:

- Hitler considered the German people as a master race, a '*herrenvolk*'. All other groups (Slavs, Jews, coloured people) were inferior according to his philosophy.

- Germany should be reunited and seize land to the east (**Lebensraum**).

Nazism *Front cover from a Nazi propaganda publication entitled 'A Battle for Germany' (1933).*

- To make Germany great again, a new leader was needed. Hitler regarded democracy as a weak system of government that should be replaced by dictatorship; he also regarded communism as evil.

- Hitler also realized that he would have to change his tactics including the organization of his party.

In 1928 the Nazis won support outside of Bavaria for virtually the first time. They began to win votes in farming areas of north Germany, as prices fell. But their big break came in 1929.

- On 3 October 1929 Gustav **Stresemann** died. He had been responsible, more than any other politician, for Germany's recovery in the 1920s.

- On 24 October 1929 Wall Street, the American Stock Exchange crashed. US bankers called in their loans to Germany. Many German companies had to close down.

The effects of the Wall Street Crash
Germany was the worst hit of all the European countries by the effects of the Depression. It had relied upon loans from the USA since 1924 and now the loans had dried up. By 1932, 6 million Germans were out of work.

From 1929 support for the Nazis rose steadily as more and more voters were persuaded that Hitler offered a real way out of the crisis. Numbers of Nazi members in the Reichstag increased from 12 members 230 members by July 1932.

'Nazi gold'
Gold owned by the Nazis, worth around £40 million, seized by the UK and the USA after the end of **World War II**. It was announced in September 1997 that holdings of Nazi gold would be switched into a fund to help victims of the **Holocaust**. The agreement, reached between the UK, USA, and France, unlocked a 50-year-old post-war reparation deal that divided the gold between governments, specifically excluding all claims from individuals whose gold was stolen by the Nazi Reich.

Nazi-Soviet pact
Another name for the Molotov-Ribbentrop pact or the Hitler—Stalin Pact, a non-aggression treaty signed by Germany and the USSR in 1939. Both countries agreed to remain neutral and to refrain from acts of aggression if either went to war. Secret clauses allowed for the partition of Poland. The pact ended when Hitler invaded Russia on 22 June 1941.
See also: *World War II.*

Nazi state

Dictatorial government established in Germany by the **National Socialist German Workers' Party (NSDAP)**, or Nazis, under Adolf **Hitler** from 1933 onwards. The Nazi state placed absolute power in the hands of an individual (the *Führer*, or 'leader') and all opposition was suppressed using violence. National Socialist Germany is also known as the Third Reich.

30 January 1933 Hitler is named chancellor and the **Weimar Republic** is swiftly dismantled.

27 February The parliament building is burned down (the **Reichstag Fire**). This is blamed on communists, but is widely believed to have been staged by the Nazis.

23 March The Enabling Act is passed, which gives Hitler sweeping powers to bypass parliament in drafting laws and conducting foreign affairs.
A vast network of secret police (Gestapo), aided by informers, enforces the new laws; political opponents are murdered or imprisoned in concentration camps.

June 1934 The Night of the **Long Knives**.

The Nazi state reached into all aspects of people's lives to ensure complete conformity and obedience.

- Indoctrination began at an early age, with schoolbooks teaching hatred against national minorities like the Jews and the Romany people.
- Books, films, and paintings that did not promote the myth of German superiority were banned, along with all work produced by Jewish artists and scientists, whatever its content.
- The press was strictly controlled, with news and diverse opinions being replaced by relentless party propaganda, and all judges and lawyers were appointed by the state.

THE EFFECTS OF THE NEP

- The buying and selling of goods was allowed once more. Soon markets developed and private trade reappeared.
- People were allowed to own small businesses with up to 25 employees. This encouraged private enterprise, especially in agriculture, leading to the emergence of the Kulaks and NEP men.
- People were allowed to make a profit and then pay taxes, instead of having goods confiscated by the state.
- Between 1921 and 1928 the Russian economy began to recover and food production rose.

NEP

Abbreviation for the New Economic Policy introduced in Russia in 1921 by Soviet leader Vladimir **Lenin**. The NEP marked a reversal of the policy of **War Communism** that Lenin had begun in 1918. It is now believed that War Communism was in fact an attempt to introduce a fully socialist society, rather than just an attempt to win the Civil War. The NEP signalled the failure of Lenin's plan.

Nicholas I (1796–1855)

A strict autocrat, he was tsar of Russia from 1825 and attempted to extend Russian territory and influence into the Balkans. This created tension with both Austria and Britain. Nicholas's Balkan ambitions led to war with Turkey from 1827 to 1829 and the **Crimean War** from 1853 to 1856.

Nicholas is credited with inventing the term 'the Sick Man of Europe', to describe the Ottoman Empire. He was hoping for the support of Britain and France in an attempt to dismember the empire, but instead found himself involved in the Crimean War.

❝ Russia has two generals in whom she can confide – Generals Janvier [January] and Fevrier [February]. ❞

Nicholas I, referring to the Russian winter, the subject of the *Punch* cartoon 'General Fevrier turned traitor', 10 March 1853.

Nicholas II (1868–1918)

Tsar of Russia from 1894 to 1917, who was heavily influenced by his wife, Tsarina Alexandra (1872–1918). She, in turn, was increasingly influenced by the religious mystic **Rasputin**, who could apparently control the haemophilia from which the tsarevich Alexei suffered. Nicholas was a weak and ineffective tsar, who had little desire for autocratic power, but believed that it was his duty to maintain the position of the Romanov family and pass it on to his son Alexei.

Nicholas's mismanagement of the Russo–Japanese War and of internal affairs led to the revolution of 1905, which he

Nicholas's insensitivity was shown in 1896. To celebrate his coronation he gave free food and drink for all in a field in Moscow. There were 1,389 fatalities as the crowd rushed forward. Nicholas continued with a ball in the evening as though nothing had happened.

suppressed, although he was forced to grant limited constitutional reforms. He took Russia into **World War I** in 1914, and assumed command of the Russian army in August 1915. He was forced to abdicate in 1917 after the February Revolution, and was executed with his family by the Bolsheviks in July 1918.

In 1995, US and Russian scientists announced that, by DNA testing, they had determined conclusively that bones found in Russia in 1991 were those of the tsar and his family. The remains were buried in 1998 in St Petersburg.

> ❝ I shall maintain the principle of autocracy just as firmly and unflinchingly as it was upheld by my ... father. ❞
>
> **Nicholas II,** declaration to representatives of the Zemstvo of Tver, 17 January 1896.

Night of the Long Knives
In **World War II**, a purge of the German **Nazi** Party, which was intended to root out possible opposition to Adolf **Hitler**. On the night of 29 to 30 June 1934 (and the following two days) the SS units under Heinrich **Himmler** were used by Hitler to exterminate the leadership of the Nazi private army, the *Sturmabteilung* (SA or Stormtroopers) under Captain Ernst **Roehm**. The SA represented the socialist element in the Nazi Party, which wanted a social revolution in Germany. Others were also executed for alleged conspiracy against Hitler including Kurt von Schleicher and Gregor **Strasser**.

The Nazi purge enabled Hitler to gain the acceptance of the German officer corps and, when President **Hindenburg** died five weeks later, to become head of state.

NKVD
Russian 'People's Commissariat of Internal Affairs', which was the Soviet secret police from 1934 to 1938, when it was replaced by the KGB. The NKVD was responsible for Soviet leader Joseph **Stalin's** infamous **purges**.

Norman
Any of the descendants of the Norsemen (to whose chief, Rollo, Normandy was granted by Charles III of France in 911), who adopted French language and culture.

- During the 11th and 12th centuries the Normans conquered England in 1066 (under William the Conqueror), Scotland in 1072, parts of Wales and Ireland, southern Italy, Sicily, and Malta, and played a prominent part in the Crusades.

- The Normans introduced feudalism, Latin as the language of government, and Norman French as the language of literature. Church architecture and organization were also influenced by the Normans, although they ceased to exist as a distinct people after the 13th century.

North Atlantic Treaty Organization (NATO)
Military alliance set up in April 1949 in response to the Soviet blockade of Berlin, which was to provide for the collective defence of the major Western European and North American states against the perceived threat from the USSR.

- In 1949 13 countries joined, including Britain and the USA.
- It led to US troops and aircraft being stationed in European countries to protect them against a possible attack by the countries of Eastern Europe.
- Since 1949 most countries of Western Europe have joined NATO and in recent years some of the former communist countries, such as Poland and Hungary, have joined. Since the alliance was set up, none of the members has been attacked.

The collapse of communism in Eastern Europe from 1989 prompted the most radical review of NATO policy and defence strategy since its inception. After the Eastern European **Warsaw Pact** was disbanded in 1991, an adjunct to NATO, the North Atlantic Cooperation Council (NACC), was established, including all the former Soviet republics, with the aim of building greater security in Europe.

The most important aspect of the alliance is that an attack on one of the member countries is considered to be an attack on all of the members.

❝ We must learn from history, not repeat it, and we must never forget that the destinies of Europe and America are inseparable. ❞

Madeleine Albright, US secretary of state, speaking at the ceremony at which Hungary, Poland, and the Czech Republic joined NATO, *Newsweek*, March 1999.

- In 1992 it was agreed that the Organization for Security and Cooperation in Europe would in future authorize all NATO's military responses within Europe.
- In 1999, the former Eastern Bloc countries of Poland, Hungary, and the Czech Republic were invited to join NATO.

November criminals
Name given by right-wing nationalists in post-1918 Germany to the socialist politicians who had taken over the government after the abdication of Kaiser **Wilhelm II** and had signed the armistice with the Western Allies in November 1918. One of the signatories, Matthias **Erzberger**, was assassinated in 1921.

Nuremberg rallies
Annual meetings of the German **Nazi** Party held during the period 1933 to 1938. They were characterized by extensive torchlight parades, marches in party formations, and mass rallies addressed by Nazi leaders such as Adolf **Hitler** and Paul **Goebbels**.

Nuremberg trials
The trials of the chief Nazi war criminals (numbering 24) from November 1945 to October 1946 by an international military tribunal consisting of four judges and four prosecutors: one of each from the USA, UK, USSR, and France. An appendix accused the German cabinet, general staff, high command, Nazi leadership corps, SS, *Sturmabteilung*, and Gestapo of criminal behaviour.

THE MAIN CHARGES IN THE INDICTMENT:

- conspiracy to wage wars of aggression;
- crimes against peace;
- war crimes: for example, murder and ill-treatment of civilians and prisoners of war, deportation of civilians for slave labour, and killing of hostages;
- crimes against humanity: for example, mass murder of the Jews and other peoples, and murder and ill-treatment of political opponents.

Fritsche, Schacht, and Franz **von Papen** were acquitted; 18 war criminals were found guilty on one or more counts.

- Funk (1890–1960) and Raeder (1876–1960) were sentenced to life imprisonment.
- Shirach (1907–74) and Speer (1905–1981) were sentenced to 20 years in prison.
- Neurath (1873–1956) was sentenced to 15 years, and Doenitz (1891–1980) to 10 years.
- The remaining 11 men were all sentenced to death by hanging, Hans Frank (1900–1946), Wilhelm Frick (1877–1946), Hermann **Goering** (who committed suicide before he could be executed), Alfred Jodl (1890–1946), Ernst Kaltenbrunner (1902–1946), Wilhelm Keitel (1882–1946), Joachim von **Ribbentrop** (1893–1946), Alfred Rosenberg (1893–1946), Fritz Sauckel, Arthur **Seyss-Inquart**, and Julius Streicher (1885–1946).

October Revolution
This was the second stage of the Russian Revolution of 1917.

- In September Leon **Trotsky** became leader of the Military Committee of the Petrograd Soviet and the Bolsheviks became the largest party in the Petrograd Soviet.

- In October Lenin returned to Petrograd and forced the Bolsheviks to seize power.

- Trotsky organized, and carried out the seizure of power. He planned the events of 24–25 October. He moved army units loyal to the Bolsheviks into Petrograd.

Since the fall of Communism and the collapse of the Soviet Union, the October Revolution has become known as the Bolshevik seizure of power.

- On 24–25 October the Bolsheviks seized power by driving the Provisional Government out of the Winter Palace.

- There were only a few thousand Bolsheviks and it took them two days to win control of the Winter Palace. The Petrograd Garrison could easily have stopped them, but it did not intervene.

Octobrists
Group of Russian liberal constitutional politicians who accepted the October Manifesto instituted by Tsar **Nicholas II** after the 1905 revolution and rejected more radical reforms. The Octobrists dominated the Third and Fourth Dumas (assembly) and became increasingly critical of Nicholas II for his failure to implement the reforms promised in the October Manifesto.

Oder-Neisse Line
Border between Poland and East Germany agreed at the Potsdam Conference 1945 at the end of **World War II**, named after the two rivers that formed the frontier.

Olivares, Count-Duke of (1587–1645)
Born Gaspar de Guzmán, Olivares was Spanish prime minister from 1621 to 1643. He overstretched Spain in foreign affairs and unsuccessfully

attempted domestic reform. He committed Spain to recapturing the Netherlands and to involvement in the **Thirty Years' War** from 1618 to 1648, and his efforts to centralize power led to revolts in Cataluña and Portugal, which brought about his downfall. His period of power marked the beginning of the decline of Spain from its dominant position in the 16th century.

Orange, House of

Royal family of the Netherlands, whose title is derived from the small principality of Orange in southern France, held by the family from the 8th century to 1713. The family held considerable possessions in the Netherlands, to which, after 1530, was added the German county of Nassau.

From the time of William, Prince of Orange, the family dominated Dutch history, bearing the title of **Stadtholder** (magistrate) for the greater part of the 17th and 18th centuries. The son of Stadtholder William V became King William I in 1815.

Orlando, Vittorio Emanuele (1860–1952)

Italian politician, prime minister from 1917 to 1919, who attended the Paris peace conference after **World War I**.

> 💧 Oratory is just like prostitution: you must have little tricks. 💧
>
> **Vittorio Emanuele Orlando**,
> *Time*, 8 December 1952.

Orlando was unable to speak English and left the conference for several weeks in protest at the failure of Britain and France to keep the promises made at the secret **Treaty of London**. Dissatisfaction with his handling of the Adriatic settlement led to his resignation.

Ottoman Empire

Muslim empire of the Turks from 1300 to 1920, the successor of the Seljuk Empire, which was founded by Osman I and reached its height with Suleiman in the 16th century. Its capital was Istanbul (formerly Constantinople).

At its greatest extent the Ottoman Empire's boundaries were: in Europe as far north as Hungary and part of southern Russia; Iran; the Palestinian coastline; Egypt; and North Africa.

The Ottomans attempted to conquer Christian Europe but were defeated by **Don John** at **Lepanto** in 1571 and **John III** (John Sobieski) at Vienna in 1683. After that the Ottoman Empire began to decline and found itself under pressure from Russia around the Black Sea and from Austria in the Balkans.

From the 18th century the empire was in decline. There was an attempted revival and reform under the Young Turk party in 1908, but the regime crumbled when Turkey sided with Germany in **World War I**. The sultanate was abolished by Kemal Atatürk (1881–1938) in 1922; the last sultan was Muhammad VI.

Overlord, Operation

Code name for the Allied invasion of Normandy on 6 June 1944 (D-day) during **World War II**.

Oxenstjerna, Axel Gustafsson, Count Oxenstjerna (1583–1654)

Swedish politician, chancellor from 1612, who pursued Gustavus Adolphus's foreign policy and acted as regent for Queen **Christina**. Oxenstierna maintained Swedish interests during and after the **Thirty Years' War**.

> ❝ At fifty you begin to be tired of the world, and at sixty the world is tired of you. ❞
>
> **Axel Gustafsson**, Count Oxenstjerna, *Reflections and Maxims*.

pact of steel
Military alliance between **Nazi** Germany and **Fascist** Italy, which was set up in 1939.

Paderewski, Ignacy Jan (1860–1941)
Polish pianist, composer, and politician; prime minister of Poland in 1919. During **World War I** Paderewski helped organize the Polish army in France. In 1919, for a short time, he was prime minister of the newly independent Poland, which he had represented at the **Versailles** peace conference.

Papal States
Area of central Italy, which stretched from Naples to Venice. This was ruled by the pope from 756 until the unification of Italy in 1870. In the Middle Ages the pope often played an important role in European affairs, but from the 16th century the papacy was increasingly overshadowed by nation states.

See also: *Pius IX.*

In 1870 the Papal States were occupied by the Italian Army and the pope lost all of his territory, this led to a rift between the Papacy and the Italian government until the **Lateran Treaties** in 1929.

Papen, Franz von (1879–1969)
German right-wing politician, who persuaded President **Hindenburg** to appoint Nazi leader Adolf **Hitler** as chancellor in January 1933. Von Papen became vice chancellor in Hitler's government, but was soon sidelined. He was envoy to Austria from 1934 to 1938 and ambassador to Turkey from 1939 to 1944. Although acquitted at the **Nuremberg trials,** he was imprisoned by a German court for three years.

Von Papen's actions in 1933 were an attempt to gain revenge on Kurt von Schleicher, who had replaced him as chancellor in November 1932. He believed that he could make use of Hitler in his efforts to supplant von Schleicher.

Paris Commune

Name given to two separate periods in the history of the French capital Paris.

The Paris municipal government from 1789 to 1794 was established after the storming of the **Bastille** and remained powerful in the **French Revolution** until the fall of **Robespierre** in 1794.

The provisional national government from 18 March to May 1871 was formed while Paris was besieged by the German troops during the **Franco-Prussian War**. It consisted of socialists and left-wing republicans, and is often considered the first socialist government in history. Elected after the right-wing National Assembly at Versailles tried to disarm the National Guard, it fell when the Versailles troops captured Paris and massacred 20,000–30,000 people from 21 to 28 May.

In 1871 the Communards, the inhabitants of Paris, kept in touch with the outside world by means of balloons. They shot every animal in the Paris zoo to try to feed the population during the Prussian siege.

Paris, treaties of

- Treaty of 1763, which ended the Seven Years' War. France gave up all claims to India, America, and Canada, while Britain retained most of her conquests in the Caribbean but returned Martinique and Guadeloupe to France.

- Treaty of 1783, which ended the War of the American Revolution. Britain recognized the independence of the American Colonies.

- Treaty of 1856, which ended the Crimean War. Russia gave up claims to the Danubian provinces and agreed that the Straits would be closed to warships in time of war.

- Treaty of 1951, signed by France, West Germany, Italy, Belgium, the Netherlands, and Luxembourg, embodying the Schuman Plan (see Jean **Monnet**) to set up a single coal and steel authority.

partitions of Poland

Dismemberment of Poland taking place in three stages at the end of the 18th century.

THE THREE STAGES OF PARTITION

▪ The First Partition was proposed by **Frederick (II) the Great** of Prussia and carried out with Austria and Russia in 1772. Poland lost a third of its territory and population and, in all but name, became a Russian protectorate.

▪ The second partition by Russia and Prussia followed in 1793.

▪ The Third Partition of the rest of Poland by Russia, Prussia, and Austria took place in 1795. King Stanislas Augustus abdicated, and died in exile in St Petersburg in 1798.

Poland ceased to be an independent country until 1919.

Passchendaele, Battle of

In **World War I**, a successful but costly British operation to capture the Passchendaele ridge in western Flanders, also known as the Third Battle of **Ypres**, from July to November 1917. The ridge, some 60 m/200 ft high, had been captured by the Germans in October 1914.

Passchendaele was fought in horrific conditions and the water-sodden battlefield soon became a quagmire. Many thousands of British and Commonwealth soldiers who drowned in the mud have no known grave. British casualties numbered nearly 400,000.

The Passchendaele ridge was protected by some 2,000 pillboxes (fortified military position). These were prefabricated in Germany and then erected on the battlefield.

The ridge was re-taken by the Germans in March 1918 and recovered again by the Belgians in October 1918.

Pavia, Battle of

Battle fought in 1525 between France and the Holy Roman Empire. The **Habsburg** emperor **Charles V** defeated and captured Francis I (1494–1547) of France; the battle marked the beginning of Habsburg dominance in Italy. Francis was held in Spain for a year. To obtain his release he signed away any claims he had to Italy (the Treaty of Madrid) but, on his return to France, disowned the treaty and organized a league against Charles V.

> ❖ Out of all I had, only honour remains, and my life, which is safe. ❞
>
> **Francis I**, King of France, letter to his mother after losing the Battle of Pavia, 1525.

Peninsular War

War of 1808 to 1814 precipitated by the French emperor **Napoleon I's** invasion of Portugal and Spain. British expeditionary forces under Sir Arthur Wellesley (the Duke of Wellington, 1769–1852) landed in Portugal and built a fortified base at the lines of Torres Vedras. Combined with Spanish and Portuguese resistance forces, the British succeeded in defeating the French at Vimeiro in 1808, Talavera in 1809, Salamanca in 1812, and Vittoria in 1813. In March 1814 Wellington invaded France.

The war tied up large numbers of French troops in Spain and meant that Napoleon's lines of supply became very overstretched. It was a major factor in the defeat of France in 1814 (leading finally to the Battle of Waterloo in 1815).

Pétain, (Henri) Philippe Benoni Omer Joseph (1856–1951)

French general and right-wing politician who became prime minister in June 1940 and head of state in July of the same year. Pétain signed an armistice with Germany on 22 June 1940 (**World War II** had begun in 1939) before assuming full powers as head of state on 16 July. His authoritarian regime, established at **Vichy**, collaborated with the Germans and proposed a reactionary 'National Revolution' for France under the slogan 'Work, Family, Fatherland'. Convinced in 1940 of Britain's imminent defeat, Pétain accepted Germany's terms for peace, including the occupation of northern France. In December 1940 he dismissed his deputy Pierre **Laval**, who wanted to side with the **Axis** powers, but bowed to German pressures to reinstate him in April 1942. With Germany occupying the whole of France from November 1942, Pétain found himself head, in name only, of a puppet state. Removed from France by the German army in 1944, he returned voluntarily and was

> ❖ To make a union with Great Britain would be a fusion with a corpse. ❞
>
> **Henri Philippe Pétain**, in response to Churchill's proposal of an Anglo-French union, 1940.

tried and condemned to death for treason in August 1945. He died in prison on the Ile d'Yeu, his sentence having been commuted to life imprisonment.

Peter (I) the Great
(1672–1725)

Tsar of Russia from 1682, Peter assumed control of the government in 1689. He attempted to reorganize the country on Western lines.

- He modernized the army and built a fleet.

- He remodelled the administrative and legal systems, encouraged education, brought the Russian Orthodox Church under state control, and built a new capital, St Petersburg.

- In order to obtain a seaport on the Black Sea coast, he declared war on Turkey and took the city of Azov in 1696, after a long siege.

Peter the Great *Tzar of Russia, and a vigorous reformer and modernizer, from 1682 to 1725.*

Peter left Russia in April 1697 and posing as Sgt Peter Mikhailov visited Western Europe.

- In the Netherlands he worked for several months as a shipwright in the dockyard.

- In London he worked for a few weeks at the Royal Naval dockyard at Deptford.

- Peter left England in April 1698, taking with him 500 English engineers, craftsmen, surgeons, and artillerymen.

At home Peter introduced many reforms, the most important of which were the abolition of the Moscow patriarchy, which controlled the Russian church, and its replacement by a synod subordinated to the tsar.

- He changed central government and set up specialised departments; reformed provincial administration by appointing provincial governors;

introduced a properly organised military and civil service open to any suitable person irrespective of origin; and introduced a poll tax.

- After the end of the Northern War in 1721 Peter was proclaimed emperor, and in 1722 promulgated a new law of succession, which stated that each monarch should nominate his own successor.

> ❝ Two things are necessary in government – order and defence. ❞
>
> **Peter I**, letter to his son Alexis, 11 October 1715.

Philip II of France (1165–1223)

King of France from 1180, he was also known as Philip Augustus. As part of his efforts to establish a strong monarchy and evict the English from their French possessions, he waged war in turn against the English kings Henry II (1133–1189), Richard I the Lionheart (1157–1199) (with whom he also went on the Third Crusade), and John (1167–1216).

Philip played a part in organizing the Fourth Crusade, and setting up the Albigensian Crusades. He built many castles, a significant number with the new-style round towers.

Against Richard he suffered setbacks at Fréteval in 1194 and at Vernon, but against John he captured Château Gaillard in 1203–04 and destroyed the Angevin Empire. He defeated John's allies, led by Emperor Otto IV (1178–1218), at Bouvines in 1214.

Philip II of Spain (1527–1598)

King of Spain from 1556, he was the son of the **Habsburg** emperor **Charles V**, and in 1554 married Queen Mary of England (1512–1558). On his father's abdication in 1556 Philip inherited Spain, the Netherlands, and the Spanish possessions in Italy and the Americas, and in 1580 he annexed Portugal. His

Philip II *King of Spain from 1556, and of Portugal, from 1580.*

intolerance and lack of understanding of the Netherlanders drove them into revolt. Political and religious differences combined to involve him in war with England (sending the unsuccessful **Spanish Armada** against them) and, after 1589, with France.

> ❧ Time and I are the two mightiest monarchs. ❧
>
> **Philip II**, attributed remark.

Philosophes
The leading intellectuals of pre-revolutionary 18th-century France, who included Condorcet (1743–1794), Diderot (1713–1784), J J Rousseau (1712–1778), and Voltaire (1694–1778). Their role in the Enlightenment (18th-century social and intellectual movement promoting rational and scientific knowledge) made them question the structures of the **ancien regime**, and they were held responsible by some for influencing the revolutionaries of 1789.

Piedmont (Italian, **Piemonte**)
Region of northern Italy, comprising the provinces of Alessandria, Asti, Cuneo, Novara, Turin, and Vercelli. It borders Switzerland to the north and France to the west, and is surrounded, except to the east, by the Alps and the Apennines.

The movement for the unification of Italy started in the 19th century in Piedmont-Sardinia, under the House of Savoy. **Cavour**, the prime minister of Piedmont, was the main leader of unification and Victor Emmanuel II (1820–1878) of Piedmont became king of Italy in 1861.

Pius IX (1792–1878)
Pope from 1846, he refused to accept the incorporation of the Papal States and Rome into the kingdom of Italy. Significant to his pontificate, the longest in history, were both his definition of the dogma of the Immaculate Conception of the Blessed Virgin Mary in 1854, which kindled Catholic devotion and, most importantly, his proclamation of papal infallibility in 1870.

Originally a liberal, he became highly reactionary as papal territories were progressively lost. He refused to set foot outside the Vatican after the Italian occupation of Rome, regarding himself as a prisoner, and forbade Catholics to take any part in politics in Italy. He centred power in the Vatican, refusing compromise with modern spiritual ideas.

- **1864** Pius attacks many contemporary ideas and claimes that the papacy should have control over culture, science, and education.

- **1870** Pius announces the doctrine of papal infallibility at the Vatican Council. Many Christians had long held that the church was infallible in its teaching of revealed truths, but Pius' definition places this infallibility with the pope.

His devotion inspired a cult following that continues to this day. The first stage in his canonization was begun in 1985.

See also; *Lateran Treaties; Papal States.*

Pius IX *The Pope from 1846, he espoused a definition of papal infallibilty that led him into conflict with politicians of the time.*

Pius XI (1857–1939)

Born Achille Ratti he was pope from 1922 and had to deal with the growth of Fascism in Italy and other European countries. His policies attracted criticism because he appeared to side with Fascist governments.

1929 Pius accepts the **Lateran Treaties** with Italian dictator Benito **Mussolini**.

1933 Pius signs a Concordat with **Nazi** Germany.

1936 Pius announces his support for **Franco** in the **Spanish Civil War**.

pogrom

Russian 'destruction'. It came to mean an unprovoked violent attack on an ethnic group, particularly Jews, carried out with official sanction. The Russian pogroms against Jews began in 1881, after the assassination of Tsar **Alexander II**, and again in 1903 to 1906; persecution of the Jews remained constant until the Russian Revolution. Later there were pogroms in Eastern Europe, especially in Poland after 1918, and during the **Holocaust** in Germany under German dictator Adolf **Hitler**.

Poincaré, Raymond Nicolas Landry (1860–1934)
French moderate republican politician, who served as prime minister and foreign minister from 1912 to 1913, from 1922 to 1924 (when he ordered the occupation of the German Ruhr in lieu of reparations for war damage), and from 1926 to 1929 (when he successfully stabilized the franc). Poincaré was president of France from 1913 to 1920.

Poland

Chronology

966	Polish Slavic tribes under Mieszko I, leader of Piast dynasty, adopts Christianity and united the region around Poznan to form the first Polish state.
1386	The Jagellonian dynasty comes to power: this is the golden age for Polish culture.
1569	Poland united with Lithuania to become the largest state in Europe.
1572	The Jagellonian dynasty became extinct; future kings are elected by nobility and gentry, who forms 10% of the population.
mid-17th century	Defeat in war against Russia, Sweden, and Brandenburg (in Germany) set in a process of irreversible decline.
1772–95	Poland is partitioned between Russia, which rules the northeast; Prussia, the west, including Pomerania; and Austria in the south-centre, including Galicia, where there is greatest autonomy.
1815	After the Congress of **Vienna**, the Russian eastern portion of Poland is re-established as a kingdom within the Russian Empire.
1918	An independent Polish republic is established after World War I, with Marshal Józef Pilsudski, founder of the PPS, elected president.
1926	Pilsudski seizes full power in a coup and establishes an autocratic regime.
1935	On Pilsudski's death, a military regime holds power under Marshal Smigly-Rydz.
1939	Invaded by Germany; western Poland was incorporated into the Nazi Reich (state) and the rest become a German colony; 6 million Poles – half of them Jews – were slaughtered in the next five years.
1944–45	Poland is liberated from **Nazi** rule by Soviet Union's Red Army; boundaries are redrawn westwards at Potsdam Conference. One half of 'old Poland' is lost to the USSR, part of Silesia, along the Oder and Neisse rivers, is added, shifting the state 240 km/150 mi westwards; millions of Germans are expelled.
1947	A communist people's republic is proclaimed after a manipulated election.
early 1950s	Harsh Stalinist rule.
1956	Poznan strikes and riots. The moderate Wladyslaw Gomulka is installed as the Polish United Workers' Party (PUWP) leader.
1980	Solidarity, led by Lech Walesa, emerges as a free trade union following Gdansk disturbances.
1981	Martial law is imposed by Gen Wojciech Jaruzelski; trade-union activity is banned, and Solidarity leaders and supporters arrested.
1983	Martial law ends.

1984	Amnesty for 35,000 political prisoners.
1988	There are Solidarity-led strikes and demonstrations for pay increases. Reform-communist Mieczyslaw Rakowski become prime minister.
1989	There is an agreement to relegalize Solidarity, to allow opposition parties, and to adopt a more democratic constitution.
1997	Poland is invited to join NATO and begins negotiations to join the European Union (EU).
1998	Full EU membership negotiations commence.
1999	Poland becomes a full member of NATO.

Polish Corridor

Strip of land designated under the **Treaty of Versailles** in 1919 to give Poland access to the Baltic. It cut off **East Prussia** from the rest of Germany. Germany resented this partition and it was one of the primary causes of tension with Poland in the build-up to **World War II**. The German government demanded to be permitted to build a road and rail connection across the Corridor, in a zone to be granted extra-territorial rights, a demand that the Poles implacably refused.

The German invasion of the Polish Corridor in September 1939 led to the outbreak of World War II in Europe. When Poland took over the southern part of **East Prussia** 1945, it was absorbed.

Pope

The bishop of Rome, head of the Roman Catholic Church, with claims to be the spiritual descendant of St Peter. Elected by the Sacred College of Cardinals, a pope dates his pontificate from his coronation with the tiara, or triple crown, at St Peter's Basilica, Rome. The pope had great political power in Europe from the early Middle Ages until the **Reformation**.

The primacy of the pope is rejected by the majority of the world's Christian denominations. In a 1995 encyclical, John Paul II called for greater unity among Christians, urging leaders to discuss the role of papal authority within the community, and indicating his willingness to consider a change in the way papal authority might be exercised.

Popular Front

Political alliance made up of liberals, socialists, communists, and other centre and left-wing parties. This policy was put forward by the Communist International in 1935 as a means of combating Fascism. It was adopted in France and Spain, where popular-front governments were elected in 1936. In France the Popular Front was overthrown in 1938 and in Spain it fell with the defeat of the Republic in the **Spanish Civil War** in 1939.

In Britain a popular-front policy was advocated by Sir Stafford Cripps and others, but rejected by the Labour Party. The resistance movements in the occupied countries during **World War II** represented a revival of the popular-front idea, and in post-war politics the term tends to recur whenever a strong right-wing party can be counterbalanced only by an alliance of those on the left.

Potsdam Conference

Conference held in Potsdam, Germany, from 17 July to 2 August 1945, between representatives of the USA, the UK, and the USSR. They established the political and economic principles governing the treatment of Germany in the initial period of Allied control at the end of World War II, and sent an ultimatum to Japan demanding unconditional surrender on pain of utter destruction.

During the conference Truman casually told Stalin about the atomic bomb. Stalin was angry with Truman for not telling him about it earlier, even though Stalin's spies had already told him all about it. Truman also refused to share atomic secrets with Stalin.

Potsdam was intended to sort out the issues that had been agreed at **Yalta**.

THE OUTCOMES OF THE POTSDAM CONFERENCE

- Germany was split into four zones.
- Berlin was divided into four sectors.
- The government of Germany was agreed. The four occupying powers would govern jointly and decisions would be unanimous. Berlin would be governed by the Joint Kommandatura of the senior military commanders.

But there were also important disagreements at Potsdam. Truman criticized Stalin for not allowing free elections in Eastern Europe. Potsdam laid the seeds of suspicion that led to the complete breakdown of relations between East and West over the next few years.

Prague Spring

The 1968 programme of liberalization, which was begun by the prime minister Alexander **Dubček,** the new Communist Party leader in Czechoslovakia.

In 1968 Czechoslovakia met the Soviet Union in the final of the Olympic ice hockey tournament. The Czechs, much to the delight of the crowd, took revenge and the gold medal.

He sought to assure the Soviets that his planned reforms would not threaten socialism. The Soviet Union rejected the changes and on 20 August 1968 Soviet tanks invaded **Czechoslovakia** and entered the capital Prague. Dubček was arrested, but released soon afterwards. He became ambassador to Turkey. Most of the Prague Spring reforms were reversed.

Protestantism
One of the main divisions of Christianity, which emerged from Roman Catholicism at the **Reformation**. The chief denominations are the Anglican Communion (Church of England in the UK and the Episcopal Church in the USA), Baptists, Christian Scientists, Congregationalists (United Church of Christ), Lutherans, Methodists, Pentecostals, and Presbyterians, with a total membership of about 300 million.

Protestantism takes its name from the protest of Martin **Luther** and others at the Diet of Spires in 1529 against the decision to reaffirm the edict of the Diet of Worms against the Reformation. Initially it denoted the position of the Lutherans as opposed to both Catholics and Reformed (Zwinglian or Calvinist), but it later came to be more generally applied.

The first statement of Protestantism as a distinct movement was the Confession of Augsburg of 1530. The most important aspects of Protestantism are the acceptance of the Bible as the only source of truth, the universal priesthood of all believers, and forgiveness of sins solely through faith in Jesus Christ. The Protestant Church reduces the importance of the priesthood and the teaching of the church of Christianity and underlines the preaching and hearing of the word of God by individuals.

Prussia
Northern German state on the Baltic coast, which was an independent kingdom until 1867. It was founded in the 17th and 18th centuries by the Electors of Brandenburg and became one of the most powerful European powers. In 1867 it became, under Chancellor Otto von **Bismarck**, the military power of the North German Confederation and part of the German Empire in 1871. The King of Prussia, **William I**, became the emperor of Germany. Prussia remained a separate state within the German Empire and had a separate government during the **Nazi** period.

purge
Removal (for example, from a political party) of suspected opponents or persons regarded as undesirable (often by violent means). During the 1930s purges were conducted in the USSR

Sergei Kirov was probably murdered on the orders of Joseph Stalin because Stalin feared that Kirov was becoming too popular. He was shot on 1 December 1934 and his assassin died mysteriously afterwards.

under Soviet leader Joseph **Stalin**, carried out by the secret police against political opponents,

1931–32 Thousands of engineers and technical experts are sacked because of the failures of the **Five-Year Plans**.
1932 850,000 party members are expelled.
1934 After the murder of Sergei **Kirov** more than 7,000,000 Soviet citizens are arrested and either executed or sent to labour camps, the Gulags.

Q–R

Quadruple Alliance

In European history the alliance which led to the defeat of **Napoleon I** in 1815. Austria, Britain, Prussia, and Russia allied in 1813 and renewed the alliance in 1815 at the **Congress of Vienna** and the Congress of Aix-la-Chapelle in 1818. This was a secret alliance established by the Allies to ensure that France did not cause trouble in the future. Plans were laid for joint military intervention. France, however, was admitted to the Alliance, which became Quintuple in 1818.

Quisling, Vidkun Abraham Lauritz Jonsson (1887–1945)

Norwegian politician and leader from 1933 of the Norwegian Fascist Party, Quisling aided the Nazi invasion of Norway in 1940 by delaying mobilization and urging non-resistance. He was made premier by German dictator Adolf Hitler in 1942, and was arrested and shot as a traitor by the Norwegians in 1945.

The term Quisling is now used to describe any traitor who aids an occupying force.

Race to the sea

In **World War I**, after the Battle of the **Marne** in September 1914, both the German forces and the Allies attempted to outflank each other in Flanders, finally reaching the sea. The trench line then expanded in the other direction until it formed a continuous front from the North Sea to the Swiss border.

Rasputin, Gregory (1871–1916)

Born Grigory Efimovich Novykh, a

Rasputin *This caricature portrays tsar Nicholas II and the tsarina as puppets in Rasputin's hands.*

Siberian Eastern Orthodox mystic who acquired influence over the Tsarina Alexandra, wife of **Nicholas II**, because of his power to ease her son's suffering from haemophilia. He was given power by the tsar to make political and ecclesiastical appointments. His abuse of this power and his notorious debauchery (reputedly including the tsarina) led to his murder by a group of nobles.

A larger-than-life character, Rasputin even proved hard to kill: when poison had no effect, his assassins shot him and dumped him in the River Neva.

Rastadt, Treaty of
In 1714, an agreement signed by Austria and France that supplemented the Treaty of **Utrecht** and helped to end the War of the **Spanish Succession**.

Rathenau, Walther (1867–1922)
German politician and, a leading industrialist who was appointed as economic director during **World War I**. After the war Rathenau founded the Democratic Party, and became foreign minister in 1922. In the same year he signed the Rapallo Treaty of Friendship with the USSR, cancelling German and Soviet counter-claims for indemnities for World War I, and soon after was assassinated.

Rathenau was killed by right-wing fanatics, who believed that he was pro-Communist. In fact the Treaty of Rapallo contained secret clauses which allowed the German armed forces to train in Russia, and so avoid the terms of the **Treaty of Versailles**.

realpolitik (German *realpolitik* 'politics of realism')
The belief that the pursuit of self-interest and power, backed up by force when convenient, is the only realistic option for a great state. The term was used to describe the German chancellor Otto von **Bismarck's** policies.

Reformation
Religious and political movement of the 16th-century Europe aimed at reform of the Roman Catholic Church, which led to the establishment of the Protestant Church. Anticipated from the 12th century by the Waldenses, Lollards, and Hussites, it was set off by German priest Martin **Luther** in 1517. The Reformation was precipitated by the corruption and worldliness of the Catholic Church during the late 15th century. In 1492 Alessandro Borgia was elected Pope Sixtus VI, despite having several children.

> ❝ The Reformation was the greatest revolution in English history. It meant that England was suddenly separated from the Europe of Western Christendom, of which it had formed an important part for more than a millennium. This was the first element in the establishment of an independent nation-state which was to be isolated from Europe until 1973. ❞
>
> **Edwin Jones**, English historian, *The English Nation: the Great Myth*, (1998).

Reichstag Fire

The burning of the German parliament building in Berlin 27 February 1933, less than a month after the Nazi leader Adolf **Hitler** became chancellor. The fire was used as a justification for the suspension of many constitutional guarantees and also as an excuse to attack the communists. There is still debate over whether the Nazis were involved in this crime, of which they were the main beneficiaries.

It is now believed that the fire was started by members of the *Sturm Abteilung* (SA) led by Karl Ernst on the orders of **Josef Goebbels**. They were subsequently shot by an SS unit.

Although three Bulgarians (Dimitrov, Popov, and Tanev) and a German, Torgler, were all indicted and tried in Leipzig, the only conviction was the Dutch communist Marinus van der Lubbe who was found at the scene of the crime and confessed.

Reinsurance Treaty

Secret treaty concluded by **Bismarck** with Russia 1887, it was designed to prevent Russia forming an alliance with France. The reason for the treaty was the refusal of Russia to extend the League of the Three Emperors for another three years.

Religion, Wars of

Series of civil wars from 1562 to 1589 in France between Catholics and (Protestant) Huguenots. Each side was led by noble families, which competed for influence over a weakened monarchy. The most infamous event was the **Massacre of St Bartholomew** in 1572, carried out on the orders of the Catholic faction led by Catherine de **Medici** and the Duke of Guise. After 1584, the heir apparent to the French throne was the

Huguenot Henry of Navarre. This prompted further hostilities, but after his accession as **Henry IV** in 1589, he was able to maintain his hold on power, partly through military victory and partly by converting to Catholicism in 1593.

He introduced the Edict of Nantes in 1598, guaranteeing freedom of worship throughout his kingdom.

Renaissance or Revival of Learning

Period in European cultural history that began in Italy around 1400 and lasted until the end of the 1500s. Elsewhere in Europe it began later, and lasted until the 1600s. One characteristic of the Renaissance was the rediscovery of classical literature, led by the writers Giovanni Boccaccio (1313–1375) and Francesco Petrarch (1303–1374).

The greatest expression of the Renaissance was in the arts and learning. The term 'Renaissance' (French for 'rebirth') to describe this period of cultural history was invented by historians in the 1800s.

In the arts, critics regard the years from 1490 to 1520 (the 'High Renaissance') as a peak, with the work of Leonardo da Vinci (1452–1519), Raphael Sanzio (1483–1520), and Michelangelo Buonarotti (1475–1564) in painting, and Michelangelo and Donato Bramante (1444–1514) in architecture being of paramount importance. The high-point of Venetian painting came some years later, with the work of Titian

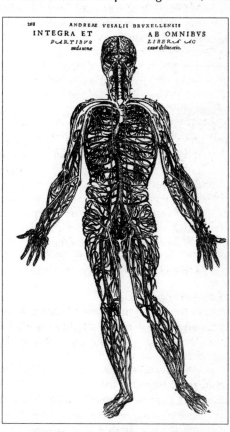

Renaissance *Anatomical diagram, a woodcut by Jan Stephan von Calcar, after a drawing by Vesalius.*

(1488–1576), Paolo Veronese (1528–1588), and Tintoretto (1518–1594). Leonardo has been described as a 'universal man' for his enormously wide-ranging studies, including painting, architecture, science, and engineering.

The enormous achievements of creative artists during the Renaissance were made possible by the patronage of wealthy ruling families such as the **Sforza** in Milan and the **Medici** in Florence; by the ruling doge of Venice; and by the popes, notably **Julius II** and Leo X.

In literature, both Boccaccio and Petrarch wrote major works in Italian rather than Latin, a trend that was continued by the creation of epic poems in the vernacular by Ludovico Ariosto (1474–1533) and Torquato Tasso (1544–1595). Progress from the religious to the secular was seen in the creation of the first public libraries, and in the many translations from the classics published in Venice in the 16th century. In philosophy, the rediscovery of Greek thought took the form of neo-Platonism in the work of such people as Marsilio Ficino (1433–1499). Niccolò **Machiavelli** in *The Prince* (1513) founded the modern study of politics.

revanche
French for 'revenge'. In French history, the term refers to those who, following the **Franco-Prussian War** 1870–71, favoured a foreign policy directed towards the recapture of **Alsace-Lorraine** from Germany.

Revolutionary Wars
Series of wars from 1791 to 1802 between France and the combined armies of Britain, Austria, Prussia, and others, during the period of the **French Revolution** and **Napoleon I's** campaign to conquer Europe. The wars began when Austria and Prussia attempted to crush the revolution in 1792 and reinstate the French monarchy. Britain declared war in February 1793 when the French occupied the Low Countries.

> ❝ Oh! The grand old Duke of York / He had ten thousand men; / He marched them up to the top of a hill, / And he marched them down again. ❞
>
> Traditional rhyme, referring to the son of George III, Duke of York, who commanded two unsuccessful campaigns against the French in the early years of the French Revolutionary Wars.

Revolutions of 1848
Series of revolts in various parts of Europe against monarchical rule, which were sparked off by an economic slump in the years 1846 to 1847.

The revolutions began in France with the overthrow of **Louis Philippe** and then spread to Italy, the Austrian Empire, and Germany, where the short-lived **Frankfurt Parliament** put forward ideas about political unity in Germany. None of the revolutions enjoyed any lasting success, and most were violently suppressed within a few months.

Rhineland

Province of Prussia from 1815, which was demilitarized by the Treaty of Versailles in 1919.

Under the terms of the Treaty of **Versailles**, following **World War I**, the Rhineland was to be occupied by Allied forces for 15 years, with a permanent demilitarized zone. Demilitarization was reaffirmed by the Treaties of **Locarno**, but German foreign minister Gustav **Stresemann** achieved the removal of the British forces in 1926. The French forces were withdrawn in 1930. Both treaties were violated when German dictator Adolf **Hitler's** troops marched into the demilitarized zone of the Rhineland in 1936. Britain and France merely protested, and the Rhineland remained under German occupation. It was the scene of heavy fighting in 1944, and was recaptured by US troops in 1945, becoming one of the largest states of West Germany after the end of the war.

Ribbentrop, Joachim von (1893–1946)

German Nazi politician and diplomat, who joined the **Nazi** party in 1932 and acted as German dictator Adolf **Hitler's** adviser on foreign affairs; he was German ambassador to the UK from 1936 to 1938. A political lightweight and social climber, Ribbentrop's loyalty was useful to Hitler since he posed no threat, although he was regarded with contempt by his colleagues. As foreign minister from 1938 to 1945, he negotiated the non-aggression pact between Germany and the USSR (the **Molotov-Ribbentrop Pact** of 1939). He was found guilty in 1946 at the **Nuremberg trials** of being a war criminal and was hanged.

> ❝ My last wish is that Germany rediscovers her unity and that an alliance is made between East and West. ❞
>
> **Joachim von Ribbentrop**, last words before being hanged, 1946.

Richelieu, Armand Jean du Plessis de (1585–1642)

French cardinal and politician who was chief minister of Louis XIII (1601–1643) from 1624. Richelieu aimed to make the monarchy absolute;

he ruthlessly crushed opposition by the nobility and destroyed the political power of the Huguenots, while leaving them religious freedom. Abroad, he sought to establish French supremacy by breaking the power of the **Habsburgs**; he therefore supported the Swedish king **Gustavus Adolphus** and the German Protestant princes against Austria and in 1635 brought France into the **Thirty Years' War**.

> ❝ Nothing is as dangerous for the state as those who would govern kingdoms with maxims found in books. ❞
>
> **Armand Richelieu**, *Political Testament.*

Risorgimento

The 19th-century movement for Italian national unity and independence which began in 1815. Leading figures in the movement included **Cavour**, **Mazzini**, and **Garibaldi**. Uprisings in 1848 to 1849 failed, but with help from France, Austria was forced out of Lombardy in 1859, and an Italian kingdom was founded in 1861. Unification was finally completed with the addition of Venetia in 1866 and the **Papal States** in 1870.

See also: *Carbonari; Young Italy.*

Robespierre, Maximilien François Marie Isidore de (1758–1794)

A lawyer who was elected to the National Assembly of 1789 to 1791. His defence of democratic principles made him popular in Paris, while his disinterestedness won him the nickname of 'the sea-green Incorruptible'. His zeal for social reform and his attacks on the excesses of the extremists made him enemies on both right and left.

Robespierre became the leader of the **Jacobins** in the **National Convention** (1792) and supported the execution of Louis XVI and the overthrow of the moderate republican **Girondins**. In July 1793 he was elected to the **Committee of Public Safety** and headed a **Reign of Terror**.

Robespierre *Portrait of Maximilien Robespierre.*

A year later a conspiracy was formed against him, and in July 1794 he was overthrown and executed by those who actually perpetrated the Reign of Terror. He was guillotined, but many believe that he was a scapegoat for the Reign of Terror since he ordered only 72 executions personally.

Robespierre tried to create a 'Republic of Virtue'. He believed that if all evil in society was destroyed, people would be good and would not need laws.

Röhm, Ernst (1758–1794)

German leader of the Nazi Brownshirts, the SA (*Sturmabteilung*), who led the socialist wing of the **Nazi Party**. After **Hitler** became chancellor, Röhm demanded the post of defence minister and command of the army. Hitler knew that this would be unacceptable to the German High Command, and so, on the pretext of an intended SA putsch (uprising) by the Brownshirts, the Nazis had some 400 SA leaders, including Röhm, killed on 29 and 30 June 1934. The event is known as the **'Night of the Long Knives'**.

Röhm represented the Socialist wing of the Nazi Party and wanted Hitler to carry out a socialist revolution in Germany. He was murdered because he was the one Nazi who might have been able to displace Hitler.

See also: *Strasser.*

Romanov dynasty

Ruling Imperial family of Russia from 1613 to the Russian Revolution 1917 when the unified state of Russia was created. Under the Romanovs, Russia developed into an absolutist empire.

The pattern of succession was irregular until 1797. The last tsar, **Nicholas II**, abdicated in March 1917 and was murdered in July 1918, together with his family.

In 1913 the Romanovs celebrated the 300th anniversary of the founding of the dynasty. A ball was held in which all the guests, including the tsar and tsarina, dressed in the costumes of 1613.

Rome-Berlin Axis

Another name for the Axis alliance of 1936 to 1940 in **World War II**.

Rome-Berlin-Tokyo Axis

Another name for the Axis alliance (from 1940) in **World War II**.

Rome, Treaties of

Two international agreements signed on 25 March 1957 by Belgium, France, West Germany, Italy, Luxembourg, and the Netherlands, which established the European Economic Community (EEC, now the **European Union** or EU) and the European Atomic Energy Commission (EURATOM).

The terms of the economic treaty, which came into effect on 1 January 1958, provided for economic co-operation, reduction (and eventual removal) of customs barriers, and the free movement of capital, goods, and labour between the member countries, together with common agricultural and trading policies. Subsequent new members of the EU have been obliged to accept these terms.

Russia

Chronology

10th–12th centuries Kiev temporarily unites the Russian peoples into its empire. Christianity is introduced from Constantinople in 988.

13th century Mongols (Golden Horde) overrun the southern steppes in 1223, compels Russian princes to pay tribute.

1462–1505 Ivan the Great, grand duke of Muscovy, throws off Mongol yoke and united lands in the northwest.

1547–84 **Ivan the Terrible** assumes the title of tsar and conquers Kazan and Astrakhan; the colonization of Siberia begins.

1613 The first Romanov tsar, Michael, is elected after a period of chaos.

1682–1725 **Peter the Great** modernizes the bureaucracy and army.

1762–96 **Catherine the Great** annexes the Crimea and part of Poland and recovers western Ukraine and Belorussia.

1798–1814 Russia intervenes in the Revolutionary and **Napoleonic Wars** (1798–1801, 1805–07); repels **Napoleon**, and takes part in his overthrow (1812–14).

1853–56 The **Crimean War**.

1861 Serfdom is abolished by **Alexander II**.

1877–78 The Russo-Turkish War

1898 The Social Democratic Party is founded by Russian Marxists; it splits into **Bolshevik** and **Menshevik** factions in 1903.

1904–05 The Russo-Japanese War is caused by Russian expansion in Manchuria.

1905 The Revolution forces the tsar to accept a parliament (Duma) with limited powers.

1914 Russo-Austrian rivalry in the **Balkans** is a major cause of outbreak of **World War I**; Russia fights in alliance with France and Britain.

1917 The Russian Revolution: the tsar abdicates, a provisional government is established; the Bolsheviks seize power under Vladimir **Lenin**.

1918 The Treaty of **Brest-Litovsk** ends the war with Germany; the tsar is murdered; the Russian Empire collapses; Finland, Poland, and the Baltic States secede.

1918–22	Civil War between the Red Army, led by Leon **Trotsky**, and White Russian forces with foreign support; the Red Army are ultimately victorious; control is regained over Ukraine, Caucasus, and Central Asia.
1922	The former Russian Empire is renamed the Union of Soviet Socialist Republics.
1924	The death of Lenin.
1928	Joseph **Stalin** emerges as absolute ruler after ousting **Trotsky**.
1928–33	The first **Five-Year Plan** and the **collectivization** of agriculture.
1936–38	The **Purges**
1939	**Nazi-Soviet** non-aggression pact is signed; the USSR invades eastern Poland and attacks Finland.
1941–45	The **'Great Patriotic War'** against Germany
1949	The Council for Mutual Economic Assistance (**Comecon**) is created to supervise trade in Soviet bloc.
1953	Stalin dies.
1955	The **Warsaw Pact** created.
1956	Nikita **Khrushchev** makes his 'secret speech' criticizing Stalin; USSR invades Hungary.
1957–58	Khrushchev ousts his rivals and becomes effective leader.
1964	Khrushchev is ousted by a new 'collective leadership' headed by Leonid **Brezhnev** and Alexei Kosygin.
1968	The USSR and its allies invade **Czechoslovakia**.
1982	Brezhnev dies; Yuri **Andropov** becomes leader.
1984	Andropov dies; Konstantin **Chernenko** becomes leader.
1985	Chernenko dies; Mikhail Gorbachev becomes leader and announces a wide-ranging reform programme (*perestroika*).
1989	Multi-candidate elections are held in a move towards 'socialist democracy'; the collapse of Soviet satellite regimes in Eastern Europe; end of Cold War.

Russian Revolution, 1905

A spontaneous protest at the rule of **Nicholas II,** beginning with the Bloody Sunday march on January 22 1905. A procession of Russian workers marched on the Winter Palace with a petition for the tsar. Troops opened fire upon the crowd. At least 200 were killed and 800 wounded, but the number of deaths may have been as high as 1,000. This led to the tsar announcing his intention to call a 'consultative assembly' on 3 March.

March	89,000 Russian soldiers are killed in the Battle of Mukden with the Japanese.
May	The Russian Baltic Fleet is destroyed by the Japanese navy at the Battle of Tsushima.
June	There is a mutiny in the navy and the battleship *Potemkin* is seized by the crew.
19 August	The tsar announces the creation of a Duma, which is to be elected on a limited franchise and is to have the power of discussing legislation. This is rejected.

20 October A general strike begins, which rapidly spreads throughout the country.

26 October The St Petersburg Soviet is formed. This is a workers' council, which is soon copied throughout Russia.

30 October The tsar publishes the October Manifesto.

Nicholas was only saved because the army remained loyal. But he did not learn his lesson.

Russian Revolution 1917
See **February Revolution** and **October Revolution**.

Sadowa, Battle of or Battle of Königgrätz

The Prussian victory over the Austrian army (German Königgrätz) on 3 July 1866 that ended the **Seven Weeks' War**. It confirmed Prussian hegemony over the German states and led to the formation of the North German Confederation 1867. It is named after the nearby village of Sadowa (Czech Sadová) in the Czech Republic.

See also: *Bismarck; Franco-Prussian War.*

St Bartholomew, Massacre of

The slaughter of Huguenots (French Protestants) in Paris, between 24 August and 17 September 1572, and until 3 October in the provinces. About 25,000 people are believed to have been killed. When **Catherine de Medici's** plot to have **Admiral Coligny** assassinated failed, she decided to have all the Huguenot leaders killed, persuading her son Charles IX (1550–1574) it was in the interest of public safety.

Catherine received congratulations from all the Catholic powers, and the pope ordered a medal to be struck.

Sakharov, Andrei Dmitrievich (1921–1989)

Soviet physicist, who was an outspoken human-rights campaigner. With Igor Tamm (1895–1971) he developed the hydrogen bomb. He later protested against Soviet nuclear tests and was a founder of the Soviet Human Rights Committee in 1970, winning the Nobel Peace Prize in 1975.

> ❝ Every day I saw the huge material, intellectual, and nervous resources of thousands of people being poured into the creation of a means of total destruction, something capable of annihilating all human civilization. I noticed that the control levers were in the hands of people who, though talented in their own ways, were cynical. ❞
>
> **Andrei Sakharov,** Sakharov Speaks,1974.

For criticizing Soviet action in Afghanistan, he was sent into internal exile from 1980 to 1986.

Sakharov was elected to the Congress of the USSR People's Deputies in 1989, where he emerged as leader of its radical reform grouping before his death later the same year.

Salazar, António de Oliveira (1921–1989)
Portuguese prime minister from 1932 to 1968 who exercised a virtual dictatorship. During **World War II** he maintained Portuguese neutrality but fought long colonial wars in Africa (Angola and Mozambique) that impeded his country's economic development as well as that of the colonies.

Until 1945 Salazar's National Union, founded in 1930, remained the only legal party. Salazar was also foreign minister from 1936 to 1947.

San Francisco conference
Conference attended by representatives from 50 nations who had declared war on Germany before March 1945. It was held in San Francisco, California, USA. The conference drew up the United Nations Charter, which was signed on 26 June 1945.

sans-culotte (French ,'without knee breeches')
In the **French Revolution**, a member of the working classes, who wore trousers, as opposed to the aristocracy and bourgeoisie, who wore knee breeches. In Paris, the sans-culottes, who drew their support mostly from apprentices, small shopkeepers, craftspeople, and the unemployed, made up a large armed force that could be mobilised by radical politicians, for example in the **Jacobin** seizure of power from the

> The sans-culottes became the most significant force in the French Revolution from 1789 to 1794. Most of the major changes in these years resulted from the actions of the sans-culottes, the Paris mob.

Girondins in June 1793. They ceased to have any real influence after the fall of the Jacobins between 1794 and 1795.

Schacht, Hjalmar Horace Greely (1921–1989)
German financier who, as president of the Reichsbank from 1923 to 1929, created a new currency that ended the inflation of the Deutschmark. In 1933 Schacht was recalled to the Reichsbank by the Nazis and, as minister of economics, restored Germany's trade balance. Dismissed from the Reichsbank after a dispute with German Nazi leader Adolf Hitler over expenditure on

rearmament, Schact was charged with high treason and interned; he was later acquitted of crimes against humanity at the **Nuremberg trials** in 1945 and cleared by the German de-Nazification courts in 1948.

Schacht's deficit budgeting enabled Hitler to bring about the economic recovery of Germany from 1933 to 1936.

Schindler, Oskar (1908–1974)

Czechoslovak industrialist, Jewish benefactor, and a flamboyantly successful businessman who set up a factory in Cracow, Poland, soon after the German invasion of 1939. Schindler established good relations with the occupying forces and, through gifts and lavish entertainment, persuaded them to let him employ Jewish workers. He saved many hundreds of Jews from death in concentration camps by bribing the Nazis to release them into his 'custody'.

His activities, which earned him the gratitude and respect of the Zionist movement (the Jewish quest for a Jewish homeland in Palestine, in response to persecution of the Jews (anti-Semitism)), were recorded in the form of a novel *Schindler's Ark* (1982), by Australian author Thomas Keneally, and later translated into an Academy Award-winning film *Schindler's List* by American film director Steven Spielberg.

Schleicher, Kurt von (1882–1934)

German soldier and chancellor who held staff posts throughout **World War I**, afterwards joining the Reichswehr ministry, where he became the link between the army and politicians. Schleicher engineered the elimination of the Socialists from government in 1930, then played a major role in Heinrich Brüning's fall two years later. He was minister of defence in 1932, and in December of the same year he became chancellor of Germany in succession to Franz **von Papen**. His government lasted only until 28 January 1933, as a result of the hostility created by Adolf **Hitler** and the Nazis. President Hindenburg refused to authorize him to dissolve the Reichstag (parliament) and appointed Hitler as chancellor, and Schleicher then retired into private life. Together with his wife he was murdered during the '**Night of the Long Knives**' on 30 June 1934.

Von Schleicher had arranged the appointment of Franz von Papen as chancellor in July 1932, but then replaced him in December. Von Papen was furious and tried to use Hitler and the Nazis as a means of forcing von Schleicher from office.

Schlieffen, Alfred von (1833–1913)

German field-marshal, who as chief of the German general staff (1891–1905) greatly developed the German Army manoeuvres, and wrote much on military matters. His *Gesammelte Schriften* were published in Berlin, Germany, in 1913. He is best known, however, for developing the military theory known as the **Schlieffen Plan**. Schlieffen was born in Berlin and distinguished himself in the Franco-Prussian War of 1870 to 1871.

Schlieffen Plan

Military plan produced in December 1905 by the German chief of general staff, Gen Count Alfred von **Schlieffen**, that formed the basis of German military planning before **World War I**, and inspired German dictator Adolf **Hitler's** plans for the conquest of Europe in **World War II**. It involved a simultaneous attack on Russia and France, the object being to defeat France quickly and then deploy all available resources against the Russians. This would be achieved by advancing in great force through Belgium and encircling Paris. Schlieffen believed that the main French forces would be massed on the German border and would be unable to prevent the collapse of France.

Although the plan was sound, it was altered by Gen von **Moltke**, who reduced the strength of the army's right wing and thus made it incapable of carrying out the plan when it was implemented in 1914.

Schuman, Robert Jean-Baptiste Nicolas (1886–1963)

French politician, who was prime minister from 1947 to 1948 and foreign minister from 1948 to 1955. Schuman was a member of the post-war Mouvement Républicain Populaire (MRP). His Schuman Declaration of May 1950, drafted by Jean **Monnet**, outlined a scheme for pooling coal and iron-ore resources. The resulting European Coal and Steel Community, established by France, Belgium, Germany, the Netherlands, Italy, and Luxembourg under the 1951 Paris Treaty, was the forerunner of the European Economic Community (the **European Union** from 1993).

Schuschnigg, Kurt von (1897–1977)

Austrian chancellor from 1934 to 1938 who succeeded chancellor Engelbert Dollfuss (1892–1934) when the latter was murdered. Schuschnigg tried in vain to prevent Nazi annexation (Anschluss), but in February 1938 Schuschnigg was forced to accept a Nazi minister of the interior, and a month later Austria was occupied and annexed by Germany. Schuschnigg was imprisoned in Germany until 1945, when he went to the USA; he returned to Austria in 1967.

Second Front

In **World War II**, the battle line opened against Germany on 6 June 1944 by the Allies (Britain and the USA). Following Germany's invasion of the USSR in June 1941 (the 'first front'), Soviet leader Josef Stalin constantly asked Britain and the USA from 1942 to invade the European mainland, to relieve pressure on Soviet forces.

Sedan, Battle of

During the **Franco-Prussian War**, the scene of a disastrous French defeat by the Prussians on 2 September 1870 at Sedan, a fortified town in northern France. The victory cost the Prussians about 9,000 casualties, but the French suffered 17,000 casualties (killed and wounded) and 104,000 prisoners of war, including Emperor **Napoleon III**. The French no longer had any effective regular army.

> When asked what he had left after his surrender to the Prussians, Napoleon III replied 'My pride'.

See also: *Alsace-Lorraine; Bismarck,*

Sevastopol, Siege of

During the **Crimean War**, a fortified Russian port on the Black Sea, which was besieged by British and French forces from September 1854 to September 1855. The Russian fleet was based in Sevastopol harbour, so the town was the prime objective of the main Allied attack in the Crimea.

After the Battle of the Alma in September 1854 the Allies closed up on Sevastopol and entrenched around it, commencing the siege on 17 October.

Little progress was made until June 1855; on 7 June the French took the Mamelon fortress, which protected the Malakoff line, the principal defensive line for the town. The British attack on the Redan, another defensive complex, a few days later was a failure. After a final assault by the Allies on 5 September, Sevastopol was evacuated and the Russians retreated inland, leaving their wounded behind.

See also: *Balaclava; Inkermann.*

Seven Weeks' War

Conflict in 1866 between Austria and Prussia, brought about by the German chancellor Otto von **Bismarck**. It was nominally over the possession of Schleswig-Holstein, but it was actually to confirm Prussia's superiority over Austria as the leading German state. The Prussian victory at the Battle of **Sadowa** was the culmination of Gen von Moltke's success.

Seven Years' War

War fought from 1756 to 1765 which marked the conclusion of the hostilities begun in the **War of Austrian Succession**. Austria and Russia attacked Prussia, which was saved by the military brilliance of **Frederick the Great** and by the accession of Tsar Peter III in 1762. Peter was a great admirer of Frederick and he withdrew from the war.

The war also marked the end of the long colonial struggle between Britain and France. All French colonies in America and Canada were seized and the French gave up all claims to India. The resentment of the French, however, led to their involvement in the American Revolution from 1778 onwards. This was a deciding factor in the American success in 1781.

1759 was called the *Annus Mirabilis*, the wonderful year, in Britain, because of the string of victories by British forces; the naval battles of Quiberon and Lagos and the armies' success at Minden in Germany and Quebec in Canada.

Seyss-Inquart, Arthur (1892–1946)

Austrian lawyer and politician, who joined the Nazi party in 1928. He was minister of the interior and security in the **Schuschnigg** cabinet from February to March 1938. Seyss-Inquart became governor of Austria in 1938 and deputy governor general of Poland in 1939. As Reich commissioner for the Netherlands he became notorious for his cruelty, and after the war was executed as a war criminal.

See also: *Anschluss*.

Sforza family

Italian family that ruled the duchy of Milan from 1450 to 1499, 1512 to 1515, 1521 to 1524, and 1529 to 1535. Its court was a centre of Renaissance culture and its rulers were prominent patrons of the arts.

- Francesco Sforza (1401–66) succeeded his father in command of the *condottiere*. He served Filippo Maria Visconti, duke of Milan, and in 1441 married his only daughter, Bianca. On Filippo's death in 1447, Francesco defeated the Venetians, hereditary enemies of Milan, and was acknowledged duke of Milan in 1450.

- Galeazzo Maria Sforza (1444–76) succeeded as duke of Milan in 1466. When he was assassinated, he was succeeded by his young son Giangaleazzo.

- Giangaleazzo Sforza (1468–94), who took the title of duke, with his mother as regent.

- Ludovico Sforza, Giangaleazzo's uncle, supplanted the regent and took power, eventually becoming duke on his nephew's death in 1494. Though he himself lost the dukedom when the French invaded in 1499, the volatile situation in the following decades meant that both his sons were, briefly, installed in Milan.

- Massimiliano (1490–1530), named after the Holy Roman Emperor, was duke from 1512 until Francis I's successful invasion of 1515.

- Francesco Maria (1492–1535) held power twice, from 1521 to 1524 and from 1529 until his death in 1535, which left Charles V in control of Milan.

show trial

Public and well-reported trial of people who were accused of crimes against the state. In the USSR in the 1930s and 1940s, Soviet leader Joseph **Stalin** carried out show trials against economic saboteurs, Communist Party members, army officers, and even members of the Bolshevik (precursors to the communists) leadership. But their main purpose was to eliminate the old Bolsheviks who had known Soviet leader Vladimir **Lenin**. In this way Stalin could destroy all who had knowledge of the real relationship between himself and Lenin.

Most of the accused at the show trials confessed to ridiculous crimes that they could not possibly have committed. They were told that their families would be protected if they pleaded guilty.

Andrei **Vyshinksy** was the Soviet prosecutor for many of the most notorious show trials of the 1930s.

See also: *Kirov; Purges.*

Sikorski, Wladyslaw Eugeniusz (1881–1943)

Polish general and politician, prime minister from 1922 to 1923, and 1939 to 1943 in the Polish government in exile in London during **World War II**. He was killed in an aeroplane crash near Gibraltar in controversial circumstances.

Some historians believe that the British government was responsible for Sikorski's death.

Following Sikorski's death, the Polish government in exile lost its sense of direction and its influence declined.

Silesia
Region of Europe that has long been disputed because of its geographical position, mineral resources, and industrial potential; it is now in Poland and the Czech Republic with metallurgical industries and a coalfield in Polish Silesia.

- The dispute began in the 17th century with claims on the area by both Austria and Prussia.

- It was seized by Prussia's **Frederick the Great**, starting the War of the **Austrian Succession**. Its seizure was finally recognized by Austria in 1763, after the **Seven Years' War**.

- In 1945, after **World War II**, all German Silesia east of the **Oder-Neisse** line was transferred to Polish administration; about 10 million inhabitants of German origin, both there and in Czechoslovak Silesia, were expelled.

Sinope, Battle of
In the Russo-Turkish war, a Russian naval victory over the Turks on 30 November 1853 off Sinope (now Sinop), a Turkish town on the southern shore of the Black Sea. The Russians wrecked a Turkish fleet and killed about 4,000 people. The British and French governments ordered their own fleets into the Black Sea to protect Turkish shipping, and so began the series of events which was to lead to the **Crimean War**.

'socialism in one country'
Policy put forward by the Soviet dictator Joseph **Stalin** in 1924, in contrast to Leon **Trotsky's** theory of permanent revolution. Stalin believed that the main emphasis should be on making socialism as secure as possible in the Soviet Union. This led to the **five-year plans**, **collectivization**, and the **purges**.

Solferino, Battle of
The scene of Napoleon III's victory over the Austrians in 1859 at a village near Verona in northern Italy. Casualties in the battle were so heavy that Napoleon decided to withdraw from the campaign to drive the Austrians out of northern Italy.

The Swiss Red Cross was set up a direct result of the heavy casualties.

Somme, Battle of the
Allied offensive in **World War I** during July to November 1916 on the River

Somme in northern France, during which severe losses were suffered by both sides. On the first day 19,000 men were killed. Originally the battle was planned by the Marshal of France, Joseph Joffre, and the British commander-in-chief Douglas Haig to be a French offensive with the British in a supporting role. But the German attack on **Verdun** caused the plan to be revised. It became a largely British offensive as a way to relieve pressure upon the French forces at Verdun. The Allies lost over 600,000 soldiers and advanced 13 km/8 mi at most. It was the first battle in which tanks were used.

Haig, the British commander did not want to fight the Battle of the Somme because he believed that it would serve no useful purpose. When the battle began on 1 July 1916, he had only about half the forces he believed he needed for success.

The German offensive around St Quentin from March to April 1918 is sometimes called the Second Battle of the Somme.

Soviet Union
Alternative name for the former **Union of Soviet Socialist Republics** (USSR).

> ❝ The market came with the dawn of civilization and is not the invention of capitalism. If the market leads to the improvement of people's daily lives, then there is no contradiction with socialism. ❞
>
> **Mikhail Gorbachev**, Soviet president, rebutting the complaints of his conservative rivals that he was attempting to restore capitalism in the Soviet Union, June 1990.

Spain

Chronology

9th century	Christians in northern Spain form the kingdoms of Asturias, Aragón, Navarre, Léon, and the county of Castile.
10th century	Abd-al-Rahman III establishes the caliphate of Córdoba; Muslim culture is at its height in Spain.
1230	Léon and Castile are united under Ferdinand III, who drives the Muslims from most of southern Spain.
14th century	Spain consists of the Christian kingdoms of Castile, Aragón, and Navarre, and the Muslim emirate of Granada.

1469	The marriage of **Ferdinand** of Aragón and **Isabella** of Castile.
1492	The conquest of Granada ending Muslim rule in Spain.
1494	The Treaty of Tordesillas; Spain and Portugal divide newly discovered America; Spain becomes a world power.
1519–56	The Emperor **Charles V** is both King of Spain and Archduke of Austria; he also rules Naples, Sicily, and the Low Countries; the **Habsburgs** are dominant in Europe.
1555	Charles V divides his domains between Spain and Austria before retiring; Spain retains the Low Countries and southern Italy as well as the South American colonies.
1568	The Dutch rebel against Spanish rule; Spain recognizes the independence of the Dutch Republic in 1648.
1580	**Philip II** of Spain inherits the throne of Portugal, where Spanish rule lasts until 1640.
1588	**Spanish Armada** attempts to invade England but is defeated.
17th century	Spanish power declines amid wars, corruption, inflation, and loss of civil and religious freedom.
1701–14	The War of the **Spanish Succession**: allied powers fought France to prevent Philip of Bourbon inheriting throne of Spain.
1713–14	The treaties of **Utrecht** and **Rastadt**: Bourbon dynasty recognized, but Spain loses Gibraltar, southern Italy, and Spanish Netherlands.
1793	Spain declares war on revolutionary France; Spain is reduced to a French client state in 1795.
1808	**Napoleon** installs his brother Joseph as King of Spain.
1808–14	The **Peninsular War**: British forces play a large part in liberating Spain and restoring the Bourbon dynasty.
1870	The offer of the Spanish throne to Leopold of Hohenzollern-Sigmaringen sparks the **Franco-Prussian War**.
1898	The **Spanish-American War**: Spain loses Cuba and the Philippines.
1923–30	The dictatorship of Gen Primo de Rivera with support of Alfonso XIII.
1931	The proclamation of the Second Republic,
1933	The Moderates and Catholics win elections; insurrection by socialists and Catalans in 1934.
1936	The left-wing **Popular Front** narrowly wins fresh elections; Gen Francisco **Franco** launches a military rebellion.
1936–39	The **Spanish Civil War**: Nationalists (with significant Italian and German support) defeats the Republicans (with limited Soviet support); Franco becomes a dictator of a nationalist-Fascist regime.
1941	Though officially neutral in World War II, Spain sends 40,000 troops to fight the USSR.
1955	Spain is admitted to the United Nations (UN).
1975	The death of Franco; he is succeeded by King Juan Carlos I.
1986	Spain joins the European Economic Community (EEC).

Spanish-American War

Brief war in 1898 between Spain and the USA over Spanish rule in Cuba and the Philippines. The war began in Cuba when the US battleship *Maine* was blown up in Havana harbour, allegedly by the Spanish. Other engagements included the Battle of Manila Bay, in which Comdr George Dewey's navy destroyed the Spanish fleet in the Philippines; and the taking of the Cuban port cities of El Caney and San Juan Heights.

The complete defeat of Spain made the USA a colonial power. The Treaty of Paris ceded the Philippines, Guam, and Puerto Rico to the USA; Cuba became independent. The USA paid $20 million to Spain. This ended Spain's colonial presence in the Americas.

Spanish Armada

The fleet sent by **Philip II** of Spain against England in 1588. Consisting of 130 ships, it sailed from Lisbon, Portugal, and carried on a running fight along the English Channel with the English fleet of 197 small ships under Howard of Effingham and Francis Drake. The Armada anchored off Calais but fireships forced it out to sea, and a general action followed off Gravelines. What remained of the Armada escaped around the north of Scotland and to the west of Ireland, suffering many losses by storm and shipwreck on the way. Only about half the original fleet returned to Spain.

Spanish Armada *English naval victory over the Spanish Armada in the Channel, July, 1588.*

Only three Spanish ships were sunk by the English fleet in the battles in the Channel and near Calais.

> ❝I know I have the body of a weak and feeble woman, but I have the heart and stomach of a king, and of a king of England too.❞
>
> **Elizabeth I**, Queen of England, speech to the troops at Tilbury on the approach of the Armada, 1588.

Spanish Civil War

Conflict that broke out in the summer of 1936 between the forces of the **Popular Front**, the elected government of Spain, and the rebel Falangists (see **Falange**), led by Gen Francisco **Franco**. The Falangists wanted to overthrow the Popular Front Republicans who had begun to undermine the power of the Church and the position of the landowners.

Franco was a Fascist and so he received aid from both Italian Fascist dictator Benito **Mussolini**, who sent 70,000 men, and German Nazi dictator Adolf **Hitler**, who sent the Condor Legion of 10,000 men. Mussolini wanted to prove that the Mediterranean was 'an Italian lake', by extending his influence. He was also trying to distract Italian opinion from his increasingly unsuccessful and unpopular domestic policies.

Hitler used the war as an opportunity to try out the strength of his new armed forces and to practise Blitzkrieg, the strategy of mobile warfare that he was to use at the beginning of **World War II**. Hitler also hoped that, by supporting Franco he would attract him into a grand Fascist alliance. This would have meant that Franco would have entered **World War II** on Germany's side.

Soviet leader Joseph **Stalin** sent financial support to the Republicans, but not soldiers or weapons. Britain and France agreed on a policy of non-intervention and tried to persuade other countries to accept this.

The Fascists won because they were supported by most of the armed forces and business. They were, therefore, much better supplied with weapons and materials. The Republicans were divided amongst themselves: at one point fighting broke out between communists and other groups. The support of Hitler proved very important. The Luftwaffe (German airforce) was able to bomb Republican areas almost unopposed.

To many people the war was a forewarning of future events. It demonstrated the terrible damage that bombing could inflict on towns and cities. The war enabled Hitler to practise Blitzkrieg and gave him a significant advantage at the beginning of World War II. It exhausted Spain and Franco, therefore, refused to enter **World War II**.

Spanish Succession, War of the

The war from 1701 to 1714 of Britain, Austria, the Netherlands, Portugal, and Denmark (the Allies) against France, Spain, and Bavaria. It was caused by **Louis XIV's** acceptance of the Spanish throne on behalf of his grandson, Philip (1683–1746), in defiance of the Partition Treaty of 1700, under which it would have passed to Archduke Charles of Austria (later Holy Roman Emperor Charles VI).

The most important feature of the war was a series of battles between the Allies (Austria, Britain, and Holland) and the French and Saxons. In these the British commander, the Duke of Marlborough, prevented all of the attempts by the French to occupy the Low Countries.

Peace was made by the Treaties of **Utrecht** (1713) and **Rastatt** (1714). Philip V was recognized as king of Spain, thus founding the Spanish branch of the Bourbon dynasty. Britain received Gibraltar, Minorca, and Nova Scotia; and Austria received the Spanish Netherlands, Milan, and Naples.

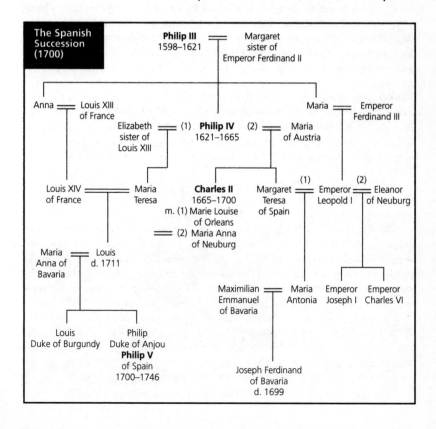

The Spanish Succession (1700)

Spartacist

Member of a group of left-wing radicals in Germany at the end of **World War I**, founders of the Spartacus League that became the German Communist Party in 1919. The league participated in

The name Spartacist came from the rebellion of slaves in Rome 73–70 BC led by Spartacus.

the Berlin workers' revolt of January 1919, which was suppressed by the socialist government. The agitation ended with the murder of Spartacist leaders Karl **Liebknecht** and Rosa **Luxemburg**.

stadtholder

Leader of the United Provinces of the Netherlands from the 15th to the 18th centuries.

Originally provincial leaders appointed by the central government, stadtholders were subsequently elected in the newly independent Dutch republic. For much of their existence they competed with the States General (parliament) for control of the country. The stadtholders were later dominated by the house of Orange-Nassau. In 1747 the office became hereditary, but was abolished in 1795.

Stalin, Joseph (Russian, 'steel') (1879–1953)

Adopted name of Joseph Vissarionovich Djugashvili, Soviet politician who, in 1928, emerged as the sole leader of the Soviet Union.

- In 1917 Stalin was editor of *Pravda*, the Bolshevik newspaper.

- In 1918 he was appointed Commissar for Nationalities in November after the Bolsheviks had seized power.

- In 1922 he became general secretary of the Bolshevik Party.

- In his political testament, Lenin had named Leon **Trotsky** as his successor, but the other Bolshevik leaders decided to keep the testament

Stalin *Stalin at a Bolshevik Congress in 1917.*

secret. Trotsky was outspoken, arrogant and unpopular with the other Bolshevik leaders.

- In 1924 the Soviet Union was ruled by a committee of **Kamenev**, Zinoviev (1883–1938), and Stalin. Stalin first allied himself with the right wing in the Communist Party, **Bukharin** and Rykov (1881–1938) so that he could get rid of Kamenev and Zinoviev.

Stalin died in March 1953. As he lay dying, Lavrenti Beriya, the head of the KGB, was summoned; he was the only man allowed to call a doctor to look at Stalin. Beriya arrived drunk and shouted: 'He is only sleeping' and staggered off to bed. Stalin died the next morning.

- Once he had got rid of the left wing, Stalin then turned on Bukharin and Rykov and in 1928 emerged as the sole ruler of the Soviet Union.
- In 1928 Stalin began a series of **five-year plans** to modernize Soviet industry.
- **Collectivization** of agriculture was introduced.
- All opposition was eliminated in Stalin's **purges** carried out between 1936 and 1938.

> ❦ It will unmake our work. No greater instrument of counter-revolution and conspiracy can be imagined. ❧
>
> **Joseph Stalin**, on the telephone, quoted in L D Trotsky, *Life of Stalin*.

Stalingrad, Siege of

In **World War II**, the German siege of the Soviet city of Stalingrad (now Volgograd) from August 1942 to January 1943. Stalingrad was the objective of the German Army Group B during the 1942 campaign to occupy the Caucasus region. The city was reinforced by the Soviets, and Gen Friedrich von Paulus (1890–1957), the commander of the German 6th Army, began attacking with units as and when they arrived instead of waiting until all his army had reached the area.

The Siege of Stalingrad was a horrific campaign, with both sides sustaining heavy casualties – the Germans lost 400,000 troops while there were 750,000 Soviet military casualties and an unknown number of civilian deaths. The Germans were finally driven out by a massive Soviet counterattack. This was launched on 19 November and swept around the flanks of the 6th Army and encircled it. Fending off German attempts to relieve von Paulus, the Soviets then set about destroying the 6th Army until it surrendered on 31 January 1943.

See also: *Barbarossa; Eastern Front.*

straits question

International and diplomatic debate in the 19th and 20th centuries surrounding Russian naval access to the Mediterranean from the Black Sea via the Bosporus (forming part of the water division between Europe and Asia). The Western powers demanded that the straits be closed to warships in time of hostilities, which would prevent the Russian Black Sea Fleet from reaching the Mediterranean.

Strasser, Gregor (1892–1934)

German politician, who took part in German dictator Adolf Hitler's **Beer-Hall Putsch** of 1923. Later he organized the National Socialist party in the Reichstag (parliament). Strasser lost favour for his radically anti-capitalist views. Hitler had him first expelled from the party, then murdered in the 1934 **'Night of the Long Knives'**.

Stresa Front

Summit meeting that took place from 11 to 14 April 1935 between the prime ministers of Britain, France, and Italy (Ramsay MacDonald (1869–1940), Pierre Flandin, and Benito **Mussolini**) with the aim of forming a common front against Germany. This followed Adolf **Hitler's** announcement that Germany would not be bound by the limitations imposed upon its armaments by the treaty of **Versailles** of June 1919. The 'front' soon broke up. In October 1935 Italy was severely criticized for launching an Abyssinian War 1935–36 to establish an east African Italian empire, and on 2 November 1936 Mussolini proclaimed the **Rome-Berlin Axis**, which brought Germany and Italy into close collaboration between 1936 and 1945.

See also: *Abyssinian Crisis; Hoare-Laval Pact.*

Stresemann, Gustav (1878–1929)

German politician of the **Weimar Republic** who was chancellor in 1923 and foreign minister from 1923 to 1929. During **World War I** Stresemann was a strong nationalist but he modified his views under the Weimar Republic. His achievements included overcoming the

Stresemann died on 4 October 1929, exactly three weeks before the Wall Street Crash which gave Hitler the opportunity to gain power in Germany. Stresemann was perhaps the only German politician who could have prevented this.

hyperinflation of 1923, reducing the amount of war reparations paid by Germany after the Treaty of **Versailles** of 1919, negotiating the **Locarno Treaties** of 1925, and negotiating Germany's admission to the **League of Nations**. He shared the 1926 Nobel Peace Prize with Aristide Briand (1862–1932).

Suvla Bay

Bay in Gallipoli, west of the **Dardanelles**, that was the scene of fierce fighting between Turkish and British and Commonwealth troops during **World War I**.

Four British divisions were landed here 6 August 1915 in an effort to follow up the landings in April at Anzac Cove and Cape Helles. Although initial progress was good and some commanding heights were taken, the opportunity to advance

The actual landing, although it took the Turks by surprise, was in total confusion. It took place under cover of dark and some officers lost contact with their units. This prevented further progress.

further in the face of weak Turkish opposition was not taken. By the time orders were given to attack, the Turks had been strongly reinforced with more troops and artillery and the attack failed. More attacks were mounted over the next few days and a fresh commander brought in to try and break the deadlock, but no impression could be made on the Turkish positions and the Allied lines settled down to defend what they had.

Sweden

Chronology

9th–11th centuries Swedish Vikings raided and settled along the rivers of Russia.

c. **1000** Olaf Skötkonung, King of the Svear, adopts Christianity and unites much of Sweden (except the south and west coasts, which remain Danish until the 17th century).

1397 The Union of Kalmar: Sweden, Denmark, and Norway are united under a single monarch; Sweden is effectively ruled by succession of regents.

1448 Breach with Denmark: Sweden alone elects Charles VIII as king.

1523 **Gustavus Vasa**, leader of insurgents, becomes king of a fully independent Sweden.

1527 Swedish Reformation: Gustavus confiscates Church property and encourages the Lutherans.

1544 The Swedish crown becomes hereditary in the House of Vasa.

17th century Sweden, a great military power under **Gustavus Adolphus**, **Charles X** , and Charles XI (1660–97), fights lengthy wars with Denmark, Russia, Poland, and the **Holy Roman Empire**.

1709	The Battle of Poltava: Russians inflict major defeat on Swedes under Charles XII.
1809	Russian invaders annexe Finland; Swedish nobles stage a coup and restore the powers of the Riksdag.
1810	Napoleonic marshal Jean-Baptiste **Bernadotte** is elected crown prince of Sweden since Charles XIII has no heir.
1812	Bernadotte allies Sweden with Russia against France.
1814	Treaty of Kiel: Sweden obtains Norway from Denmark.
1818–44	Bernadotte reigns in Sweden as Charles John.
1905	Union with Norway dissolves.
1940–43	Under duress, neutral Sweden permits the limited transit of German forces through its territory.
1995	Sweden becomes a member of the **European Union** (EU).

taille

In pre-revolutionary France, the term referred to either of two forms of taxation. The personal taille, levied from the 15th century, was assessed by tax collectors on an individual's personal wealth. Nobles, clerics, and many other groups were exempt from this tax and its burden fell disproportionately on the peasantry. During a similar period the 'real' taille was levied on common land in central and southwestern France and produced more revenue for the crown.

Talleyrand-Périgord, Charles Maurice de (1754–1838)

French politician and diplomat who, as bishop of Autun from 1789 to 1791, supported moderate reform during the French Revolution and was excommunicated by the pope. Talleyrand fled to the USA during the **Reign of Terror**, but returned and became foreign minister under the **Directory** from 1797 to 1799 and under **Napoleon** from 1799 to 1807. He represented France at the **Congress of Vienna** in 1814 and 1815.

Tannenberg, Battle of

In **World War I**, the victory of German forces led by field marshal Paul von **Hindenburg** over Russian forces under Gen Alexander Samsonov (1859–1914) in August 1914 at a village in East Prussia (now Grunwald, Poland). The Germans took 90,000 prisoners and several hundred guns. Along with the Battle of the **Masurian Lakes**, Tannenberg stopped the Russian advance into Germany.

The Russian generals Samsonov and Rennenkampf (1853–1918) hated each other and refused to co-operate. They were in fact racing each other to see who could achieve victory first. Samsonov committed suicide after the defeat.

Tehran Conference

Conference held in 1943 in Tehran, Iran, between the Allied leaders Churchill, Roosevelt, and **Stalin** constituting the first meeting of **World War II**. The chief subject discussed was co-ordination of the Allied strategy in Western and Eastern Europe.

Terror, Reign of

The phase of the **French Revolution** when the **Jacobins** were in power (October 1793 to July 1794) under **Robespierre** and began to systematically murder their political opponents. The Terror was at its height in the early months of 1794. Across France, it is thought that between 17,000 and 40,000 people were executed, mainly by **guillotine**, until public indignation rose and Robespierre was overthrown and executed in July 1794.

The Reign of Terror began with the Jacobin seizure of power from the more moderate **Girondins** in June 1793. The **Committee of Public Safety**, with **Robespierre** at the helm, assumed dictatorial powers and liquidated anyone regarded as a threat to the state. One of the most prominent of the Terror's victims was the revolutionary minister of justice Georges **Danton**.

third estate or tiers état

In pre-revolutionary France, the order of society that comprised the common people as distinct from members of the first (noble) or the second (clerical) estates. All three met collectively as the Estates General.

See also: *ancien regime.*

Third Reich

Third Empire Germany, which existed during the years of German Nazi Adolf **Hitler's** dictatorship after 1933. The idea of the Third Reich was based on the existence of two previous German empires: the medieval Holy Roman Empire, and the second empire of 1871 to 1918.

The term was coined by the German writer Moeller van den Bruck (1876–1925) in the 1920s and was used by the **Nazis**.

See also: *Nazi State.*

Thirty Years' War

Major war from 1618 to 1648 in central Europe, which began as a German conflict between Protestants and Catholics, it was gradually transformed into a struggle to determine whether the ruling Austrian **Habsburg** family could gain control of all Germany. The war caused serious economic and demographic problems in central Europe. Under the Peace of **Westphalia** the German states were granted their sovereignty and the emperor retained only nominal control.

thousand-bomber raid

The name of a massive air raid during **World War II** that devastated the German city of Cologne on 31 May 1942. Some 898 RAF (British air force) bombers actually arrived over Cologne and dropped 1,455 tons of bombs, starting 1200 fires; 18,440 buildings were destroyed and over 56,000 people made homeless.

It was followed by two similar attacks, one on the town of Essen and one on Bremen, which were less successful.

The raid was organized by Air Marshal Harris (1892–1984) shortly after he took over Bomber Command as a means of reviving the morale of the Command and demonstrating the ability of the RAF as a strategic bombing force. His plan involved extensive training and the deployment of spare aircraft; crews were drafted in from different commands to make up the required numbers. Cologne was selected as the target because it was well known and lightly defended.

Tilsit, Treaty of

Peace treaty between **Napoleon I** and **Alexander I** on 7 July 1807, also a treaty between Prussia and France on 9 July 1807. The treaties marked the end of hostilities between France and Prussia and Russia. Russia also agreed in principle to the **Continental System**.

The treaty between France and Russia was signed on a raft in the middle of a river, because neither leader was prepared to cross over.

Tito (1892–1980)

Adopted name of Josip Broz, the Yugoslav communist politician who effectively controlled Yugoslavia from 1943. In World War II he organized the National Liberation Army to carry on guerrilla warfare against the German invasion of 1941, and was created marshal in 1943. Tito became prominent as a communist and as partisan leader against the Nazis during **World War II**. He established a provisional government and gained Allied recognition (previously given to the Chetniks) in 1944, and with Soviet help proclaimed the federal republic in 1945.

Tito was able to hold together Yugoslavia, which was made up of six republics, by the force of his personality. But after his death the separatist elements were so great that the Balkans became extremely unstable.

As prime minister, he settled the Yugoslav minorities question on a federal basis, and in 1953 took the newly created post of president (for life from 1974). In 1948 he was criticized by the USSR and other communist countries for his successful system of decentralized profit-sharing workers' councils, and became a leader of the non-aligned movement. He followed a foreign policy of 'positive neutralism'.

See also: *Balkans*.

Torquemada, Tomás de (1420–1498)
Spanish Dominican monk, confessor to Queen **Isabella I**, who in 1483 revived the **Inquisition** on her behalf. At least 2,000 'heretics' were burned. Torquemada also expelled the Jews from Spain in 1492, with a resulting decline of the economy.

Trafalgar, Battle of
During the **Napoleonic Wars**, the victory of the British fleet, commanded by Admiral Horatio Nelson (1759–1805), over a combined French and Spanish fleet on 21 October 1805; Nelson was mortally wounded during the action. The victory laid the foundation for British naval supremacy throughout the 19th century. It is named after Cape Trafalgar, a low headland in southwest Spain, near the western entrance to the Straits of Gibraltar.

The Battle of Trafalgar ended **Napoleon's** plans of an invasion on Britain.

> 6 England expects every man will do his duty. 9
>
> **Horatio Nelson**, at the Battle of Trafalgar, 1805.

trench warfare
Hostilities conducted from defensive long, narrow, deeply dug trenches, which were first used widely during the American Civil War in 1864. Trenches were commonly used from the advent of mechanized war until increased mobility provided by the aeroplane and the motor car enabled attacking armies to avoid such large-scale, immobile forms of defence.

It was most famously used during **World War I**, when tactics included wire entanglements, bombing raids, armour-plated loopholes for snipers, listening posts, the provision of close-range shotguns, clubs and knives for raiding parties, and mining enemy trenches.

Trent, Council of
Conference held from 1545 to 1563 by the Roman Catholic Church at Trento, northern Italy, which was an important stage in the Counter-Reformation. Its aim was to reform the church, which was under pressure from the Protestants. The Council was dominated by the 'Society of Jesus', which had been set up in 1540.

- The supremacy of the pope was reasserted.
- The Tridentine Mass was published in Latin for use in all churches.
- Internal abuses and corruption were tackled.

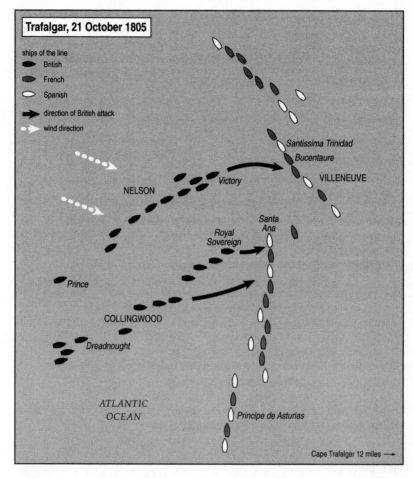

Battle of Trafalgar *Map showing the plan of battle.*

Triple Alliance
An extension in 1882 of the **Dual Alliance,** with the inclusion of Italy. While these agreements gave German chancellor Otto von **Bismarck** some security, they isolated Russia, so that in 1881 he had arranged the Alliance of Three Emperors, between Germany, **Austria-Hungary**, and Russia. This was based on the **Dreikaiserbund**, but this time contained a series of terms. This agreement was renewed in 1884, but in 1887 Russia refused to sign.
  See also: *Reinsurance Treaty.*

Triple Entente

An agreement signed by Britain and Russia in 1907. As in the case of the *Entente Cordiale*, its most immediate effects were the settlement of outstanding disputes between the two countries in Persia: Afghanistan and Tibet. But the agreement also drew Britain into the system of alliances, which had dominated European politics since 1870. Britain was now clearly aligned with France and Russia against the powers of the **Triple Alliance** – Germany, **Austria-Hungary**, and Italy. The Triple Entente, as it came to be known, did not commit Britain to defend or support the other two powers, but it did make British support for them much more likely in the event of war.

Trotsky, Leon (1879–1940)

Born Lev Bronstein, Trotsky became the second most important figure in the Russian Revolution after Vladimir **Lenin**. He was a Menshevik until September 1917, then joined the **Bolsheviks** (precursors of the communists) and masterminded the seizure of power in October.

Trotsky organized the Red Army during the Russian Civil War, recruiting tsarist officers to take charge of the units. He was chosen by Lenin to succeed him, but had made enemies amongst the other Bolshevik leaders and they decided to ignore Lenin's political testament.

Stalin hated Trotsky, partly because of his sudden rise to prominence in the Bolsheviks, but also because of Trotsky's policy of 'Permanent Revolution'. He believed that the only way to ensure the success of communism was to encourage revolutions in other countries. This clashed with Stalin's **'Socialism in one country'**.

In 1926 Trotsky was stripped of his offices and in 1929 he left the Soviet Union for exile. He settled in Mexico, where he was murdered by one of Stalin's agents, Ramon Mercado, in 1940

Truman Doctrine

An offer of US support, in March 1947, for any country being threatened either from without or within. In February 1947 the British government had announced that it could no longer afford to support the Greek government in its fight against communist rebels. The US president, Harry Truman (1884–1972), offered Greece $400,000,000 of aid and also decided to issue a warning to the Soviet Union.

Truman had visited Europe in 1945 and had seen the devastation caused by the war. He was keen to offer US aid to help European recovery.

In March 1947 the Truman Doctrine was published. Truman did not say what support the USA would give and he did not mention any country by name, but it was assumed that he meant the Soviet Union.

> ❝I believe it must be the policy of the United States to support free peoples who are resisting attempted subjugation by armed minorities or by outside pressures. I believe that we must assist free peoples to work out their own destinies in their own way.❞
>
> The text of the Truman Doctrine.

tsar

Russian imperial title in use from 1547 to 1721, derived from the Latin *caesar*, the title of the Roman emperors.

Ivan (IV) the Terrible, the grand duke of Muscovy, was crowned the first tsar of Russia in 1547. In 1721 **Peter (I) the Great** officially changed the title to 'emperor of all Russia' as part of his efforts to reorganize and modernize his country on Western lines. However, the title of 'tsar' continued in popular use for subsequent Russian rulers until **Nicholas II** was deposed by the **Russian Revolution** in 1917.

United Kingdom of Great Britain and Northern Ireland (UK)

Chronology

9th–11th centuries	The Vikings raid the British Isles, conquering north and east England and northern Scotland.
1066	The Normans, led by William I defeat the Anglo-Saxons at the Battle of Hastings and conquer England.
1215	King John of England is forced to sign Magna Carta, which places limits on royal powers.
1265	Simon de Montfort summons the first English parliament in which the towns are represented.
1284	Edward I of England invades Scotland; the Scots defeat the English at the Battle of Stirling Bridge in 1297.
1314	Robert the Bruce leads the Scots to victory over the English at the Battle of Bannockburn; England recognizes Scottish independence in 1328.
1513	The Battle of Flodden: the Scots are defeated by the English; James IV of Scotland is killed.
1529	Henry VIII founds the Church of England after the break with Rome; the Reformation is effective in England and Wales, but not in Ireland.
1536–43	The Acts of Union unites Wales with England, with one law, one parliament, and one official language.
1541	The Irish parliament recognizes Henry VIII of England as king of Ireland.
1603	Union of crowns: James VI of Scotland also becomes James I of England.
1607	The first successful English colony in Virginia marks the start of three centuries of overseas expansion.
1610	James I establishes the plantation of Ulster in Northern Ireland with Protestant settlers from England and Scotland.
1642–52	The English Civil War between king and Parliament, with Scottish intervention and Irish rebellion, results in victory for Parliament.
1649	The execution of Charles I; Oliver Cromwell is appointed Lord Protector in 1653; the monarchy is restored in 1660.
1689	The 'Glorious Revolution' confirms the power of Parliament; the replacement of James II by William III is resisted by the Scottish Highlanders and the Catholic Irish.
1707	The Act of Union between England and Scotland creates the United Kingdom of Great Britain, governed by a single parliament.

c. **1760–1850**	The Industrial Revolution: Britain becomes the first industrial nation in the world.
1775–83	The American Revolution: Britain loses 13 American colonies; the empire continues to expand in Canada, India, and Australia.
1793–1815	The period when Britain is at war with revolutionary France, except for 1802 to 1803.
1800	The Act of Union that creates the United Kingdom of Great Britain and Ireland, governed by a single parliament; effective from 1801.
1880–90s	A period of rapid expansion of the British Empire in Africa.
1914–18	The UK plays a leading part in World War I; the British Empire expands in the Middle East.
1931	A National Government coalition is formed to face a growing economic crisis; unemployment reached 3 million.
1939–45	The UK plays a leading part in World War II.
1945–51	The Labour government of Clement Attlee creates the welfare state and nationalizes major industries.
1947–71	Decolonization brings about the end of the British Empire.
1973	The UK joins the European Economic Community (EEC).
1991	British troops take part in a US-led war against Iraq under a United Nations (UN) umbrella. Following the economic successes of the 1980s there is a period of severe economic recession and unemployment.

United Provinces

Federation of states in the northern Netherlands that endured from 1579 to 1795, comprising Holland, Zeeland, Friesland, Gelderland, Utrecht, Overijssel, and Groningen. Established by the Union of Utrecht, its aim was to assert independence from the Spanish crown.

Urban V (*c.*1310–1370)

Born Guillaume de Grimoard in France, he was pope from 1362–1370 as the successor to Innocent VI. Urban V was a zealous reformer; he also founded the great medical school at Montpellier. Urban was beatified by Pius IX in 1870.

Utrecht, Treaty of

Treaty signed in 1713 that ended the **War of the Spanish Succession**. Philip V (1683–1746) was recognized as the legitimate king of Spain, thus founding the Spanish branch of the Bourbon dynasty and ending the French king **Louis XIV's** attempts at expansion; the Netherlands, Milan, and **Naples** were ceded to Austria; Britain gained Gibraltar; the duchy of Savoy was granted Sicily.

Valmy, Battle of

During the French **Revolutionary Wars**, the scene of a comprehensive French victory over the Prussians on 20 September 1792, near Valmy in France. The victory was largely a result of French superior artillery. This forthright defeat of a powerful army by the previously despised revolutionary forces set the seal upon the authority of the revolutionary French government.

See also: *Barras; Directory; Napoleon.*

Vasa dynasty

Swedish royal house founded by Gustavus Vasa (1496–1560). He liberated his country from Danish rule, suppressing local uprisings of nobles and peasants from 1520 to 1523. By 1544 he was secure enough to make his

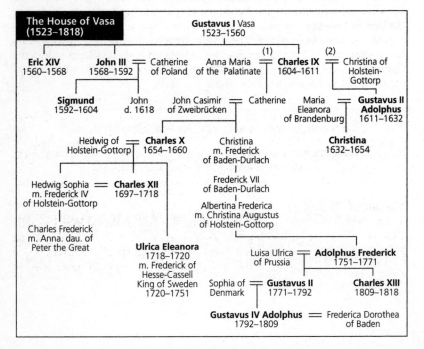

The House of Vasa (1523–1818)

title a hereditary one. His grandson, **Gustavus Adolphus**, became king in 1611 and led the armies of the Protestant princes in the **Thirty Years' War** until his death. The dynasty ended in 1809 when Gustavus IV (1778–1837) was deposed by a revolution and replaced by his uncle Charles XIII (1748–1818). With no heir to the throne, the crown was offered in 1810 to one of Napoleon's generals, **Bernadotte**, who became King Charles John until his death in 1844.

See also: *Charles X.*

Verdun

Fortress town in northeast France in the *département* of the Meuse, which during **World War I,** became a symbol of French resistance. It was the centre of a series of bitterly fought actions between French and German forces, finally being recaptured in September 1918.

Verdun became a first-class fortress after the experience of the **Franco-Prussian** war in 1870, its ring of modern forts being one of the principal French frontier defences. In 1916 the Germans attacked it in great strength; it had great psychological value to the French, and the Germans assumed that they would throw large masses of troops into battle rather than lose it. The German plan was not necessarily to capture Verdun but to decimate the French army by constant bombardment and attack. The battle continued for the rest of the year, both sides moving back and forth capturing and re-capturing forts and ground, until the fighting finally died away early December 1916. The French lost an estimated 348,300 troops and the Germans 328,500.

See also: *Somme.*

❝Whatever you do, you lose a lot of men.❞

Charles Mangin, French general in World War I, remark on comparing casualty figures from each division at Verdun, 1916.

Versailles, Treaty of

Treaty signed on 28th June 1919 marking the end of **World War I** exactly five years to the day after the assassination of the Archduke **Franz Ferdinand**. The treaty compelled Germany to accept specific terms of peace and was also intended to make sure that such a war could never happen again.

THE TERMS GERMANY WAS FORCED TO ACCEPT:

- a national army of 100,000 men and no conscription;
- a national navy of six ships and no submarines;
- an airforce with no warplanes;
- the loss of all its overseas colonies;
- the loss of **Alsace-Lorraine** to France and the '**Polish Corridor**' to Poland;
- other territory to Belgium and Denmark;
- the blame for the war, the 'War Guilt Clause';
- reparations (the cost of rebuilding France and Belgium after the war); the final bill was set at £6,600,000,000.

The Treaty was very unpopular in Germany and led to unrest in the years from 1919 to 1923.

Vichy government

In **World War II**, the French right-wing government that controlled unoccupied France after its defeat by the Germans in June 1940. It was named after the spa town of Vichy, France, where the national assembly was based under Prime Minister **Pétain** until the liberation of 1944. Vichy France was that part of France not occupied by German troops until November 1942. Authoritarian and collaborationist, the Vichy regime cooperated with the Germans even after the latter moved in to the unoccupied zone in November 1942.

The Vichy government imprisoned some 135,000 people, interned another 70,000, deported some 76,000 Jews, and sent 650,000 French workers to Germany.

See also: *Laval.*

Victor Emmanuel II (1820–1878)

First king of united Italy from 1861, who became king of Sardinia on the abdication of his father Charles Albert in 1849. In 1855 Victor Emmanuel allied Sardinia with France and the UK in the **Crimean War**. In 1859 in alliance with the French he defeated the Austrians and annexed Lombardy. By 1860 most of Italy had come under his rule, and in 1861 he was proclaimed king of Italy. In 1870 he made Rome his capital.

See also: *Cavour; Garibaldi; Mazzini.*

Victor Emmanuel III (1869–1947)

King of Italy from the assassination of his father, Umberto I (1844–1900), he acquiesced in the **Fascist** regime of Benito **Mussolini** from 1922 and, after the dictator's fall in 1943, relinquished power to his son Umberto II (1904–1983), who cooperated with the Allies during World War II. Victor Emmanuel formally abdicated in 1946.

Victor Emmanuel was an admirer of Mussolini and helped him become prime minister in 1922 by refusing to allow the existing prime minister, Facta, to declare martial law. This would have allowed him to use the army against the Fascists.

See also: *Fascism; March on Rome.*

Vienna, Battle of

Turkish defeat by a Christian army on 12 September 1683. It was the last attempt by the Turks to occupy Christian Europe. The Ottoman Turks had launched a fresh invasion of the West, and Mustapha Pasha was besieging Vienna with about 138,000 troops facing a force of about 40,000 in the city. King **John III** of Poland assembled a relief army of 30,000 of various nationalities and advanced on the Turkish lines. After a day of severe fighting the Turks were routed with enormous losses, and retired to the east.

Vienna, Congress of

International conference held from 1814 to 1815 that agreed the settlement of Europe after the **Napoleonic Wars**. National representatives included the Austrian foreign minister **Metternich, Alexander I** of Russia, the British foreign secretary Castlereagh (1769–1822), the military commander the Duke of Wellington (1769–1852), and the French politician **Talleyrand**.

The Treaty of Vienna tried to create a balance of power in Europe.

- Germany had been carved up into more than 300 small states in 1789; in 1815 this was reduced to fewer than 40.

- The Rhineland was given to Prussia so that the Prussian army could act as a barrier to France.

- Poland was given to Russia and remained under Russian control until 1920.

- The United Netherlands, comprising the modern countries of Belgium and the Netherlands, was established in an effort to prevent future French aggression.

- Northern Italy was put under Austrian control and the remainder of Italy was restored to its former rulers.

- **Louis XVIII** was confirmed as king of France.

In fact the decisions made at Vienna created problems. Many people found themselves being governed by a foreign ruler and this led to revolutions later in the 19th century.

> ❖ *Le Congres ne marche pas, il danse*/The Congress is going nowhere; it dances. ❯
>
> **Prince de Linge Charles-Joseph**, Austrian diplomat, referring to the Congress of Vienna.

Vittorio Veneto, Battle of

Official Italian name for the third battle of the Piave, the Italian victory over Austria between October and November 1918, which heralded Austria's final defeat in **World War I**.

This was virtually the first Italian victory of the war, but the Armistice on 11 November prevented the Italian forces from following it up.

Vyshinsky, Andrei Yanuaryevich (1883–1954)

Soviet politician, who as commissar for justice acted as prosecutor at Soviet leader Joseph Stalin's **show trials** from 1936 to 1938. Vyshinksy was foreign minister from 1949 to 1953 and frequently represented the USSR at the United Nations.

> ❖ Confession is the queen of evidence. ❯
>
> **Andrei Vyshinsky**, quoted in D Burg and G Teifer, *Solzhenitsyn*.

W–Z

Wagram, Battle of

During the **Napoleonic Wars** the scene of the decisive French victory on 6 July 1809 over the Austrians led by the Archduke Charles near Wagram, an Austrian village. Austria was forced to concede general defeat to French emperor **Napoleon I**.

See also: *Marie Louise.*

Wallenstein, Albrecht Eusebius Wenzel von (1583–1634)

German general who, until his defeat at **Lützen** in 1632, led the **Habsburg** armies in the **Thirty Years' War**. Wallenstein was assassinated.

War Communism

In 1918, after the end of Russia's participation in **World War I**, the term referring to the policies introduced by the **Bolshevik** government in Russia. Tight controls were imposed on industry and agriculture in an effort to maintain supplies, factories came under government control, workers were centrally directed to where their labour was most needed, and food was rationed. Despite such directives, millions of workers left the towns and industrial areas for the countryside and production slumped. The revolutionary policy of the socialization of all means of production and the centralized planning of the economy, together with the effects of the civil war and the Allied blockade, led to the virtual collapse of the economic system by 1921. Faced with a severe crisis, the Communist Party adopted the **NEP** (New Economic Policy).

See also: *Kronstadt uprising, Lenin.*

Warsaw ghetto

Area in the centre of Warsaw, Poland, established by the Nazis in 1939 into which some 433,000 Jews were crowded.

In July 1942 shipments of Jews to the extermination camp at Treblinka began. On 19 April 1943 a detachment of SS (Nazi elite corp) were sent into the ghetto to round up the remaining inhabitants and destroy the buildings. Rather than submit, the Jews fought back with small arms and grenades they had managed to acquire. Resistance ended on 16 May when the main synagogue was blown up. Many Jews escaped via the sewers and joined the Polish Home Army.

Warsaw Pact

The shortened name of the Eastern European Mutual Assistance Pact, military alliance in existence from 1955 to 1991 between the USSR and East European communist states. It was originally established as a response to the admission of West Germany into NATO. Its military structures and agreements were dismantled early in 1991; a political organization remained until the alliance was officially dissolved in July 1991.

Czechoslovakia, Hungary, and Poland announced in January 1991, and Bulgaria in February, that they would withdraw all cooperation from the Warsaw Treaty organization from 1 July 1991. In response, the USSR announced that the military structure of the pact would be wound up by 31 March 1991, and a meeting of member countries convened for this purpose in February 1991. The organization was formally dissolved at a meeting held in Prague on 1 July 1991.

Warsaw rising

In **World War II**, an uprising against the German occupation of Warsaw during the period of August to October 1944 organized by the Polish Home Army. The rebellion was brutally quashed when anticipated Soviet help for the rebels did not arrive.

The German army had begun their withdrawal from Warsaw in anticipation of the arrival of the Soviets when the Polish Home Army rose to keep the German troops occupied and so make it easier for the Soviets to enter the city. Street fighting began on 1 August, but on the following day the Soviet attack was halted and the Germans were free to turn their full power against the rebellion.

In spite of appeals for assistance from the Polish army the Soviets made no move to assist the Poles and also prohibited the landing of supply aircraft on Soviet territory.

Home Army detachments from outside Warsaw that attempted to go to the city's aid were surrounded and disarmed by the Soviets. Eventually the Poles realized the Soviets were waiting for the Poles and Germans to exhaust each other so they could impose their own regime with no resistance and the Poles surrendered on 2 October 1944.

Waterloo, Battle of

Final battle of the **Napoleonic Wars** on 18 June 1815 in which a coalition force of British, Prussian, and Dutch troops under the Duke of Wellington (1769–1852) defeated French emperor **Napoleon I** near the

Wellington's choice of a battlefield in the shape of a funnel with woods on either side, was virtually the same as that chosen by Henry V (1387–1422) of England at Agincourt in October 1415.

village of Waterloo in Belgium. **Napoleon** found Wellington's army isolated from his allies and began a direct offensive to smash them, but the British held on until joined by the Prussians under Marshal Gebhard von **Blücher**. Four days later Napoleon abdicated for the second and final time.

Wellington had 67,000 soldiers (of whom 24,000 were British, the remainder being German, Dutch, and Belgian) and Napoleon had 74,000. The French casualties numbered about 37,000; coalition casualties were similar, including some 13,000 British troops.

❝ Every man meets his Waterloo at last. ❞

Wendell Phillips, US reformer, lecture, at Brooklyn, 1859.

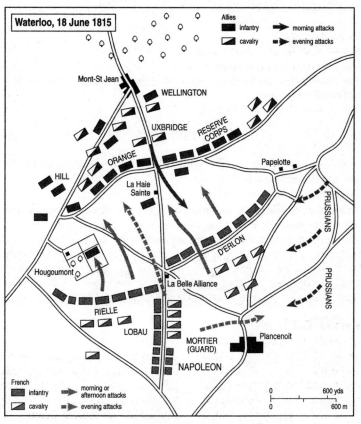

Battle of Waterloo *Map showing the plan of battle.*

Weimar Republic

Constitutional republic in Germany from the end of **World War I** in 1919 to 1933, which took its name from the city where, in February 1919, a constituent assembly met to draw up a democratic constitution.

The Weimar constitution was based upon proportional representation. This meant that it was very difficult for one party to gain an overall majority in the Reichstag, the lower house of the German parliament. The Allies (Britain and its empire, France, and Russia) hoped that this would prevent a strong German government coming to power. In fact it meant that all German governments were weak and were unable to take decisions.

The Weimar constitution was one of the most democratic in the world, but it created difficulties. Proportional representation meant that it was worthwhile setting up new parties and the result was that no one party ever had a majority in the Reichstag. All governments had to be coalitions and these were frequently changing.

Because Berlin was in chaos, the new democratic government met in the small town of Weimar.

The constitution stated that:

- Everyone over 20, male and female, had the vote. Freedom of speech and religion were guaranteed.

- There was an elected parliament, called the Reichstag. The chancellor, (as the prime minister was called), had to have the voting support of the Reichstag.

- There was a president, elected every 7 years. It was expected that the president would just be a figurehead, but there were plans for the president to rule without democratic support in the Reichstag in a crisis.

- Elections were held on the basis of proportional representation. This gave numbers of delegates in the Reichstag in proportion to the numbers of votes cast for their party in elections.

  See also: *Beer-Hall Putsch; Erzberger; Hitler; hyperinflation; Rathenau; Stresemann; Versailles.*

Westphalia, Treaty of

Agreement in 1648, which brought to an end the **Thirty Years' War**. The peace marked the end of the supremacy of the **Holy Roman Empire** and the emergence of France as a dominant power. It recognized the sovereignty of the German states, Switzerland, and the Netherlands; Lutherans, Calvinists, and Roman Catholics were given equal rights.

Wilhelm II (1859–1941)

Kaiser of Germany from 1888, Wilhelm was the son of **Frederick III** and Victoria, daughter of Queen Victoria (1819–1901) of Britain.

- In 1890 he forced Chancellor Otto von **Bismarck** to resign in an attempt to assert his own political authority. The result was a period of domestic and international political instability.

    Wilhelm II's left shoulder was dislocated at birth and never grew properly. He was disabled for the rest of his life.

- He encouraged the development of the German Empire and the **_Drang nach Osten_**, 'the drive to the east'.
- In 1905 he visited Morocco and sparked the first of the **Moroccan Crises**.
- He was an enthusiastic supporter of Admiral Tirpitz's plans for naval expansion.
- In 1914 he first approved Austria's ultimatum to Serbia and then, when he realized war was inevitable, tried in vain to prevent it.
- In 1918 he fled to Doorn in the Netherlands after Germany's defeat and his abdication.
    See also: _Agadir Incident; Algeciras Conference._

> ❝ Though he would have hated to be told so, he was a bourgeois monarch. ❞
>
> **Michael Balfour**, _The Kaiser and his Times._

William the Silent (1859–1941)

Prince of Orange from 1544, he led a revolt against Spanish rule in the Netherlands from 1573. He became the national leader and first **Stadtholder** (the chief magistrate of the United Provinces of the Netherlands). William briefly succeeded in uniting the Catholic south and Protestant northern provinces, but the former provinces submitted to Spain while the latter formed a federation in 1579 (Union of Utrecht) which repudiated Spanish suzerainty in 1581. He was known as 'the Silent' because of his absolute discretion. He was assassinated by a Spanish agent.

Winter King, the

Name given to **Frederick V** because he was king of Bohemia for one winter (during the period 1619 to 1620).

Witte, Sergei Yulevich, Count (1849–1915)

Russian politician and prime minister of Russia from 1903 to 1906. Witte's industrial and trade policies included securing massive foreign loans (especially from France) and imposing protectionist tariffs to favour Russian goods.

* As minister of transport (in 1892) and finance (from 1892 to 1903), he developed the railway network (including the vast Trans-Siberian Railway, built between 1891 and 1905) and helped make Russia a major industrial power.

* In 1905, he negotiated the Treaty of Portsmouth that ended the Russo-Japanese War, and tried to quell civil unrest by granting limited reforms. Notable among these were the establishment of a constitution and a representative parliament, the **Duma**.

World War I

Conflict from 1914 to 1918 between the Central European Powers (Germany, Austria-Hungary, and allies) on one side and the Triple Entente (Britain and the British Empire, France, and Russia) and its allies, including the USA (which entered in 1917), on the other side. An estimated 10 million lives were lost and twice that number were wounded. It was fought on the eastern and western fronts, in the Middle East, in Africa, and at sea.

World War II

Conflict from 1939 to 1945 between Germany, Italy, and Japan (the **Axis** powers) on one side, and Britain, the Commonwealth, France, the USA, the USSR, and China (the Allied powers) on the other. The main theatres of war were Europe, the USSR, North Africa, and the Pacific and Atlantic seaboards. An estimated 55 million lives were lost, including 20 million citizens of the USSR and 6 million Jews killed in the **Holocaust**. Germany surrendered in May 1945, but Japan fought on until the USA dropped atomic bombs on Hiroshima and Nagasaki in August.

See also: *Eastern Front; Hitler; Kursk; Operation Barbarossa; Operation Overlord; Stalingrad.*

Yalta Conference

Conference held at Yalta in the Crimea in February 1945, which was attended by US president Franklin Roosevelt (1882–1945), English prime minister Winston Churchill (1879–1965), and Soviet leader Joseph **Stalin** to plan the end of the **World War II**.

* Stalin agreed to accept France as one of the powers. They agreed to divide Germany into four zones, each one would be occupied by one of the four Allies. The German capital Berlin would also be split into four sectors.

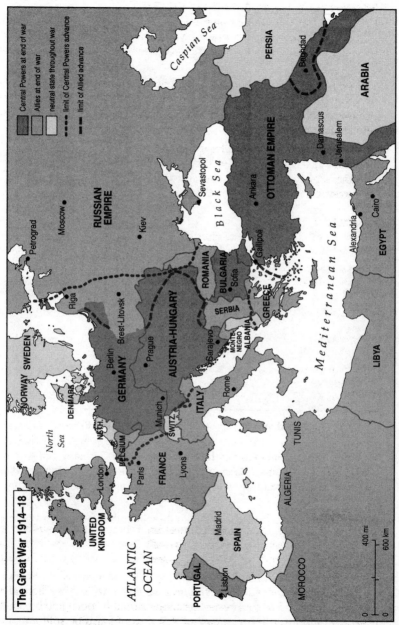

World War I *Map of Europe during the 'The Great War'.*

World War II *Map of Europe during World War II.*

- Poland would be given land in the west, taken from Germany, but would lose land to the USSR. Stalin promised to allow free elections in the countries of Eastern Europe that had been occupied by the Soviet army, including Poland.

- The USSR would declare war on Japan three months after the end of the war with Germany.

Young Italy

Italian nationalist organization founded in 1831 by Giuseppe **Mazzini** while in exile in Marseille, France. The movement, which was immediately popular, was followed the next year by Young Germany, Young Poland, and similar organizations. All the groups were linked by Mazzini in his Young

Europe movement, but none achieved much practical success; attempted uprisings by Young Italy in 1834 and 1844 failed miserably. The movement was superseded in Italy by the **Risorgimento**.

Ypres, Battles of

Flemish city called Ieper, which was the site of three major battles during the period 1914 to 1917 in the course of **World War I**. Neither side made much progress in any of the battles, despite heavy casualties, but the third battle in particular (also known as **Passchendaele**) from July to November 1917 stands out as an enormous waste of life for little return. The Menin Gate (1927) is a memorial to British and Commonwealth soldiers lost in these battles who have no known grave.

October–November 1914 A British offensive aimed at securing the Channel ports of Dunkirk and Ostend clashed with a German offensive aimed at taking those ports. The subsequent fighting was extremely heavy and ended with the Germans gaining the Messines Ridge and other commanding ground, but with the British and French holding a salient (projection into enemy troops) around Ypres extending into the German line. German losses were estimated at 150,000 troops; casualties to the British and French were put at about the same number.

> Ypres formed a salient in the frontline surrounded by German held hills and was of no strategic importance. It would have made military sense to have evacuated it in 1914, but the British army did not want to retreat in case this weakened morale.

April–May 1915 Hostilities opened with a German chlorine-gas attack; this made a huge gap in the Allied lines but the Germans were unprepared for this success and were unable to exploit it before the Allies rushed in reserves. More gas attacks followed, and the British were driven to shorten their line, so making the Ypres salient a smaller incursion into the German line.

July–November 1917 An Allied offensive, including British, Canadian, and Australian troops, was launched under British commander-in-chief Field Marshal Douglas Haig, in an attempt to capture ports on the Belgian coast held by Germans. The long and bitter battle, fought in appalling conditions of driving rain and waterlogged ground, achieved an advance of only 8 km/5 mi of territory that was of no strategic significance, but the Allies alone lost more than 300,000 casualties.

Zhukov, Georgi Konstantinovich (1896–1974)

Marshal of the USSR in **World War II** and minister of defence from 1955 to 1957, who in his first year as Chief of Staff from 1941 defended Moscow. Zhukov also organized the counterattack at **Stalingrad** (now Volgograd) in 1942 and the relief of Leningrad (now St Petersburg) in 1943. He led the offensive from the Ukraine in March 1944, which ended in the fall of Berlin, Germany.

Zhukov forged a close relationship with Nikita **Khrushchev** during the Siege of Stalingrad, facilitating the latter's quest for the leadership of the Soviet union after the death of Joseph Stalin.

Zimmerman, Arthur (1864–1940)

German politician who as foreign secretary sent the notorious Zimmermann Telegram to the German minister in Mexico in January 1917. It contained the terms of an alliance between Mexico and Germany, by which Mexico was to attack the USA with German and Japanese assistance in return for the 'lost' states of New Mexico, Texas, and Arizona. Publication of the message in March 1917 finally brought the hesitant USA into the war against Germany, and Zimmerman was forced to resign shortly afterwards.

Zinoviev, Grigory Yevseyevich (1883–1936)

Russian communist politician whose name was attached to an alleged forgery, the Zinoviev letter, inciting Britain's communists to rise and thus helping to topple the Labour government in 1924.

A prominent **Bolshevik**, Zinoviev returned to Russia in 1917 with Vladimir **Lenin** and played a leading part in the Revolution. He became head of the Communist International 1919. As one of the 'Old Bolsheviks', he was seen by Soviet leader Joseph **Stalin** as a threat. Zinoviev was accused of complicity in the murder of the **Bolshevik** leader Sergei **Kirov** in 1934, and was tried and shot.

❝ Armed warfare must be preceded by a struggle against the inclinations to compromise which are embedded among the majority of British workmen. ❞

Grigory Zinoviev, letter to the British Communist Party, 15 September 1924, quoted in *The Times*, 25 October 1924, alleged by some to be a forgery.

Zollverein

A 19th-century German customs union that was set up by Prussia in 1828; the union included most German-speaking states by 1834, except Austria.

Although designed to remove tariff barriers and increase trade within the German confederation, the Zollverein also had a political effect in isolating Austria. The Austrians were committed to trade tariffs to protect their agriculture and industry; so their inability to join the Zollverein increased Prussian power in the confederation.

Although it was economic in origin, the Zollverein was the basis for the unification of Germany under **Bismarck**.

See also: *Franco–Prussian War; Seven Weeks' War.*

Appendix

Europe: Chronology

BC

850000	Stone Age hunter-gathering peoples arrive in Europe.
6500	Britain separated from continent by rising sea levels.
3000	Bronze Age civilizations of the Mediterranean: Minoan and Mycenaean.
1000	Start of Iron Age.
6th–4th centuries	Greek civilization at its height.
594	Solon gives laws to Athens which formed basis of democracy.
490	Greeks defeat Persians at Battle of Marathon.
336–323	Alexander the Great, king of Macedonia, makes conquests as far east as India.
3rd century	Rome takes control of the Italian peninsula.
218–203	Second Punic War: Carthaginians under Hannibal invade Italy but fail to defeat Rome.
146	Greece a Roman province and Carthage destroyed.
27	Augustus takes title of Caesar; birth of imperial Rome.

AD

1st century	Expansion of Roman Empire to northern frontiers on Rhine and Danube; Roman conquest of Britain.
2nd century	Roman Empire ceases to expand.
323	Emperor Constantine the Great professes himself a Christian and divides empire into east and west.
4th–6th centuries	Europe overrun by Goths, Franks, Lombards, Anglo-Saxons; fall of Rome; start of the Dark Ages.
7th–8th centuries	Christendom threatened by the Moors (Moslem Arabs) via Mediterranean countries. Beginnings of feudalism.
800	Charlemagne given title of Holy Roman Emperor by the Pope.
9th–11th centuries	Viking raids on coastal regions at their height.
1073	Gregory VII begins two centuries of conflict between the papacy and the empire.
1096	First Crusade sets out to take Jerusalem.
12th century	Beginnings of the German, Flemish, and Italian city states.
13th century	Teutonic Knights conquer Prussia.
14th–15th century	Renaissance begins in northern Italy.
1453	Constantinople falls to the Turks, bringing an end to the Byzantine Empire.
1517	Martin Luther starts the Reformation.
1519	Habsburg emperor Charles V unites crowns of Austria and Spain, leading to prolonged wars with France.

1533–84	Ivan the Terrible makes Russia powerful.
17th century	Absolute monarchy comes to prevail in most of Europe.
1618	Start of Thirty Years' War in Germany between Protestants and Catholics.
1648	Treaty of Westphalia secures French dominance in Europe.
1683	Turks besiege Vienna, but are repulsed.
1703	Peter the Great founds St Petersburg as new capital of Russian Empire.
1741–8	War of the Austrian Succession; rise of Prussia as a military power.
1756–63	Seven Years' War; France loses colonies to Britain.
1789	Start of the French Revolution; revolutionary wars follow.
1804	Napoleon Bonaparte crowns himself emperor of the French.
1815	Battle of Waterloo ends Napoleonic Wars.
1821–29	Greek War of Independence.
1848	The Year of Revolutions.
1861	Unification of Italy by King Victor Emmanuel I and Cavour.
1871	Unification of Germany under Prussian leadership by Bismarck.
1878	Treaty of Berlin brings independence to Serbia and Romania and Bulgarian autonomy.
1912	Turkey-in-Europe collapses in the Balkan War.
1914–18	First World War arises from Austro-Russian and Franco-German rivalries; it ends in German defeat and destroys the Austrian and Russian empires.
1917	Bolsheviks seize power in Russia, leading to creation of USSR.
1919	Paris Peace Conference: Poland and Hungary regain independence; Czechoslovakia and Yugoslavia are created.
1933	Adolf Hitler comes to power in Germany.
1939–45	Second World War arises from German aggression; it results in decline of European power and emergence of USA and USSR as "superpowers".
1945–48	"Iron Curtain" established as USSR imposes communist regimes on Eastern Europe; Germany divided; start of Cold War.
1957	Treaty of Rome founds the European Economic Community (EEC).
1973	First enlargement of EEC to include Britain, Denmark, and Ireland.
1989	Collapse of communism in eastern Europe and fall of the "Iron Curtain".
1990	Reunification of Germany; end of the Cold War.
1991	Breakup of USSR and Yugoslavia.
	Maastricht Treaty on European Union.
1992	Civil war breaks out in Bosnia-Herzegovina.
1993	European Single Market comes into effect.
	Czech Republic and Slovakia are created by division of Czechoslovakia.
1994	Channel Tunnel links Britain to the continent.
1995	Bosnian peace agreement negotiated at Dayton, Ohio.
1997	Plans for expansion of the European Union into Central and Eastern Europe.
1998	Euro monetary zone created within the European Union countries.

Some Key Dates in the Growth of the European Union

17 March 1948 Benelux Treaty enters into force.

1948 Creation of the Organization for European Economic Cooperation (OEEC) to administer Marshall Plan aid.

1949 Creation of the Council of Europe based in Strasbourg.

9 May 1950 Schuman Declaration; Robert Schuman proposes pooling Europe's coal and steel industries.

18 April 1951 European Coal and Steel Community (ECSC) Treaty signed.

1952–54 Development and failure of the plan for a European Defence Community (EDC).

25 March 1957 Signing of the Treaties of Rome establishing the European Economic Community (EEC) and European Atomic Energy Community (Euratom).

1967 Merger of the executive institutions of the three European Communities (ESCS, EEC, and Euratom).

1 July 1968 Completion of the Customs Union 18 months early.

1 January 1973 Denmark, Ireland, and the United Kingdom join the European Community (EUR 9).

13 March 1979 European Monetary System (EMS) becomes operative.

1 January 1981 Greece joins the European Community (EUR 10).

29 June 1985 European Council endorses "White Paper" plan to complete single market by the end of 1992.

1 January 1986 Spain and Portugal join the European Community (EUR 12).

1 July 1987 Single European Act enters into force.

26–27 June 1989 Madrid European Council endorses plan for Economic and Monetary Union.

3 October 1990 Unification of Germany; the states of the former German Democratic Republic enter the European Community.

7 February 1992 Signing of the Maastricht Treaty setting up the European Union.

2 May 1992 European Community and European Free Trade Association (EFTA) agree to form the European Economic Area (EEA).

1 January 1993 European single market is achieved on time.

1 November 1993 Treaty on European Union (Maastricht) enters into force after ratification by the member states.

1 January 1994 Establishment of the European Economic Area.

1 January 1995 Austria, Finland, and Sweden join the European Union (EUR 15).

17 June 1997 Treaty of Amsterdam is concluded.

12 March 1998 European Conference in London launches Europe-wide consultations on issues related to Common Foreign and Security Policy and Justice and Home Affairs.

30–31 March 1998 EU opens membership negotiations with Cyprus, Czech Republic, Estonia, Hungary, Poland, and Slovenia.

2 May 1998 Eleven EU member states qualify to launch the euro on 1 January 1999: Austria, Belgium, Finland, France, Germany, Republic of Ireland, Italy, Luxembourg, the Netherlands, Portugal, and Spain.

1 July 1998 European Central Bank inaugurated in Frankfurt, Germany.

1 January 1999 EMU and euro launched in the 11 qualifying EU countries.

1 May 1999 The Amsterdam Treaty enters into force after ratification by the member states.

European Union: Central Organs

European Commission

membership	20—two each from France, Germany, Italy, Spain, and the UK, and one each from Austria, Belgium, Denmark, Finland, Greece, Ireland, the Netherlands, Portugal, and Sweden, plus the president, from Luxembourg. The members are nominated by each state for a four-year, renewable term of office. One member is chosen as president for a two-year, renewable term.
	The post of president is a mixture of head of government and head of the European civil service
operational methods	the commissioners are drawn proportionately from member states, and each takes an oath on appointment not to promote national interests. They head a staff of 13,000, with 20 directorates-general, each responsible for a particular department
base	Brussels

Council of Ministers of the European Union

membership one minister from each of the 15 member countries

operational methods it is the supreme decision-making body of the Union. The representatives vary according to the subject matter under discussion. If it is economic policy it will be the finance ministers, if it is agricultural policy, the agriculture ministers. It is the foreign ministers, however, who tend to be the most active. The presidency of the Council changes hands at six-monthly intervals, each member state taking its turn

base Brussels

Committee of the Regions

membership 222 regional or local

representatives France, Germany, Italy, and the UK 24 each; Spain 21; Austria, Belgium, Greece, the Netherlands, Portugal, and Sweden 12 each; Denmark, Finland, and Ireland 9 each; Luxembourg 6

operational methods to advise on regional policy, as a direct result of the Maastricht Treaty, with its emphasis on "subsidiarity"

Committee of Permanent Representatives (COREPER)

membership a subsidiary body of officials, often called "ambassadors", who act on behalf of the Council. The members of COREPER are senior civil servants who have been temporarily released by member states to work for the Union

operational methods COREPER receives proposals from the Council of the European Union for consideration in detail before the Council decides on action

base Brussels

Economic and Social Committee

membership representatives from member countries covering a wide range of interests, including employers, trade unionists, professional people, and farmers

operational methods a consultative body advising the Council of the European Union and the Commission

base Brussels

European Parliament

membership

determined by the populations of member states.

The total number of seats is 626, of which Germany has 99, France, Italy, and the UK 87 each, Spain 64, the Netherlands 31, Belgium, Greece, and Portugal 25 each, Sweden 22, Austria 21, Denmark and Finland 16 each, Ireland 15, and Luxembourg 6.

Members are elected for five-year terms in large Euro-constituencies. Voting is by a system of proportional representation in all countries except the UK

role and powers

originally mainly consultative, but it does have power to reject the Union budget and to dismiss the Commission if it has good grounds for doing so. It debates Union present and future policies. As well as expanding its membership, the Maastricht Treaty increased its powers, giving it the right to be consulted about the appointment of the Commission, and in particular its president

base

Luxembourg and Strasbourg